How To Build A *Successful* One-Person Business

Veltisezar B. Bautista

Bookhaus Publishers

Copyright © 1994 by Veltisezar B. Bautista

Library of Congress Catalog Card Number 93-74798
International Standard Book Number 0-931613-09-4

Publisher's Cataloging in Publication
(Prepared by Quality Books Inc.)

Bautista, Veltisezar B., 1933 -
    How to build a successful one-person business: a common-sense guide to starting
& growing a company / by Veltisezar B. Bautista.
        p. cm.
    Includes bibliographical references and index

    Preassigned LCCN: 93-74798.

    ISBN 0-931613-09-4

    1. New business enterprises -- United States. 2. Entrepreneurship --
United States. I. Title.

    HD62.5.B38 1994   658'.041
                                   QBI94-79

This book is printed on recycled, acid-free paper.

Printed in the United States of America

Distributed to the trade by Publishers Group West
1 (800) 788-2123

Address mail orders to:

Bookhaus Publishers, P.O. Box 3277
Farmington Hills, MI 48333-3277 U.S.A
(810) 489-8640 Fax: (810) 489-8155

Dedication

I dedicate this book to the light of my life,
Genoveva Abes-Bautista;
to my beloved children,
Hubert, Lester, Melvin, Ronald, and Janet;
to my daughter-in-law,
Maria Cecilia Asi-Bautista;
and to all dreamers who will read this book.

Contents

Introduction

With American corporations continuing to practice the fine art of downsizing, streamlining, and belt-tightening simply to remain competitive in the '90s, the writing is on the wall for the would-be one-person work forces: smaller is not only better, it's the way of the future. This book draws both on author Veltisezar Bautista's personal experience and on examples from case studies to create strategies for success as a solo business person.

Revolutions in technology and communications have fueled the increase of one-person businesses, most of which are operated at home. By 1995, it's estimated that 44 percent of all U.S. households will support some kind of home office activity.

While large and small companies are engaging in what is known as *partnering*, smart one-employee companies are now making alliances with other independent contractors and small, medium-sized, and large companies to have their products manufactured quickly, promoted nationally, and distributed effectively to the marketplace.

Today, cheaper but advanced machines, computers, and software are now available to entrepreneurs to do jobs such as desktop publishing, computer-aided design, and other functions in business operations.

Also, single-person companies have access to commercial data bases through computers and modems, putting in their hands a vast store of facts that used only to be at the disposal of large and well-oiled companies with huge business libraries.

While there's a glut of books, manuals, and cassette and video tapes generally directed at the burgeoning small-business field, there's a dearth of material ideal for solo operators.

To show the secrets of avoiding failures and financial disasters and to attain real success, *How to Build a Successful One-Person Business* was written and published for the one-person operation. Instructive as well as inspiring, the book appeals not only to those who have long-time dreams of establishing businesses of their own, but also to the victims of corporate downsizing, retirees, and people looking to break from their current careers.

Among other things, the book contains:

❑ Key points for developing entrepreneurial traits.

❑ Ideal one-person businesses.

❑ Reasons for using the single-entry *cash system* instead of the double-entry *accrual system* of accounting.

❑ A Directory of Microloan Lenders

❑ How to start and operate a mail order business.

❑ How to build a successful one-person newsletter and/or book publishing business.

❑ How to establish a network of subcontractors, distributors, wholesalers, dealers, and sales representatives.

❑ How to target a niche market and/or a general market.

❑ How to select and use smart technology to run your business.

❑ The seven-point success formula for solo operators.

In a nutshell, the book provides an easy-to-follow prescription for achieving entrepreneurial potential that integrates ingenuity, technology, common sense, and simple know-how.

Why Start & Grow a One-Person Company?

London calling? Yes...this is the customer service.

Spawned by improved technology and corporate downsizing, there's now a growing trend of establishing a new type of company. These companies have only a single employee, maintain a low overhead, and work with a network of subcontractors, distributors, wholesalers, and dealers. Some of them are called "virtual corporations."

If you want to build such a company or any other type of one-person company, this is the right book for you!

More than ever, now is the right time to establish a one-person business.

Today's advanced technology, from computers to modems to voice mail, can provide you with the necessary tools to communicate nationally or internationally with your dealers, suppliers, contacts, and customers.

Nowadays, with the help of modern technology and other forces, distribution systems have become more efficient. Thus, small companies, including one-person enterprises, are getting their products to market faster and easier.

Says Mark Mendel, retail analyst for Solomon Brothers (in an article published in *Nation's Business*): "The ongoing restructuring and downsizing of many large corporations and advances in telecommunications should increase the number of home workers and spur small-business formation."

I. The Great Organizer

Here's the true story of a man whom we may call John Doe, a former executive, who successfully formed a one-person company that became an ultimate "virtual corporation."

The Idea

Doe conceived the idea of inventing a new kind of boat made of recycled plastic. Knowing enough of manufacturing, materials, labor, and money to produce such a boat (without the $1 million he might need to push through the project by himself), Doe founded a one-person company and formed alliances with a designer, a packaging expert, an accountant, a banker, a lawyer, a manufacturer, and several distributors—making them "partners" for success.

His Alliances

Starting from scratch, Doe began to research the market for his small boat. He talked with boaters, boating organizations, and dealers.

Armed with a business plan, he formed an alliance with a designer who could give him a good design in order that his product would be superior to other boats in this category available on the market. Then he searched for a company that was an expert in molding plastics who would actually manufacture the boat. Then followed his alliances with other professionals.

Sales Projections

In 1993, he expected to sell about 1,000 units at $390 per unit as compared to other prices in the market ranging from $400 to $2,500. In 1994, he predicted to sell at least 3,000 units.

Thus, an ultimate "virtual corporation" was born.

II. The Solo Operator

Here's another true story of a solo operator who does his business in Carmel, Indiana. Let's just call him Melvin Funk and his company, International Communications.

Workload

As an entrepreneur, Funk's one-person company arranges commercial sponsorship and marketing support for sporting events. He does all the work. He is the president, the sales manager, the messenger, and the janitor.

$1 Million Sales

An entrepreneur who never travels without his laptop computer, Funk, 42, married and the father of three, works an average of 11 hours a day and his work week often covers the full 7 days. Although his work schedule is hectic, he really enjoys it, considering the fact that he generates a sponsorship sales volume of about $1 million a year.

A self-confident man, Funk used to be a salesman for a manufacturing company in Traverse City, Michigan. But it took him 13 years to be a one-person business owner. "Now that I'm independent, I know I can take the credit for every reward that comes my way," he says.

III. Small Businesses

The stories above are examples of successful one-person companies formed by ambitious individuals, some of whom have been fired, laid off, or forced to resign by corporate America because of tough economic times. You can find this type of company throughout the United States.

Why Form a One-Person Company?

There are many reasons why many entrepreneurs want a one-person business.

The major reasons include the following advantages:

■ They are their own bosses and are in control of their careers and destinies.

■ They have little overhead—no problem of meeting a payroll or covering the fixed monthly costs of a big operation, especially if they operate out of their own homes.

■ They form partnerships with distributors, wholesalers, retailers, and other professionals. They don't worry about managing employees.

■ They increase production of their products by assigning manufacturing to a single contractor or to various contractors, paying them for every product. If they themselves are contractors, they seek the help of subcontractors.

Pursuing the Dream

Different people at different times have engaged in or contemplated to launch businesses to pursue their dreams.

While some of them were born entrepreneurs, some have no business background whatsoever and others have no jobs at all.

The reasons for launching a business are generally varied; some people want to become millionaires, others want to be just rich—having a big house by the sea or the lakefront, with a luxurious boat and a few expensive cars. Still, others just want to earn enough money—the amount of money they are earning in their jobs so that they can say goodbye to their supervisors and be their own bosses.

You're one of them. Maybe you have launched your business or are just planning to start a new one. You want to work for yourself, maybe out of your home—somewhere in the basement, in the kitchen, or under the stairs of your second floor.

If you're to be a one-person business owner, you'll be engaging in a *small business.*

A *small business,* as defined by the Small Business Act of 1953, is one that is independently owned and operated and not dominant in the field of its operation. The same act authorized the U.S. Small Business Administration (SBA) to formulate a more detailed definition of a small business based on its sales volume and the number of employees.

The SBA, therefore, has set guidelines to determine which businesses are considered small as far as applying for loans is concerned. Its definition of a small business is based on the number of employees and the amount of annual sales. Its established *upper limits* for small companies are defined in following paragraphs:

1. *Manufacturing.* A small manufacturing company should have 250 or fewer employes. (If the employment is between 250 and 1,500, another size standard is used for a particular industry.)

2. *Wholesaling.* A small wholesale firm should have up to $9.5 million to $22 million in annual sales, depending on the line of wholesaling involved. That means different wholesalers may have different upper limits.

For instance, a department store grossing up to $13 million in annual sales can still be considered a small business. On the other hand, firms selling nursery products should sell less than $500,000 to be considered a small business.

3. *Retailing. A small* retail business in this industry is one annual sales up to $2 million to $7.5 million, depending on the line of retailing. In other words, firms in different lines of retailing have different upper limits.

4 *Service Business.* A small service business has annual sales up to $1.5 million to $10 million, depending on the line of service.

Based on its own criteria, the SBA considers 90 percent of all businesses throughout the country as *small businesses.*

Of course, there's no doubt that if you are a single-person business owner, your business is considered small.

IV. Status of Businesses

Small Businesses

In the 1880s, the number of small businesses (as defined by the SBA increased tremendously.

In 1981, according to "The State of Small Business: A Report of the President" (1992), 13.7 million small businesses filed tax returns. By 1991, the annual figure had increased by almost 50 percent, to 20.5 million. This number covers all forms of business activity, including millions of part-time "hobby" businesses. (These businesses are undertaken part-time by individuals with regular jobs while others are operated by full-time entrepreneurs.) Of the 20.5 million small businesses, only 5.8 million of them had employees in 1991, up from 4.7 million in 1981. That was a compound rate of growth of approximately 2 percent a year. All except about 7,000 of these are small businesses with fewer than 500 employees.

One-Person Businesses

The SBA, in a response to our inquiry, estimated that in 1993 there were about 17,000,000 registered sole proprietorship businesses. Of this number, 15,000,000 were one-person businesses. Therefore, of the 17,000,000 registered sole-proprietorship businesses, only 2,000,000 had more than one employee. (Also see, "The State of Small Business," page 33.

The majority of these one-person operations were based at home.

Meanwhile, a market research firm, BIS Strategic Decisions (based in Norwell, Massachusetts), predicts 44 percent of all U.S. households will support some kind of office activity in 1995.

Way back in 1984, a survey made by AT&T showed that about 13 percent of all U.S. households were home to businesses.

Of these businesses, more than half were being operated full time. A home-based business is run from some space in a home; which can be an apartment, a boat, a condo, a mobile home, a single-family residence, etc. The space can be an attic, a kitchen, a basement, a bedroom, or under the stairs. Of course, you can rent an office outside your home. But that's expensive, especially for someone just starting out. It's more economical and convenient to have the office in the home because of low overhead expenses.

Woman Entrepreneur

In an article published in the May 1989 issue of *Nation's Business*, it was cited that almost one-third of the small businesses in the U.S. belonged to women. From 1980 to 1986, sole proprietorships owned by women rose from 2.5 million to 4.1 million—a 62.5 percent jump during a period when the number of male-owned business receipts nearly doubled, from $36 billion to $71.5 billion. (Of course, some single-proprietorship businesses have employees.)

This jump was attributed to the fact that women who stay at home with kids often want to do something besides raising children and doing household chores. Hence, they start their part-time or full-time businesses.

V. Why Enter a Business?

In general, you want to go into business because going into business is part of the American Dream for men and women. This is possible because in our free enterprise system, anyone who has the ambition, the money (from a few hundred to thousands or millions of dollars), the time, and the knowledge can engage in business.

The following paragraphs offer some good reasons why you may want to go into a one-person business.

Freedom

You're your own boss if you are in a one-person business. There's no one to tell you, "Hey! Will you do this for me?" or "Didn't I tell you that you have to finish that today?"

However, on the other hand, there's no one to tell you, "Here's your paycheck!" (That is, if you're employed by someone, you get a regular paycheck periodically.)

Moreover, being home alone, you can:

■ *Think freely*. There's no boss to tell you, "I don't think you're right; let's do it my way."

■ *Set your own schedule*. There's no one to instruct you, "You can take a break at 3:00 p.m.and come back at 3:15."

Work in comfort. There are no more worries about what to wear. If you like to work in pajamas, in a sport shirt or in a suit (even if you're all alone or with kids at home), it's fine. But then, you can't expect someone to say, "That's a nice suit!"

■ *Go on vacation whenever you want.* You schedule your own vacation.

Job Security

You're secure in your own job as owner, manager, and janitor. And no one to shock you with "You're fired!" or "You're laid off!"

Big Money

If you're employed by someone else or the government, your pay is fixed—earning probably $15,000, $25,000 or $35,000 a year. But when you're self-employed, you can really make it big!

You can earn $20,000, $50,000, $100,000, or $500,000 or more, depending on the business you're in.

"I'm Free! I'm Free!"

Business Write-Offs and Tax Deductions

When you're employed by someone else, you have to worry about payments of bills for telephones, electricity, and more. But as a self-employed business person, you can deduct a part, or all in some instances, of the expenses you incur by using home office space or your car. When you have a salary from someone else, say $30,000 a year, that's considered as your net income by Uncle Sam (and only about $25,000 of it will actually pass through your hands after tax deductions—if you're lucky. That is, you're to pay your tax based on a $30,000 income. You can't deduct any cost for gasoline and other personal expenses.

On the other hand, if you're running your own enterprise and your gross income is about $100,000, that's not your net income. That amount will pass through your hand, but your net income probably will be only about $30,000. The tax will be based on this net income. Why? Because many business expenses, such as costs of equipment, office supplies, business trips (which sometimes on your part can also be considered as a pleasure trip) can be deducted from your gross income. In other words, a big portion of the gross income from business would have to be used in the purchase of office equipment, land, or buildings, all of which can be considered as tax advantages. Depreciation will further reduce your business income, while the cost of equipment may depreciate. On the other hand, the cost of land or buildings appreciate in value, which is to your advantage in the future.

Also, you can deduct a portion of your home (office space) that is used for business, including a percentage of your cost of utilities, provided it's your principal place of business.

Traffic! Traffic! Traffic!

You waste a lot of time in going to and from the office or the factory where you work. You probably spend about one or two hours every day in commuting. But when you're working at home, you won't yell, "Hey, don't blow your horn!"

In other words, you don't only save time, but you also save money in the cost of gasoline, clothes, etc.

Closer to Your Kids or Spouse

Many people complain about not being with their loved ones more of the time. But when you're engaged in a one-person business working at home, there's no need to call from your office and ask Mom (or Dad), "How are the kids?"

Pa, I Like It Here!

Yes, you will have the time to be with your kids to watch them grow. You can develop a good relationship with them. For instance, you can be with your wife or husband at home, if he or she doesn't work outside the home. You can take your break or day off as you wish.

Enhancing Your Self-Esteem

If you're in business and are successful at it, you'll enhance your self-esteem. When you meet with your friends or relatives, you'll feel at ease, confident, and beam with pride. You can tell them that you are happy because you enjoy being a self-employed person. Also, you'll be known in your own community.

The Challenge

While working alone (or with kids) at home, you'll be challenged to use all of your skills and mental resources. You'll have to plan, to organize, to dream, and to set goals to accomplish your American Dream. "The sky's the limit!" as far as you're concerned. You're the master of your own destiny! No one to blame but yourself if you don't succeed in life. But if you follow the instructions in this book or get ideas from it, you'll be on your way to success.

Most successful business persons enjoy the competition.(I like it, too!) When you compete, you work and think hard to make your products or services better than others' products or services. You've got to do that because you want to get a larger share of the market. And there's so much joy when you compete and—win!

Dreaming of Retirement

Some people engage in business, many while holding full-time jobs, to prepare for their retirement. While in retirement, you can reap the rewards of having operated your own business. Or you can still run your one-person business (after your retirement from your employment job) while you're fishing or enjoying the company of your co-retirees, or even traveling around the world. How you can do that is revealed in this book.

An advantage to having your own business is that you can set a retirement plan for yourself. For instance, under the Keogh plan as a self-employed person, you can allocate 13.5 percent of your net income (at the time of this writing) to such a plan and pay no taxes on that allocated money. However, since a Keogh is a tax-deferred plan, you'll have to pay taxes after you withdraw the money. But at that time, you'll probably be in a lower tax bracket.

Meet New People

When you operate a business from your home, it doesn't mean that you won't go out except to the Post Office, the United Parcel Service or the bank. There probably be occasions when you will attend a conference in or out of your state. At seminars, for instance, you may meet new people with whom you can network.

VI. Think Big, Start Small

As a would be single-person business owner, you have to think big but start small! Have a dream and chase it! However, your growth should be steady in order to succeed. Think of the career you'll build, the money you'll accumulate, or the fame you'll achieve! And you'll have the enthusiasm to work for the success of your own business!

Have a Dream and Chase It!

Moreover, you don't need millions of dollars, or even a hundred thousand, to build a successful one-person business. You can start with just a few hundred dollars.

Most one-person businesses start small because small entrepreneurs have an opportunity to learn the business as it grows and prospers.

You can run your business while still working for someone else and make your business a part-time endeavor. Then later, you can engage in it, full time.

When I quit my regular job in 1988, my supervisor asked me why I was quitting. I happily answered, "I'm making my own destiny!"

$50 Capital

Sometime in 1983, I started with a $50 capital in publishing a booklet about postal examinations. I titled the booklet *How to Score 95-100% on Postal Exams and How I Did It!*

A book entitled *The Book of U.S. Postal Exams* (based on the booklet) and another book entitled *Improve Your Grades* garnered more than $100,000 in net sales in 1990, realizing for the first time my long-time dream of making more than $100,000 a year as a one-person business owner.

Since then, I've written and published several other successful books.

Success Stories

There are amazing stories of one-person successful business owners who run their businesses out of their home.

Many of them start small and grow into big-time businesses.

VII. Bottom Line

■ Now is the best time to start and run a one-person company because of today's advanced technology, from computers to modems to cellular phones.

■ Any one-person company may form partnerships with distributors, wholesalers, retailers, and other professionals. In that way, a group of people and companies work for you.

How to Develop Your Entrepreneurial Traits

2

■ Is an entrepreneur born or self-made? There are those born as entrepreneurs—they are the naturals who have the knack in selling goods or services; there are those who are born to parents who are entrepreneurs; then there are those who become entrepreneurs because they lost their jobs or they can't find positions working for others.

If you engage in business, you'll be called a business owner, a businessman or a businesswoman, a business person, or the most commonly known name, an *entrepreneur.* An entrepreneur is a person who establishes, manages, and assumes the risks of a business undertaking for the purpose of making a profit.

Sometimes, maybe, you wonder whether you're a natural, or maybe you don't know if you can even become a successful entrepreneur.

For this reason, let's examine what the personal traits are of those who become successful business owners.

I. Entrepreneurial Traits

In general, entrepreneurs bound to be successful possess the major traits of *desire, vision, self-confidence, diligence, persistence, organizational skill, competitiveness,* and *determination.*

Desire

Desire should be the starting point of those who want to be somebody, to accomplish something big, or to make big money. Desire breeds an idea or a dream; it is an urge or an itch to do something for yourself and not for someone else. Desire makes you think; it is invisible in your head. You can't see it, yet you feel you have it.

Go for It!

Ambitious people have an abundance of desire; that's why they have larger dreams than most people. They are not satisfied with their present situation in life; they want to pursue further education to make money so they can be rich and afford the luxuries of life. They want not only money, but also fame and whatever power and nice things that money can bring. Many of them say (even to themselves), "I want to be somebody!" "I want to be a millionaire!" or "I want to be rich!"

Desire something and make it produce dreams! Let your imagination soar to the heights of the sky; let it seek the destination you want. Then ask questions from yourself: *What do I want from life? What can I do to live comfortably, to send my children to school, to contribute to the community? How can I be rich? How can I accomplish these things: by working for others or for myself?*

Then, probably, you may think that you can accomplish these things by engaging in a business of your own!

Let your desire be not a *weak one,* but rather a *burning desire.* This burning desire can breed ideas and dreams. You'll have the enthusiasm to work with vigor and energy for long hours—from the wee hours of the morning to the late hours of the night.

Vision

Vision is the ability to see the future where one wants to be and how he or she can be there at the proper time. Successful entrepreneurs, in general, can visualize on the screen of their imagination what their businesses will be in the years to come. Individuals with vision formulate their business plans in writing—reviewing those plans week by week, month by month, year by year, making adjustments to cope with the present political situation or economic condition.

Forecasting the Future

To forecast the future, you must know the past and the present. Study past and present business trends to forecast what may happen in the years to come. Set short- and long-term goals so that you'll know when to start, how to proceed, and how to get to your destination. While many people see dark clouds in the sky, with your vision, you may see a clear horizon behind those clouds. There are times, too, when you have to use not only your common sense, but also your gut feelings when you decide what to do or how to solve business problems. Sometimes you may say,

"I'll do it! I just feel this is the right thing to do!"

Having a timetable for accomplishing your goals in life can help you clearly see in your mind the path to your destiny. Hence, your vision pushes your thoughts towards your dreams!

Self-Confidence

Successful entrepreneurs are self-confident people. They believe in themselves and in what they plan or do. They don't wait for any approval from other people, such as friends or relatives.

A Self-Confident Man

In the past, you might have completed difficult tasks that you thought you might not have accomplished. For instance, the first time you attempted to walk (an occasion only your parents remember), you often stumbled; yet you stood up and tried again. When you finally walked a few steps, you then had the confidence that you could walk, and you did!

Look back at small and large successes you've had in the past, and you'll feel confident that you'll attain more successes in things you do. Lay out your plans well and make an all-out effort to clear the roads to your destination, although there may be some bumpy rides along the way.

Diligence

Successful entrepreneurs are hard-working and persevering people. They are careful in their work and make most of available opportunities and options. They know their strengths and weaknesses. They know what further education to pursue or what skills to develop.

To develop diligence, sustain your strengths and strengthen your weaknesses. If you lack enough education in the particular industry or service you've chosen, then develop new skills or go back to school at night. Work hard and always think that there's nothing worthwhile that is easy to do.

Persistence

When they suffer failures, successful entrepreneurs consider them as temporary setbacks and make them their stepping stones to success. They may even see them as "learning opportunities." They remain inwardly optimistic and are not heartbroken by frequent turndowns. Instead, they may say, "I can make it!"—repeating this phrase, day in and day out.

Optimistic people, entrepreneurs or not, apply the trial-and-error method. Thomas Edison failed a thousand times before he perfected an incandescent lamp. Colonel Sanders was rejected by over 1,000 restaurants before he got an order for his recipe for fried chicken. Abraham Lincoln suffered many failures before he was elected as president of the United States. The list goes on and on.

You can follow the examples of outstanding people who persisted and finally did it!

Persistence Pays

To develop persistence when you are working toward your goals, take one small step at a time, repeating each small step until you take bigger steps. It's like going upstairs; you take the first step, then the second step, then the third step.In business, you can't go from the first step directly to the third or fifth step.

These steps can be summed up in a few lines (reprinted from *The Great-*

est Salesman in the World by Og Mandino. Copyright 1968 by Og Mandino. Used by permission of Frederick Fell Publishers, Hollywood, Florida):

"I will persist until I succeed.

"Henceforth, I will consider each day's effort as but one blow of my blade against a mighty oak. The first blow may cause not a tremor in the wood, nor the second, nor the third. Each blow, of itself, may be trifling, and seem of no consequence. Yet from childish swipes, the oak will eventually tumble. So it will be with my efforts of today.

"I will be likened to the raindrop which washes away the mountain; the ant who devours a tiger; the star which brightens the earth; the slave who builds a pyramid. I will build my castle one brick at a time for I know that small attempts, repeated, will complete my undertaking.

"I will persist until I succeed."

Organizational Skill

Successful entrepreneurs usually have the skill to organize things. The one-person business owner, like yourself, having no associates or employees, should be a great organizer and should know how to apply systems in the daily conduct of business (for instance, organizing the office, such as in record-keeping and work priorities). You should plan your work and work your plan.Always set deadlines for accomplishing your goals.

Competitiveness

Entrepreneurs love to compete, simply because fellow entrepreneurs are rivals for certain segments of the market. They are not afraid of competition; in fact, competition makes them work harder to have the edge in selling products or services.

To be competitive, learn what your competitors are doing or what products they are producing or what services they are offering and how they are marketing them. Always try to produce better products and better services—using effective marketing methods.

We are all competitors because we are in competition with other people— whether in school, for jobs, in the workplace, or in business. To beat the competition, you have to catch up with your opponents. Don't stop running. If you look back, someone will pass you.

Don't Stop Running...

Determination

Determination is the one trait that successful entrepreneurs must have. It simply means that having belief in

themselves and in their plans, they are determined to chase their dreams. No setbacks or obstacles can stop them from continuing their efforts to attain their goals.

Being determined, success-conscious entrepreneurs focus their attention on how they run their businesses. They are committed to implementing their projects—whatever time is needed and whatever effort is exerted.

If you develop a good business plan and you have a burning desire to succeed, you'll have the courage to face the challenges of business opportunities and to proceed with determination to continue whatever you've started.

II. New Entrepreneurs

The one-person business owners, whether they are based at home or in an outside office, are a "special" breed of entrepreneurs. Although they must have the general qualities of successful entrepreneurs previously cited, they have certain qualities and problems different than those other entrepreneurs (who run businesses with their associates and employees). In short, their management style may be different from entrepreneurs who have associates and employees.

Some additional qualities of successful single-person business owners are *self-discipline, self-motivation, independence,* and *smart working ability:*

Self-Discipline

Single-person business owners must discipline themselves. They don't receive orders from any supervisors because they give orders—to themselves.

To be sucessful, you must discipline yourself to do any needed tasks. Applying self-control, you must exercise self-discipline in time management, cash management, decision-making, and other matters. Decisions must be made, not on emotional outbursts, but on the careful analysis of problems, based on available study and information.

Self-Motivation

You're not a business owner to motivate your employees, because you have none. You're not an employee to be motivated by any supervisor. You're your own boss and your own employee. Therefore, you must motivate yourself. Of course, it's a plus if your spouse can motivate you.

You can say to yourself, "You can do it! "You can do it!" "You can do it!" This kind of self-talk is called *affirmation.* Affirmation is the process by which you talk to yourself, confirming what good things you have done or what good thoughts you have. When these thoughts are repeated again and again, your mind eventually accepts them as true. Then they make you feel good, giving you the enthusiasm and inspiration to push toward your goals.

Independence

Single-person business owners must be independent. Since most of them are home-based, these entrepreneurs should enjoy being alone— working at home with no associates to help decide certain matters and no

employees to whom work can be delegated.

So although you may seek advice from other people—experts or friends—you must make your own decisions on many matters.

Smart Working Ability

More than anyone else, the one-person business owners should work not only harder, but also smarter. Having the ability to build an organized effort—cementing beneficial relationships between suppliers, distributors, wholesalers, customers, business contacts, and other businesses and entrepreneurs— you can establish business operations that can extend from the basement or any corner of your house or apartment to all corners of the United States and perhaps many parts of the world.

III. Bottom Line

■ Entrepreneurs bound to be successful must possess the major traits of desire, vision, self-confidence, diligence, persistence, organizational skill, competitiveness, and determination.

■ Entrepreneurial traits can be developed and dreams can be pursued by setting short- and long-term goals.

■ Vision is the ability to see the future where you may want to be and how you can be there at the proper time.

Vision!

How to Determine Which Business Is Right for You

3

■ Choosing the right business is one of the most important steps you're going to take to be a successful entrepreneur. If you choose the right one, then it may be your first step towards business success; if you select the wrong one, then it may be your path to disaster, both emotional and financial.

I. The Major Factors

Basically, the major factors to consider in choosing the right business for you are your *experiences, interests, lifestyle, ability, personality* and *the amount of money you have or are willing to invest in your business.*

Experiences

You have many experiences in life. You may recollect some of those experiences.

■ *School Class Experience.* What is your educational background? Are you a high school graduate, a college dropout, or a college graduate? What were your favorite subjects? What course did you study? Engineering? computer science? teaching? architecture? interior decorating?

It doesn't matter whether you're a high school or college graduate. What matters is that you must have at least some background in basic academic subjects—subjects that you can use in running your one-person business, such as math, reading, and writing.

Your past and present educational pursuits and work experiences can be the foundation of a business that you can start and grow.

■ *Work Experience.* What is your present job, if you have one? What jobs have you held in the past? Do you have cooking experience? Possibly you can be a cookbook author. Have you been a secretary? Then you can probably establish a home typing service. Have you worked in an advertising agency? If so, maybe you can establish a one-person advertising agency. Have you worked as a bookkeeper or an accountant in a certain company? Then why not establish your own accounting service company?

What Is Your Present Job?

In other words, your past and present educational pursuits and work experiences can be the foundation of a business that you can start and grow. So right now, review the nature of work activities—both past and present. What you've learned in such activities can be a wealth of knowledge that you can use in running your own one-employee company.

What Is Your Present Job?

Interests

What are your likes and dislikes? Do you like music? Do you love books? Do you like carpentry? Think about your interests—the things that you enjoy doing. Knowing your interests can help you choose the right business for you. What are your hobbies? Any of your hobbies can be the basis for a one-person business. For instance, if you're making small dolls as a hobby, you can probably start a doll company and find a distributor that can sell the dolls to wholesalers and retailers.

Lifestyle

Do you like traveling? As an entrepreneur, you can go to far-away places that you've not gone before and deduct the expenses from your income tax returns. But the trip must be business-related. You must attend a seminar or a conference, for instance. You may stay in an expensive hotel, have some fun, meet with different kinds of people, and hobnob with those successful in the particular industry you're in.Traveling, while tiring, is enjoyable, and it can energize your outlook and enthusiasm.

Are you loner? Perhaps it's ideal for you to have a home business. If you like writing, maybe you can write books and publish them yourself. Or how about publishing a newsletter? Or engaging in a mail order business? How about an import-export business? With today's technology, even if you operate from your basement, or from a space in the corner of your bedroom, you can cover the entire United States and even the whole world. By mail, fax, or phone, you can communicate with your distributors or customers, from Michigan to Hawaii, from Texas to Maine, from the Virgin Islands to Australia.

Ability

What things do you do well? In other words, what do you do best? Do you enjoy tinkering with small things or small machines? Are you a good speaker? What are your personal strengths? Do you like to be with people? How do you spend your vacation every year? You can use your skills and strengths that are compatible with your interests. Know yourself and your skills and you'll know what can be the right business for you.

Personality

The business that you select should be compatible with your personality. Each of us has different personality traits.

According to psychologists, personality traits are formed at an early age which can be shaped by the environment we are in and by those people with whom we are frequently with or by those other people around us. Then such experiences can be the foundation upon which we decide on what types of people, things, or events we like.

Generally, the two major personality groups are *extroverts* and *introverts*. (The degree of being extrovert and introvert varies. We can be categorized as truly an extrovert or an introvert or we can be a combination of these two personality groups.)

■ *Extroverts*. Extroverts are outgoing people. They are energized by the outer world of people and they go where the action is. They like laughter and the outward expressions of emotions. In other words, they like being with people. For instance, if you're an extrovert, you probably prefer to include as many people as possible in your projects or activities. You enjoy meetings and networking. You want to dominate conversations, because you want to be the center of attention. In short, you prefer talking to listening. You also like sharing your ideas with other people for feedback. You need affirmation from others on what you're doing.

■ *Introverts*. On the other hand, introverts are energized by the inner world of ideas and thoughts. In general, they prefer to be alone. They enjoy peace and tranquility. That doesn't mean that they are lonely when they are alone. Actually, most of them are happiest when they are alone—especially when they are engrossed in their work or while they recollect the past and think about the future. They are reserved, and are good listeners. They can concentrate well on whatever they think or do.

If you are an introvert, you enjoy being with one other person or a few close friends.

If you are an introvert, you can make decisions on your own. You don't rely on approval from other people as to what you think, what you say, or what you do. Even if your relatives or friends are against what you do, you're bent on following your own decisions and instincts based on your knowledge, available information, feelings, and past experiences.

Many experts agree that introverts are usually more suited to engaging in single-person businesses operating out of their homes.

The Amount of Money for Business

The amount of money you have or are willing to invest in business will play a big role in deciding which business is the right one for you. It's just common sense that you can't engage in a business that will require a big investment if you don't have enough money to finance it.

If you're a retired person, then decide how much of your savings you feel that you can allocate to your business.

II. Kinds of Businesses

Basically, there are only two kinds of businesses: the *product oriented* and the *service oriented*.

Product-Oriented Businesses

Product-oriented businesses are involved in products that are self-created or products manufactured by others but purchased and resold by other businesses until the products reach the consumers. In other words, these businesses are involved in *manufacturing, wholesaling,* and *retailing.* Some businesses are just involved in manufacturing, while others are in wholesaling, and still others are in retailing.

However, some businesses are engaged in three facets: manufacturing, wholesaling, and retailing. In addition, they offer their products to other wholesalers and retailers. (Some of them also sell goods with the purpose of servicing them, too.)

In general, manufacturers may sell or consign goods to distributors and/or to wholesalers. In turn, the distributors and/or wholesalers sell goods to retailers.

(See Chapter 11, *Selling Products: An Ideal One-Person Business,* page 99.)

fig. 2

Making a Liquid Product

Service-Oriented Businesses

Service-oriented businesses are offered or run from home or from outside the home. Examples of such services are accountants, photographers, computer programmers, and private teachers.

These one-person business owners offer services to individuals and to other businesses. (See Chapter 12, *Offering Services: Another Great One-Person Business,* page 107.)

Product/Service Businesses

There are businesses that sell both products and services. They sell products and then continue serving the customers.

III. Case Histories

The Executive Turned Entrepreneur

Jane Applegate, in her syndicated "Small Business" column, tells of the story of a career changer. (Used by permission of Jane Applegate of the Los Angeles News Syndicate.)

When Baer lost his job as an advertising sales executive for General Media in Manhattan, he didn't have the time or money to feel sorry for himself.

He began driving a "gypsy" cab in Harlem and worked as a front desk clerk in a budget hotel catering to foreign tourists.

"People would ask me how to get to the airport, and I would say 'I'll be back in the morning with my cab.' That's when it struck me to begin some sort of an airport shuttle business."

Today Baer's Shuttle Bus Plus owns one 15-passenger van, leases another and is contracting with a bus company to help shuttle tourists to Kennedy, La Guardia and Newark airports.

The Colonel

Colonel Sanders retired as a cook from the U.S. Navy and opened his first store while in his sixties. Not wanting to retire from life, and using his talent as a cook, he thought of selling a different kind of fried chicken. With his own recipe, he fried chicken in his store.

As they say, the rest is history. His business, Kentucky Fried Chicken has been franchised, not only in the United States, but also throughout the world!

IV. Knowing Your Market

Of course, before you engage in a business, you have to know your market.

The term "market" means a particular segment of the population or businesses that need your products or services and who have the money to buy them. The two major markets are the *general market* or *mass market*, and the *single-target market*. (See Chapter 13, *Savvy Marketing: How to Sell Your Products or Services*, page 113.)

What Is Your Market?

To be successful in business, you have to define your market: whether to focus on the mass market or to target the single market. But you can do both with good distributors and wholesalers. (See Chapter 15, *Distributors, Your Lifelines to Profits and Growth*, page 135.)

Don't Just Imitate Others!

The mistake that many people make is choosing a business based on what they see: hot businesses around them that sprout everywhere until the market is saturated with their products or services. When someone becomes successful in a business and is making big money in it, other friends, relatives, and entrepreneurs start a similar business—only to fold up in a short period of time!

Ideal One-Person Businesses

In other chapters of this book, ideal one-person businesses are featured. You may select one of them, or you may have an idea of your own (even establishing a new business or an old business with a new approach) that will serve a general market or a niche market. The time is now!

V. Bottom Line

■ The major factors to consider in choosing the right business for you are your *experience, interests, lifestyle, ability, personality*, and *the amount of money you have or are willing to invest in your business*.

■ Product-oriented businesses are involved in *manufacturing, wholesaling*, and *retailing*. Manufacturing is the best because if engage in it, you can mass produce your products and distribute and sell them through distributors, wholesalers, and retailers.

■ Service-oriented businesses are offered or run from home or from outside the home. As a one-person business owner, you can increase your service-oriented business by subcontracting some of your work.

Subcontract Your work to Me!

Creating a Business Plan Tailored to You Alone

4

■ Why do you need a business plan? You need it because it's the map you're going to use when you go along the sometimes winding, bumpy road to success. But a plan, especially for a one-person enterprise, to be effective and workable, should be clear, simple, and practical.

Entrepreneurs should create their business plans before starting a business venture. Many of them do so—writing elaborate plans, especially when they apply for bank loans to finance their endeavors. Others just keep their plans in their heads.

But many of those with written plans just keep their plans in the drawers. Some look at them often; some once every six months or once a year; some don't look at them at all.

Others just keep their plans in their memory, retrieving them when they encounter some problems in running their businesses. "What went wrong?" they ask.

What I'm going to discuss is a plan tailored to you alone; it's not a plan to be presented to the bank, venture capitalists, or prospective investors.

Anyway, if yours is a newly established endeavor, the bank most likely will not grant you a loan, since you are just starting and have no profit history. Of course, if you've been profitably in business for a few years and want to expand, you may request a bank loan. If you want a more elaborate business plan, you may obtain free counselling services from the Service Corps of Retired Executives (SCORE) and Small Business Development Centers (SBDCs), two programs sponsored by the Small Business Administration. (There may be a branch office in your area.)

I. Ingredients of a Good Plan

Here's an outline of a business plan that may get you organized and give you the blueprint for building a successful one-person business.

I. The Business

   A. Industry background
   B. Business description
   C. Business objectives

II. Products and Services

   A. Products and services list
   B. Consumer benefits
   C. Product uniqueness

III. Product Development

   A. Manufacturing process
   B. Subcontractors
   C. Suppliers

IV. The Market

   A. Target market
   B. Market size and trends
   C. Market research
   D. Marketing strategy
   E. Distribution methods

V. The Competition
   A. Major competitors
   B. Direct competitors

VI. Financial Data

   A. Capital sources
   B. Operating costs
   C. Projected income

VII. Operational Plan

   A. Location
   B. Organization
   C. Management
   D. Consultants
   E. Goal setting
   F. Goal deadlines

I. The Business

A *Industry Background.* Write a clear, brief description of the industry your business represents. What is the status of the industry compared to other industries? Is it still a hot industry? What are the current trends of the industry? Where is the industry heading? Who are the leaders of the industry?

When I was a neophyte in the self-publishing business, the first thing I did was to learn of the leaders of the self-publishing industry. I bought their books and attended seminars, even in New York or Las Vegas. By attending such seminars, I tapped their experiences and learned how they were operating their own businesses. Then I used their proven strategies and techniques and created my own tactics and systems to achieve success in my business.

B. *Business Description.* Write something about your business, presenting a summary of your business idea. Know why you think your new or improved idea or approach will work or how it fits into the marketplace. Predict the future of your business.

C. *Business Objectives.* Your business must have a mission. You may wish to help the poor to raise their living standards; participate in the education of children, or help travelers enjoy their vacations. As you can see, profit is not the only thing that you want; you also want to help other people. If you can't help other people, then they can't help you either—to put money in your pocket. As the saying goes, "There's no something for nothing!"

To achieve your mission, your business should have a major goal broken down into minor goals. Then you use strategies to fulfill those objectives to reach your destination.

Write Your Business Plan

II. Products and Services

A. *Products and Services List.* List the products you wish to sell or the services you wish to offer. What will be your major product or service? Secondary product? Minor product? If your products are not yet in production, when will they be available? (See Chapter 11, *Selling Products: An Ideal One-Person Business,* page 99.)

B. *Consumer Benefits.* How will consumers benefit from your business or service? Will your products make their work easier? Will your products make them thinner or healthier? Without benefits, they won't buy your products and services!

C. *Product Uniqueness.* How are your products different from other products? Emphasize their uniqueness in your promotion.

III. Product Development

A. *Manufacturing Process.* If you create or manufacture your products, you'll be a manufacturer. How will your products be manufactured? What raw material will you use? Paper? Plastics? Wood?

B. *Subcontractors.* If you don't manufacture your own products, you must pay those who do manufacture them. Those people and companies have the expertise and facilities to make your products at a lower cost. (See Chapter 14, *Wise Ways to Manage Subcontracting & Partnering,* page 125.)

For instance, if you wish to publish a book, you don't have to buy a printing press. You only must secure the services of a book manufacturer: the printer. If you wish to sell products, you may have them made by people in their homes or by a manufacturing firm that has the necessary tools and facilities to produce them.

C. *Suppliers.* If you are not a manufacturer and you wish to resale products to the general public, you will need a list of suppliers who will furnish the products.

IV. The Market

A. *Target Market.* Where will you sell your products or services? To a *general market* (or *mass market*) or to a *single target* or *a niche market?* Make a survey of the market. (See

Chapter 13, *Savvy Marketing: How to Sell Your Products or Services,* page 113.)

B. *Market Size and Trends.* How large is the market? How crowded is it. Is the current market growing or declining? How will political or economic conditions affect your market, now and in the future?

C. *Market Research.* Before you go into business, you should conduct a market research. Do you think your products or services will sell? Is there a real need for them?.

D. *Marketing Strategy.* How will your products be promoted and sold? Do you intend to use newspaper or magazine advertising? Direct mailings? Radio spot announcements? Mail order? What is your pricing strategy? Estimate your sales and market share for the first three or five years.

E. *Distribution Methods.* Since you are a single-person business owner, *distributors, wholesalers,* and *retailers* are your greatest partners. (See Chapter 15, *Distributors: Your Lifelines to Profits & Growth,* page 135.)

Before you obtain your products, you should know who your distributors will be. Research national, regional, and local distributors. Know the big wholesalers in your particular business. And don't forget the retailers (grocery or discount stores) in your area that can test market your products.

V. The Competition

A. *Major Competitors.* Know your major competitors and their products.

These are usually the large, established companies dominant in the industry. Determine how they market their goods and services. Try to locate segments of the markets they're not serving. Visit their stores as a customer and ask questions about their products.

Know Your Competition

B. *Direct Competitors.* These are small businesses in your industry. How successful are they? Why are they successful? Join the national, state, and local organizations of your industry so that you will know what they're doing and how they're doing it. (See Chapter 24, *Effective & Smart Networking,* page 245.)

Beat the Competition!

VI. Financial Data

A. *Capital Sources.* Where will you get your capital? From your savings? The sale of your stocks? Your spouse? Some of your relatives?

B. *Operating Costs.* Operating costs include start-up costs and expenses incurred while operating your business. These costs are *fixed or indirect costs* and *variable* or *fluctuating costs.*

1. *Fixed costs* or *indirect costs* are expenses not directly related to the production of your products (*fixed or indirect costs*). They may include rent, utilities, license fees (which you incur whether you have customers or not), and office expenses.

2. *Variable or fluctuating costs* are the expenses of producing and selling your products (*costs of goods* plus *direct expenses*). Such expenses are inventory purchases, packaging, freight, commissions, etc.

C. *Projected Income.* Expenditures are easier to calculate than projected income. Some books suggest that in calculating projected income, you should prepare a profit-and-loss statement and a cash flow chart that includes your monthly projected sales. But that's easier said than done, particularly if you engage in business on a part-time basis with a limited capital.

As you probably know, most single-person businesses are part-time before they graduate to full-time. Naturally, you must estimate your monthly or yearly income, because without seeing future income, you're not likely to start a business. But it's hard to make a cash flow chart when you're just beginning. If you can do it, that's fine, but if you can't, don't be disappointed. However, it's necessary to make a calculated guess on how much money you should expect to earn in a month or a year. As you go down the road, however, you must eventually prepare a cash flow chart and a profit-and-loss statement at least at the end of every quarter. (See Chapter 23, *Smart Ways to Manage Your Company's Cash Flow,* page 235.)

VII. Operational Plan

A. *Location.* Decide the location of your business. Should it be in the basement? The bedroom? Outside your home?

B. *Organization.* Determine whether your business will be a single-proprietorship, a partnership, or a corporation. (See Chapter 5, *Choosing a Business Structure,* page 33.) Of course, if you intend to be a single-person business owner, you'll have either a single proprietorship or a corporation. Even if you are a single-person business owner, your business can be a corporation—but not a partnership.

C. *Management.* As a one-person business owner, you'll be wearing many hats: owner, general manager, advertising director, finance officer, marketing director, secretary. In short, you're all of them in one person. Of course, you'll make your own decisions.

However, if you're acting as the marketing director and want to do a major promotion, you'll ask the financial officer (another of your roles), "Do we have the money?" Then you may answer your own question, "Not now. We have to wait for some of our accounts receivables to come in."

Hire a Consultant

D. *Consultants.* There are times when you may have some operational problems that you can't solve. Perhaps that will be the time to seek the advice of a consultant in your industry. You may pay consulting fees by the hour or by the project. Before contracting a consultant, be sure you have a written agreement, specifying the exact fee, the specific work to be done, and the time frame in which the work is to be completed.

As much as possible, use professionals in other aspects of your business. (See Chapter 25, *Using Other People's Brains,* page 251.)

E. *Goal Setting.* You should set *long-term, mid-term,* and *short-term goals.* In goal setting, go straight to your long-term goals and work backward to your short-term goals.

1. *Long-term goals* may include strategic and financial plans from *three to five years.* To accomplish these goals, you need to make good operational plans. For instance, when you imagine where your business will be after five years, you can focus your attention on what you have to do to fulfill your dream.

2. Your *mid-term goals* may cover from *one to three years.* They may include plans on how you can launch new products or cover new sales territories—your state or neigh-

boring states and the whole country in general.

3. *Short-term goals* may cover from *one month to one year.* They may include your daily plans and activities.

F. *Goal Deadlines.* You need to set deadlines to accomplish each goal. For example, you may set this goal: "In five years' time, I'll have a yearly income of $100,000 from my business." Be definite in your goals; pinpoint the exact dates when you intend to accomplish your goals and the exact amount of money you plan to accumulate.

Type these goals, with their deadlines of accomplishment on heavy paper stock. Frame and hang it on the wall in your office where you can look at it every day of the year.

Never mind if some people think you're crazy. Never mind if they don't understand what you're doing. Just remember, you're your own boss and you're the one only who knows what you want from life!

This chapter has discussed your practical, but complete, business plan. But remember—it's not cast in stone. It's subject to modifications from time to time, even after you become successful in business.

II. Bottom Line

■ You need a business plan because it's the map you're going to use when you go along the sometimes winding, bumpy road to success.

■ You need this question to answer if you wish to introduce a product or a service: "Who will buy it?"

■ You must know where you will get your capital. From savings? Sale of stocks? Your spouse? Your relatives?

Choosing a Business Structure   5

■ Choosing the right business structure in order to register the name of your business with the proper agency should be made carefully. Registering your company name is the first step to starting your business as soon as possible.

Whether your business is a sole proprietorship, a partnership, or a corporation, it will have an important impact on your business' success. In fact, it can "make" or "break" your business. Each of type of business has its advantages and its disadvantages.

Speaking of statistics, here's how small businesses in the United States were organized in 1991 according to "The State of Small Business: A Report of the President, 1992":

Sole Proprietorships: 14,300,000 (IRS Schedule C)

Partnerships: 1,700,000 (IRS Form 1065)

Corporations: 4,500,000 (IRS Forms 1120 and 1120S)

These figures were based by U.S. Small Business Administration on statistics published by the Internal Revenue Service. (Also see *One-Person Businesses,* page 7.)

As you can see, proprietorships dominate business organizations.

I. Business Structure

Your selection of a business structure should depend on the kind of business you're entering and your current circumstances or situations.

Sole or Single Proprietorship

If your business is a sole proprietorship, you are the only owner and the only employee. Of course, you can hire employees, but since this is a book about businesses run by one person, we'll presume that you are the sole employee.

Sole proprietorship is the simplest and most common form of business ownership. Being the lone owner, you are the only financier and you can do what you want and retain all the profits. You also shoulder all the losses that may incur in your business.

The One-Person Business Owner

Since you are the business, all your personal assets are at risks. For instance, if a customer is taken ill or is hurt by any of your products, he or she can sue you, resulting in damage claims against any and possibly all of your personal assets.

As the sole owner of your business, you must file a tax form, IRS Schedule C or C-EZ, reporting your income or losses. The income is subject to the regular personal income tax (individual rate), the maximum federal tax rate of which was 31 percent of the net in 1992. The losses, if you have any, are deducted from your income from any regular job you may have.

A One-Person Business Operator

Partnerships

Although you probably won't consider this option because you'll be a one-person business owner, we'll discuss it briefly.

A partnership may be composed of two or more persons who agree to form a business for the purpose of receiving profits. Of course, they'll agree to share the losses, too. The profits and losses of the partnership will be divided by an agreed-upon percentage by the partners, depending on their investment and involvement in the business.

Although it is not required by the government, the partners should have a written agreement on the amount of money each of them should invest and how much time each of them should devote to the business.

Perhaps one partner will act as the managing partner and the others may have limited involvement in the business, except in their own expertise and in the amount of money to be invested. In short, you can't just say to your prospective partner: "We're friends, so let's just do it!" Without an agreement, you may later end up disputing a lot of matters. Who knows? You may end up in court, too.

Income and loss from the business are "passed through" to the individual partners and they are taxed at the individual rate, like that in the sole proprietorship.

There are two types of partnerships: the *general partnership* and the *limited*.

General Partnership. As in the sole proprietorship, the partners in a *general partnership* are *not* protected from liability; that is, their personal assets are at risk in case anyone sues the partnership, whether they are creditors or customers.

Limited Partnership. Under the *limited partnership*, the so-called *general partners* are the only ones subject to all legal obligations to the partnership. For this reason, their personal property can be taken or seized as a result of unpaid bills or other liabilities. On the other hand, the other partners, who may be considered as *silent partners,* are liable only to the extent of their investments; therefore, their personnel assets are exempted from seizure for any corporate obligations. The silent partners may be your friends, relatives, or any investors who invest their money in your partnership.

A Form of Partnership

Corporations

There are two types of corporations: the *C-Corporation* (otherwise known as the regular corporation) and the so-called *S-Corporation.*)

When you form a corporation, you're creating a new entity, having all the legal rights of an individual. For instance, it can sue or be sued, or own or sell property.

You can form a corporation even if you're the sole owner and employee. In a corporation, your personal assets are free from any corporate liabilities. This feature of the corporation is the major reason why some people choose to incorporate their businesses.

If you wish to incorporate, you should choose either the C-corporation or the S-corporation.

Both of these corporations protect you from corporate liabilities; that is, your personal assets can't be touched by creditors or damage claimers.

Here are some differences between the two types of corporations:

■ *C-Corporation.* The C-corporation, otherwise known as the regular corporation, is taxed for its corporate earnings, whether profits are distributed or not to you or to other shareholders. Under the current law, the corporate income tax rate is divided into three brackets: a 15-percent rate on the first $50,000 of taxable income, a 25-percent rate on the next $25,000, and a 34-percent rate in income above $75,000. If your one-person corporation can generate a taxable income between $100,000 and $335,000, you'll pay an additional 5-percent surtax. The corporate income tax rate above $335,000 is a flat 34 percent.

If earnings are distributed, they are again subject to your federal personal income tax (up to 31 percent) or any shareholder's personal income tax. That's considered as *double taxation,* and it really is.

The C-corporation, however, *can* pay fringe benefits, such as medical, life, and accident insurance and pension contributions.

These are deductible expenses that can lower your corporation's profit. This fact and the exemption from business liabilities prompt some entrepreneurs to incorporate.

■ *The S-Corporation.* The S-corporation, is not taxed on corporate earnings. Like in partnerships, profits or losses are "passed through" to you or to individual shareholders. In other words, profits are only taxed once at the federal individual rate up to 31 percent. Losses can be deducted immediately from any of your other income, thus lowering your income and tax. (Losses from the C-corporation, on the other hand, are *not* deducted the year they are made; rather they are carried forward, year to year, until they are offset by corporate earnings.)

Furthermore, as in a sole proprietorship, the S-corporation *cannot* pay your insurance premiums (as mentioned above). You can, however, as in sole proprietorship, set up your own retirement plan, such as a Keogh plan.

II. Your Decision

Sole Proprietorship or Corporation? We shall limit the discussion on which type of business to select: a sole proprietorship or a corporation.

Entrepreneurs who are swayed to choose the corporation over sole proprietorship want limited liability. Furthermore, they want to retain the profits in the business to avoid distributions of these earnings, thus avoiding *double taxation* (corporate and personal income taxes).

In fact, some people consider that they can avoid double taxation with a C-corporation by avoiding the distribution of these gains as dividends, especially closely held corporations where the owners control the distribution of profits. They may invest some of the money in the corporation to buy equipment or to expand the business. So a portion or all of the profits may be allocated for the business, provided the purpose is reasonable. In other words, there are certain limits in such a right. For example, the IRS may question whether the amount is to be added to the capital or left untouched in the corporation. The IRS has the power to get hold of these funds by imposing an *accumulated earnings tax,* which imposes a tax on undistributed earnings left in the corporation for no practical reason. As a result, double taxation also occurs.

In a corporation, you *can't* just get any funds anytime. The corporation pays you with a check. Even if you're the sole owner and employee of your corporation, you can't use company checks for payments of personal bills. For instance, your spouse can't just say, "Honey, can you buy this ring with your company check?"

If you run your corporation like a sole proprietorship, getting cash from the corporation, not through your paycheck (salary) or dividend, you're liable to violation of tax laws. Such withdrawal to reduce profits, and therefore taxes, is tantamount to tax fraud. Thus, you may be fined and imprisoned. Moreover, if you run your corporation like that of a sole proprietorship, it may be declared null and void, thus depriving you of the liability protection that you sought.

In other words, such liability protection is questionable, under certain circumstances, if your business is not run as a corporation. You cannot mix personal and corporate matters.

In a recent case, the IRS accused a corporation's owner of taking cash from the business. The business owner, when charged in court, refused to produce his personal and business papers, saying that the IRS could not make him incriminate himself. The court ruled that self-incrimination applies only to personal records. He was ordered to produce his corporate financial documents because a corporation has no right against self-incrimination.

If your business is a sole proprietorship, you can use your company checks to pay personal bills. In fact, you can use your checks to withdraw money from your bank at anytime, and for any amount. (However, if you do that often, you may wake up one morning to learn that your business is out of cash—and out of operation.) This is considered as a *draw* or *a withdrawal*. Such draws, however, are *not* deductible expenses. It's pure common sense, though, that sole proprietorship owners withdraw cash or use checks for personal bills. This is not a violation of the law, provided they are not deducted for income tax purposes and are recorded accordingly.

In choosing between a sole proprietorship and a corporation for your business, you must realize that as a single proprietorship, you have to pay the so-called *self-employment tax*, which at the present time is 13.02 percent of your net income.

But, also, as the owner and only employee of your corporation, you must pay the worker's compensation on your behalf as the employer and the employee. That amounts to 15.02 percent. Therefore, as a proprietorship, you can save 2 percent of the tax.

Here's another important thing. If you receive a salary of $25,000 or $30,000 a year from your corporation, you'll pay a personal income tax for this amount, whether it has profits or losses. It's kind of weird: your corporation loses money and yet you pay an income tax for your salary. And remember, your losses can't be deducted immediately, they are forwarded from year to year. On the other hand, if yours is a sole proprietorship, since you yourself are the business, and you lose money, then you can deduct it at once from your other income.

The Joy of Being Your Own Boss

ADVANTAGES AND DISADVANTAGES OF TYPES OF BUSINESSES

BUSINESS	ADVANTAGES	DISADVANTAGES
Sole Proprietorship	1. Sole owner. 2. Easy to establish. 3. Simple to operate. 4. Simple accounting procedures. 5. Receive all financial profits. 6. Taxed on individual tax rate.	1. No one else to answer to. 2. Responsible for all financial risks/losses. 3. Liabilities unlimited. 4. Assets at risk. 5. Insurance/fringe benefits not deductible for tax purposes. 6. No continuity at death/retirement.
C-Corporation	1. Protection from unlimited liabilities. 2. Can pay for insurance/fringe benefits. 3. Unlimited number of shareholders. 4. Earnings possibly used for equipment/expansion without paying corporate taxes.	1. Costly to form. 2. Double taxation. 3. Regulated and taxed by states. 4. Accounting complex and costly. 5. Losses cannot be subtracted from other income. 6. Losses forwarded, year to year, to offset future profits.
S-Corporation	1. No double taxation. 2. Profits/losses passed to owners or shareholders. 3. Profits taxed on individual tax rate. 4. Losses deducted from other income lowers net income and taxes. 5. Limited liability, only money and property of corporation at risk.	1. Costly to form. 2. Lot of paperwork. 3. Accounting complex and costly. 4. Insurance/fringe benefits payments not tax deductible. 5. Maximum of 35 shareholders. 6. Limited kind of stock purchases. 7. Not recognized by all states; taxed there as regular corporations. 8. Profits cannot be used for expansion without being taxed as earnings.

The Way to Go

Most entrepreneurs start as sole-proprietorships. If their net income is high enough, say from $50,000 to $100,000 a year, they may consider incorporating.

In choosing the right business structure, you may consider the following facts (which are mentioned again for clarification):

■ *Sole Proprietorship.* As a start-up and you expect to operate at a loss for the first year or two, you may consider this option. Losses are deducted immediately from your other income to lower your taxes.

■ *C-Corporation.* If you want protection from business liabilities and want fringe benefits, such as medical and life insurance, and want to flow your profits into buying equipment and expanding without being taxed, a regular corporation may be the choice.

■ *S-Corporation.* An S-corporation has no corporate tax. Profits and losses are passed through to shareholders and earnings are taxed on an individual tax rate. But, like the C-corporation (regular corporation), the S-corporation protects shareholders from unlimited liabilities. If you want to protect your personal assets from any lawsuits and you expect to operate at a loss for the first or year or two, you may consider the S-corporation.

After weighing the advantages and disadvantages of the three options (sole proprietorship, C-corporation and S-corporation), you have to decide which one is best for you. It would be better if you ask the opinion of an accountant or a lawyer on what business structure to select, based on your current circumstances.

The choice is yours, of course.

III. Bottom Line

■ Sole proprietorship is the simplest and most common form of business organization.

■ As a sole proprietorship, you have to pay the so-called *self-employment tax* of about 13.02 percent of your net income. On the other hand, as the owner and only employee of a corporation, you must pay the worker's compensation on your behalf as the employer and the employee, which is about 15.02 percent of the net income.

Home Alone

What's in a Name?   6

■ What's in a name? Why bother thinking about an appropriate name for your business? It's because you must select a suitable and effective name for your enterprise to be able to signify the right image that you want to convey to your customers or clients. Select a name that tells what the company does or offers.

I. Commercial Names

The commercial name of a business is commonly called a *trade name.* Other commercial names are *trademark* and *service mark.*

1. Trade Name

A trade name is given to a sole proprietorship, a partnership, or a corporation. (Example: *Greenhills Carpet Distributors.*) A *trade name* may be a *corporate name*—the name of a corporation that is registered with the secretary of state (or its equivalent in other states). Usually, a corporate name is followed by an identifier, such as *Corp.* or *Inc.* (example: *Chrysler Corporation.*)

Another form of trade name is the *fictitious* or *assumed name* which is used when a sole proprietorship or a partnership uses a name not their own. You can register your fictitious or assumed name with the city, county, or state government, depending on the law in your state. There is a registration fee (the average is $10). Some localities require publication of the business name in a widely circulated newspaper before the name is approved. (Example: *The Corner Bookshop.*)

What's the Name?

41

2. Trademark

A trademark is the name given to a company's product or products. (Example: *Diet Coke*, a product of *Coca-Cola*.)

A Trade Mark

The *trademark*, as well as the *service mark*, is registered with the U.S. Patent and Trademark Office, Box Trademark, Washington, DC 20231. The current registration fee for each trademark or service mark is $175.00.

3. Service Mark

A Service mark is given to the services that a business provides to the public. (Example: *National Bookkeeping Service*.)

While the trade name is the name of the business itself, the product name is the trademark. Many businesses use at least a part of their trade name as their trademark and/or as their service mark.

Service marks and trademarks are sometimes used interchangeably. Symbols and names are called trademarks when they are used for product names and service marks when they are used for marketing goods. For instance, when a business such as *Northeast Typesetting Service* uses its name on a letterhead, a brochure, or a signboard, it uses its trade name as a mark—a service mark.

A trademark or a service mark may consist of a symbol, a word, a picture, a color scheme, initials, etc. In short, it may consist of anyone or a combination of some or all of the above.

According to experts, simple names are better than complex or tricky names for a company or a product. Moreover, choosing the right name for your business is a challenge. In fact, American firms register about a million business names a year, according to Naseem Javed, president of ABC Namebank International, Inc., a New York company that researches trade names. He advises that entrepreneurs choose names that are memorable and distinctive, but which won't pose legal problems.

A Service Mark

Choosing a product name (trademark) is also a challenge. According to David Placek, president of Lexicon

Naming, in Sausalito, California, when naming a product line, one should build equity in one or two names by adding "descriptors" to a root name, such as what McDonald's Corporation does with its products.

It is very important to know that with just a few words, the company name must conjure up a good image which is distinguishable from the competition. In short, a trade name is an ad itself—a marketing tool that will sell your products or services.

II. The Logo

Large businesses spend a lot of money in designing eye-catching, attractive logos to accompany their names. As a single-person business owner, you must do the same. A logo may contain a symbol or a drawing along with the first word or the first letters of each word of the trade name. Study logos created by big companies and you'll have an idea as to what kind of logo you can create.

A Logo

Since it may contain well-designed letters or symbols, you may seek the help of an advertising agency or a commercial artist to create a simple, but easy to remember, logo.

If it isn't possible to get such help, you may design it with the assistance of the print shop where you have your letterhead or calling card printed. Usually, it can be developed from word graphics, using the name or initials of your business along with a symbol or a drawing. For instance, letters or initials (with the same or different kinds of typefaces) can be placed inside a circle, a square, or a triangle. As an example, the "M" in McDonald's represents the golden arch for which it is known.

III. Name Choices

There are several ways you can select your trade name.

1. Entrepreneur's Name

An entrepreneur's name should seldom be used as a trade name. Use your real name only when you're a consultant in a certain field or a well-known person in your community offering your products or services.(Example: *James Richardson's Company.*) The name identifies your name but it doesn't indicate what your business is.

2. Entrepreneur's Name Along with What the Business Does

This type of name denotes who you are and what you do. This is a good choice only if you're known in your community and if you don't expect to expand your business to other states. (Example: *Julia Roberts' Beauty Products.*)

3. Name That Describes the Company's Main Activity

This type of name gives you the opportunity to cite what your business does. (Example: *Statewide Plumbing Service*s.)

4. Made-up Name

This type of name may consist of initials, a word, or a combination of words that you may invent. (Example: *The ABC Company.*) The name doesn't say what it does, but it may indicate a company engaged in various commercial activities. (Another example: *Interstate Real Estate Consultants.*) In this case, the made-up name says what the business does.

IV. Your Business Name

As a one-person business owner, you should avoid using your name unless you are a well-known person or professional. For example, avoid using a trade name such as *John A. Smith's Word-Processing Service.* Of course, if you're a well-known cook with a television show of your own, you may name your business after your name. (Example: *Helen Beltz' Cookbooks.*)

In other words, don't announce to the world that you are a one-person business, especially if you plan to cover the entire country or the entire world as your market. If you engage in an export-import business, you must not reveal that you are a one-person enterprise. You may name it *American Importers-Exporters* instead of *Roy Hamilton's Import-Export Business.* Another example is my business name, *Bookhaus Publishers*; it doesn't say it's a single-person business or a corporation. But by the name itself, people may think that it's a company that publishes books. (The addition of an "s" after publisher indicates that it's a big company.) To cite an example, I received a call from a man who would like to buy one of my books. I answered, "Good morning, this is Bookhaus Publishers."

"Can you connect me to customer service?" the man asked.

"This is customer service. What can I do for you?" I replied.

Then he placed his order.

Once in a while, I receive inquiries from different parts of the world seeking information about my books for publication in their countries. Such inquiries are addressed to the Foreign Rights Department or the Foreign Rights Director, Bookhaus Publishers.

Needless to say, when you have a nice, appropriate name and a good image, the more customers or clients will have trust in your company.

Name Search

After you have decided what name to use, you must check with your county, or several counties in your locality, or with your state fictitious-name registry, to see if there's such a name already. Be sure that the name you use will not have the name of a business that already exists.

To cite an example, I first named my business *Bookhouse,* which I registered with our county. Later on, I discovered that there's a company here in Michigan by that name; it also is engaged in books. Not wanting to completely change my trade name, I changed the "house" to "haus" and added the word "Publishers." Thus, the company became *Bookhaus Publishers.*

In Search of a Name

In some states, fictitious names are registered with a centralized fictitious or assumed names registry. Those names are usually checked against a state list of assumed names before registration. A few states also check fictitious names against the names of corporations and limited partnerships. If yours is a one-person corporation, check your business name with every state of the nation.

Well-Known Names

Also, avoid using well-known commercial names or names of well-known persons as part of your business name. This is to avoid any legal problems that may arise. As an example, if you are in publishing and even if your last name is McMillan, you should not name your business *McMillan's Book Publishing,* because *McMillan's Publishing* (a major

national publisher based in New York) may sue you. Even if your name is Cindy Crawford, you must not use a name such as *Cindy Crawford's Modeling* or Cindy Crawford may see you in court.

After you have selected your name, register it with the proper agency or agencies: city, county, or state government to obtain the necessary permit or license to operate your business.

V. ID Number

All businesses, even one-person businesses, are required to have a federal identification number, called an *employer identification number* (EIN). To obtain this number, file form SS-4 with the Internal Revenue Service. A copy of this form may be acquired from the IRS or your bank.

VI. Bottom Line

■ You should not use your own name as your trade name unless you are a famous person.

■ To have a good image, you should select a name that signifies that it's a big company, not a one-person business.

■ You should select a trade name that tells what the company does or offers.

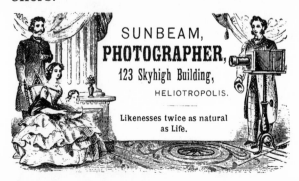

Setting Up Your Office   7

■ Setting up your office in your home is the smartest way to start and run your one-person business. By doing this, you'll save office or shop rent, eliminate travel time, and, most of the time, be with your children (if you have any at home), especially when they are not yet of school age.

Owners of many successful businesses started their operations from a space in their home: attic, bedroom, garage, or basement.

I. First Steps

Zoning Ordinances

Before you establish a home office, visit your city hall or courthouse and learn the local zoning ordinances. Typically, property is zoned in one of four ways: *residential, commercial, industrial,* or *agricultural.*

If you live in a residential area, you find out what types of businesses are allowed to be conducted from homes, with or without restrictions.

For example, in Los Angeles, home-based businesses are banned in residential neighborhoods. The

prohibition covers even professions such as artists, freelance writers, and others who often work from home. But despite this ban, many home businesses exist in the city. In fact, Darryl Fisher, associate zoning administrator in Los Angeles, was quoted in the *Nation's Business* magazine as saying, "Lots of (home-based businesses) are out there, but they're not creating a problem. If they do create problems, people complain, and they're put out of business." However, the city allows employees to work at home and to communicate with the office via computer and modem.

In Chicago, businesses operated from home are technically prohibited. The only home offices allowed are those for professional consultation or emergency treatment. But Graham C. Grady, the city's zoning administrator, was quoted, also in a *Nation's Business* article, as saying, "Lots of people operate businesses regardless of what the ordinance says. It's rarely enforced unless a neighbor complains."

In other communities around the United States, there are movements to revise zoning codes to cope with the times. This is a result of the increase of home-based businesses, due to the wish of parents to try it as a way of balancing career and family.

Estimates of the total number of home-based entrepreneurs vary. *Entrepreneur* magazine puts it at more than 12 million and estimates the growth of the industry at 12 percent yearly. On the other hand, Link Resources, a New York City research and consulting firm, has found out that about 12.1 million Americans operate their businesses from their homes full-time and another 11.7 million work part-time.

Things to Do

If you live in a residential neighborhood where businesses are not allowed, you may choose to operate out of your home and hope no neighbors complain, or move to an area that welcomes home-based businesses, or rent an outside office.

Should you decide to have an office in a restricted residential area, know the penalties and other consequences. It's pure common sense, however, that if you have no business signboard and no 18-wheel trucks or a large number of people coming to your place, none of your neighbors may file a complaint against you. It is best to make product

deliveries through United Parcel Service (UPS) instead of using big trucks. The decision is yours, of course.

II. Where to Set up Office

Now it's time to decide where to find a space in your home for your office.

Kitchen

The kitchen may be a suitable place for business. In fact, many entrepreneurs have worked their way to business success through their "kitchen tables." The beauty of this is that you can work there even if you're cooking or watching television. The disadvantage, however, is that the refrigerator may often call your name, "Come on! Come on!"

(If the kitchen is not your primary place for your endeavor, it may become your secondary office, especially at night, if you don't want to be alone in the attic or the basement.)

Dining Room.

You may have an office space in the dining room, if it's a large one.

Bedroom

You can have an office space in your bedroom, particularly if you're a writer. For instance, when you wake up in the middle of the night and great ideas pop out of your mind, you don't have to go downstairs or upstairs to put your ideas on paper or onto your computer disks.

With a closed door, you'll have peace and tranquility in the bedroom. However, during the day, the bed may often call you and say, "That's enough!"

When you work before midnight, there may be some distractions. If you see your spouse asleep while you're working, you may also be inclined to go to bed, as it's really hard to see him or her asleep while you're still awake.

The Bed May Often Call You

Living Room

Some entrepreneurs use living rooms as their offices. Of course, your office should occupy only a small portion of the living room. There, you can listen to the stereo or watch television. But this is an open space and you'll be distracted by your kids or your spouse and maybe some of their visitors.

Den

If you have a den, perhaps you may convert it into an office. I first had the den as my office. I thought that it would be a good idea to see people coming into my house from where I worked. It was there where I wrote my books and packed orders. Later, however, I found it to be too small for my computer workstation and office supplies.

Under Stairs

In some houses, there may be an office under the first-floor stairway. The disadvantage, however, of using this space as your place of work is that you'll be disturbed when your kids chase each other going up and down the stairs. "Stop it! Stop it!" you may yell.

Lofts

The loft may also be used as an office. A loft, often built under a cathedral ceiling, is an open space, up and away from rest of the living space. It is often used as a bedroom for house-guests.

Closet

A closet is another space you may convert into an office, especially if it's a large one. To have this type of office, install a work surface and some book-shelves. Also, set up a shelf for your computer monitor and a sliding key-board tray. Then place your computer in a suitable location. When you don't use the office, you can close the door and it's out of sight!

Attic

Some people use the attic as an office. However, it's not an ideal place; it's hot in the summer and cold in the winter. It's better to insulate it well.

Basement

The basement is an ideal home office. For instance, when I found that the den was too small for my computer workstation and office supplies, I moved to the basement. I set up my office in a nook, with a five-piece computer workstation (shaped like an L) positioned against two adjoining walls. On the workstation I have two computers (a 386 computer system and an IBM PC, a dot matrix printer, a Hewlett-Packard Laserjet 4 printer, an electric typewriter, a modem, a FAX machine, and a telephone attached to an answering machine. From this space, I work night and day (without any fixed hours). This where I write and typeset my books through my desktop publishing program. I communicate through telephone and other electronic devices with my distributors, wholesalers, and other contacts in my one-person business, covering the whole United States and some other parts of the world.

Garage

The garage, usually attached to the house, may be used as an office by some entrepreneurs, especially if it is for making or assembling products. However, during the winter, it's a freezing place in snowbelt areas and a very hot place in the Deep South.

Library

If you have a library in your house, you may use it also as your office.

Attached or Unattached Office

If you're not comfortable using a space in your house, you may have your office made to order. Make an addition to your house, if you can afford it.

This is Not a Modern Office

III. Office Furniture

Computer Workstation

If you have a computer and other electronic devices, you need to buy a workstation instead of connecting standard office desks. An L-shaped workstation is an ideal choice because it can be positioned against two adjoining walls in a nook in a room or the basement, saving space. A U-shaped, four- or five-piece workstation can be placed against four adjoining walls, depending on the size of the area.

Computer Rack

A computer rack may be installed on the wall or it may have wheels so that it can be moved into the closet or around your office. This holder may consist of a rolling metal stand with surfaces for a monitor and a keyboard and a rack that holds the computer itself on its edge. Or the rack may be installed permanently on the wall.

Open Cart

If you wish, you may buy an open cart with rollers, containing a rack, a desk, and a cabinet. Some open carts can accommodate your computer, monitor, printer and paper. You may move the unit anywhere, anytime, for your convenience.

Computer Cabinet

The computer cabinet, usually with rollers, is similar to the open cart. However, it has some sort of doors hiding the computer processing unit (CPU), the keyboard, the monitor and maybe the printer. The doors are closed when the computer is not in use.

Tables

Table sizes must depend on the size of the area you will have them in.

Chairs

The best working chair for a one-person business owner is the swivel chair with wheels. You can easily maneuver around your office space. It's best to select a chair that can be raised or lowered to whatever height you want.

Don't buy a chair just because it's good looking. Comfort is the name of the game! If you're comfortable with it, then perhaps you should have it. Try to avoid buying chairs by mail. Go to a discount or furniture store and try a swivel chair, lowering or raising it to the height you desire.

(I purchased my first swivel chair by mail. It looked good in the catalog and it had a bargain price, so I bought it. However, it continuously squeaked whenever I moved—squeaks that irritated my ears! So I changed it for a swivel chair that I bought at a local store.)

In addition, you may buy some office chairs for clients if you are in a service-oriented business.

Filing Cabinet

As a start, it's best to buy a standard, four-door steel filing cabinet. If you wish, you may buy the so-called lateral file cabinet which accommodates legal-size folders. You can use this for your permanent files.

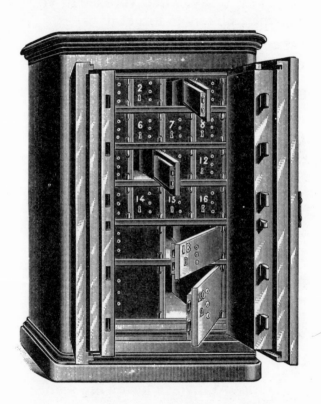

An Old-Type Filing Cabinet

Rolling File Bins

For files you often use, you may obtain all types of sliding and rolling file bins or cabinets. It's easier to retrieve files from folders hung from file bins. Select a simple rolling file bin that glides right under a standard desk.

File Trays

File trays made of steel or plastic are usually placed on top of desks for easy access. Most of the files here are for immediate action.

Bulletin Board

Buy a bulletin board made of cork and hang it on the wall by your desk. There, stick your schedules, price lists, important letters to be answered, and often-called telephone numbers. Needless to say, when you see it, you are not as likely to forget it.

IV. Office Supplies

Stationery

If you have already registered your company's name, you may now order your letterhead stationery, envelopes, and business cards. You may also include a post office box number, which you may rent if you want to get your mail early in the morning. You may have both your residential address and your postal address printed on the stationery, such as Amazon Product Distributors, 5832 Lovers Lane, P.O. Box 312, Fairfax, VA 22033.

Invoices

Standard invoice forms are available in three-, four-, or five-part sets. Generally, they contain the seller's name and address; buyer's name, billing address, and shipping address; date of invoice; date of shipment; method of shipment (USPS Fourth Class Mail, UPS, etc.); invoice number; customer's purchase order number; quantity and description of goods shipped; unit price and total amount, plus shipping charges; and terms of payment (such as Net 30 days or Net 60 days).

Purchase Orders

If you will be ordering products from suppliers, then you need a purchase orders. Also, you'll be receiving purchase orders from customers. Upon receipt, you need to ship the product as soon as possible.

Packing Lists

A packing list, contained in a clear plastic covering, is usually attached to the top or one side of the shipping box or carton. It describes the unit's contents. The packing list forms, in three- or four-part sets, contain information similar to that on the invoice, with the addition of the number of cartons and the name of the shipping company.

Computer Software

If you have a computer, then you purchase software, such as simple accounting software or fulfillment software that will automatically produce invoice and customers' and sales reports, and will adjust your inventory as you prepare each invoice. In my publishing business, I use the fulfillment software called PIIGS, a user-friendly program produced by Upper Access, Inc. With it, I've computerized my operations. You may also produce a spreadsheet that may be used for a simple listing of your sales and expenses if you use a single-entry accounting system. If you use the double-entry system, then buy a sophisticated accounting software.

If you don't yet have a computer, then you can probably buy some simple accounting forms or ledgers at any office supply store.

Other Office Supplies

Also order bond paper, transparent tape, pens, pencils, and other supplies you may need for your office.

Workstations, other furniture, office supplies, and equipment may be purchased in discount stores, such as Office Max, and catalog houses, such as Quill Corporation and The Drawing Board. Other supplies such as invoices, purchase orders, and packing slips, may be bought from these catalog houses. You should prepare your promotional materials. This includes an announcement of the opening of your business.

V. Bottom Line

■ If you live in a residential area, find out what types of businesses are allowed to be conducted from homes, with or without restrictions. If they are not allowed, then move to a community that welcomes home-based businesses. Or rent an outside office.

■ Although you may set up an office in different areas of your home, it's best to have it in the basement, the den, or the library if you have one.

Seed Funds for Small Start-ups from Microloan Lenders

8

■ Let's face reality: You have to spend money to make money. To start a business, you need to raise capital from a few hundred dollars to a few thousand dollars.

I. Loan Sources

Microloan Lenders

Today's seed funds for small start-ups can come from the so-called *microloan lenders*. Of course, you can get money from a savings account, a second mortgage, or an insurance policy, or even a loan using your Keogh money as your collateral.

Bank Loans

There are moneyed banks. But most start-up companies have two things in common: a few assets and a high risk of failure. Banks rarely give loans to start-up businesses. Unless your company has been in business for three to four years (with a history of profits), look for other loan sources instead of banks. So if you're entering a start-up business, you had better not approach the bank unless the chairman of the board is your mother-in-law. Of course, even that relation-

ship is not a guarantee that you'll get a bank loan!

But if your company has been in business a few years and you need money for expansion, for inventory, or for buying equipment, then you may try the banks, submitting a business plan with details on how you plan to repay the loan.

As a new one-person business owner, you may try the so-called *microenterprise* groups that offer support and modest loans to low- and moderate-income individuals who want to start or expand a business.

Microenterprise Groups

More than one hundred micro-enterprise agencies have been formed throughout the country in the past several years, and more are being formed every year. The intention of these microenterprises is to give management and financial support to disadvantaged entrepreneurs—among them, women, low-income groups, welfare recipients, and minorities. They give loans from a few hundred dollars to a few thousand dollars.

Case History

Here's an example of how a woman was helped by one of these groups. Let's just name her Michelle Brooks.

Brooks, who lost a job when her boss closed the day-care center where she was working, wanted to establish a day-care center in a former church building in a Maine city. However, with train tracks running a few yards behind the back lawn of the church, she needed money to build a fence between the yard and the railroad. She also wanted to purchase a swing set.

So Brooks tried to obtain a loan from local banks and credit unions. But none of them would grant her a loan.

Then she approached one of the agencies offering microbusiness programs. She was able to get a $1,500 loan at 12-percent interest, enabling her to open the day-care center.

Most of these microenterprise groups get their funding from private and public sources.

The Origin of Microloans

Previously, the U.S. Government had given $75 million a year to fund such microloan programs in other parts of the world through its AID program.

Then microenterprise agencies, funded by grants from foundations, sprouted up in different parts of the country. Many more are in the planning stage.

The SBA Microloan Program

In June 1992, the Small Business Administration (SBA) launched a 5-year demonstration project to provide $75 million in funds to 47 existing nonprofit microloan agencies that have been in business for at least a

year. The purpose, is of course, to provide loans to new and fledgling entrepreneurs who have no access to conventional loans from banks and other funding institutions. While conventional loans are given based on collateral, equity, credit history, or some business success, microloans are based on a belief in the borrowers' character and integrity and the soundness of their business ideas.

"Home-based businesses are most likely to benefit from this type of loan," Mike Stamler of the SBA public affairs office was quoted to have said.

Individual or Group Loans

Some agencies give only loans to individuals; some others to groups only. Still, others grant loans to both individuals and particular groups. With regard to so-called groups of entrepreneurs, they are formed so that they can network and help each other. Members of a group are granted loans one at a time.

Usually, loans range from $250 to $50,000, the average of which is about $7,000. In some instances, small loans start at $500, with the tendency of increasing it with each successful payback. Interests range from 5 to 16 percent. The time allowed for paying off loans ranges from 3 months to 6 years.

Technical Assistance

Loans are not the only the help provided. Most programs give technical assistance in the form of individual counselling, seminars, and courses. Some agencies require or recommend the completion of a training program before a loan is given. Usually, the loans given are for renovation, working capital, supplies, inventory, and equipment. Some microenterprise groups give only technical assistance in the form of advice or a business training program.

Among businesses granted loans are desktop publishing, day care, computer training, and tax services.

The SBA increased its microloan program to 110 lenders in 1993. These microenterprise agencies give priority to businesses in their local territories.

II. The Bottom Line

■ Banks rarely give loans to start-up business. So unless your company has been in business for three to four years (with a history of profits), look for other loan sources instead of the banks.

■ Microloan agencies are the right sources for possible start-up funds. So look for the microloan lenders in your locality. Call or write the agencies and inquire about who are eligible to receive microloans.

■ If there's no microloan agency in your locality listed in the following directory, call a small-business center in your state to locate an agency that might have recently been formed or is about to be organized.

Directory of Microloan Lenders

Community Enterprise
    Development Corp. of Alaska
1577 C St., Ste. 304
Anchorage, AK 99501
(907) 274-5400

The Arkansas Enterprise Group
605 Main St., Ste. 203
Arkadelphia, AR 71923
(501) 246-9739

Good Faith Fund
400 Main St., Ste. 118
Pine Bluff, AR 71601
(501) 535-6233

Chicanos Por La Causa, Inc.
501 W. Pache
Phoenix, AZ 85003
(612) 646-3808

Micro Industry Credit
    Rural Organization
802 E. 46th St.
Tucson, AZ 85713
(602) 622-3553

P.P.E.P. Housing
    Development Corporation
Micro Industry Credit Rural
    Organization
802 East 46th St.
Tucson, AZ 85713
(602) 622-3553; (602) 622-1480

Areta Economic Development
    Corp.
100 Ericson Ct., Ste. 100
Arcata, CA 95521
(707) 822-4616

The Center for Southeast Asian
   Refugee Resettlement
875 O'Farrell St.
San Francisco, CA 94109
(415) 855-2743
Coalition for Women's
   Economic Development

   (CWED)
315 W. Ninth St., #705
Los Angeles, CA 90015
(213) 489-4005

Community Ventures, Inc.
   Child Care Revolving Loan
   Program
512 Front St.
Santa Cruz, CA 95060
(408) 425-7708

Santa Cruz Community
   Credit Union
Community Development
   Loan Program
512 Front St.
Santa Cruz, CA 95060
(408) 425-7708

San Francisco Mayor's Office
   of Community Development
Self-Employment and Economic
   Development Program
10 United Nations Plaza, Ste. 600
San Francisco, CA 94102
(415) 554-8765

Self-Employment and Enterprise
   Development Program
10 United Nations Plaza, Ste. 600
San Francisco, CA 94102
(415) 554-8765

Valley Small Business
   Development Corp.
955 N St.
Fresno, CA 93721
(209) 268-0166

The WEST Company
   Women's Economic Self-
   Sufficiency Training
413 North State St.
Ukiah, CA 95482
(707) 462-2348

The West Enterprise Center
367 North State Street, Ste. 206
Ikiah, CA 95482
(707) 468-3553

Women's Economic Growth
325 Miner St.
P.O. Box 391
Yreka, CA 96097
(916) 842-1571
and
423 Main Street
P.O. Box 605
Etna, CA 96027
(916) 467-3100

Women Entrepreneurs
   Self-Employment Training
   Opportunities
445 West Weber St., Ste. 140
Stockton, CA 95203
(204) 467-4803

Women's Initiative for
   Self-Employment (WISE)
P.O. Box 192145
San Francisco, CA 94119-2145
(415) 624-3351

Greater Denver Local
   Development Corp.
P.O. Box 2135
Denver, CO 80201-2135
(303) 296-9535

Mi Casa Resource
   Center for Women
The Business Center for Women
571 Galapago St.
Denver, CO 80204
(303) 573-1302

Office of Business/Small Business
    Center
Colorado Leading Edge
1625 Broadway, Ste. 1710
Denver, CO 80224
(303) 892-3840

Cooperative Fund of
    New England
108 Kenyon St.
Hartford, CT 06105
(203) 523-4305

Greater Hartford Business
    Development Center, Inc.
15 Lewis Street
Room 204
Hartford, CT 06103
(203)-527-1301

Hartford College for Women
    Entrepreneurial Center for
    Women
50 Elizabeth St.
Hartford, CT 06105
(203) 236-1215

Community Equity
    Investments Inc.
302 N. Barcelona St.
Pensacola, FL 32501

Greater Atlanta Small Business
    Project
The Microloan Program
10 Park Place St. Ste. 305
Atlanta, GA 30303
(404) 659-5955

Small Business Assistance Corp.
31 W. Congress, Ste. 100
Savannah, GA 31401
(912) 232-4700

Panhandle Area Council
11100 Airport Dr.
Hayden, ID 83835
(208) 772-0584

Institute for Social and Economic
    Development
The Economic Development
    Council for the
    Peoria Area
124 SW Adams
Peoria, IL 61602
(309) 676-7500

The Neighborhood Institute
1750 E. 71st St.
Chicago, IL 60649
(312) 684-4610
Women's Economic Ventures
    Enterprise
229 16th St.
Rock Island, IL 61201
(309) 788-9793

Women's Self-Employment
    Project
Entrepreneurial Training Program
    Group Lending Program
166 West Washington, Ste. 730
Chicago, IL 60613

YWCA
Women's Economic
Ventures Enterprise (WEVE)
229 16th Street
Rock Island, IL 61201
(309) 788-9793

Eastside Community
    Investment, Inc.
Self-Employment Loan Fund
26 N. Arsenal St.
Indianapolis, IN 46201
(317) 637-7300

Institute for Social and
    Economic Development
    (ISED)
1901 Broadway, Suite 313
Iowa City, IA 52240
(319) 338-2331

Iowa Department of
    Economic Development
Self-Employment Loan
Program
200 East Grand Ave.
Des Moines, IA 50309

Siouxland Economic
    Development Corp.
400 Orpheum Electric Bldg.
Sioux City, IA 51101
(712) 279-6286

Human/Economic Appalachian
    Development Corporation
HEAD Community Loan Fund
P.O. Box 504
Berea, KY 40403
(606) 986-3283

Kentucky Highlands
    Investment Corp.
P.O. Box 1738
London, KY 40743
(606) 864-5175

Aroostock County Action
    Program, Inc.
Maine Job Start Program
P.O. Box 1116
Presque, ME 04769
(207) 764-3721

Coastal Enterprises, Inc.
Water St.
P.O. Box 268
Wiscasset, ME 04578
(207) 882-7552

Council for Economic
and Business
    Opportunity
800 N. Charles St.,
Suite 300
Baltimore, MD 21201
(401) 576-2326

ACCION International
130 Prospect St.
Cambridge, MA 02139
(617) 492-4930

Hilltown Community
    Development Corporation
Hilltown Enterprise Fund
P.O. Box 17
Chesterfield, MA 01012
(413) 296-4536

Massachusetts Department of
    Employment and Training
The Enterprise Project
19 Stanford St.
4th Floor, Hurkey Bldg.
Boston, MA 02114
(617) 727-1826

Neighborhood Reinvestment Corp.
Commercial and Economic
    Development Department
Neighborhood Enterprise Center
    Program
80 Boylston St. Ste. 1207
Boston, MA 02116
(617) 565-8240

Valley Community
    Development Corporation
Valley CDC Enterprise Fund
16 Armory St.
Northampton, MA 01060
(413) 586-5855

The Western Massachusetts
    Enterprise Fund
324 Wells St.
Greenfield, MA 01301
(413) 774-7204

Working Capital/ICCD
99 Bishop Richard Allen Dr.
Cambridge, MA 02139
(617) 576-8620

Ann Arbor Community
    Development Association
2008 Hogback Road, Ste 2A
Ann Arbor, MI 48105
(313) 677-1400

Ann Arbor Community
    Development Corporation
Women's Initiative For
    Self-Employment
815 Taylor
Ann Arbor, MI 48105
(313) 769-7573

Grand Rapids Opportunities
    for Women
233 East Fulton,
Ste. 108
Grand Rapids, MI 49503
(616) 458-3404

Northern Economic
    Initiatives Corporation
Small Business Development
 Center
1500 Wilkinson
Marquette, MI 49855-5367
(906) 227-2406

Minneapolis Consortium
    of Nonprofit Developers, Inc.
2600 E. Franklin Ave.
Minneapolis, MN 55406

Northeast Entrepreneur
Fund, Inc.
Olcott Plaza
820 Ninth St. N.
Virginia, MN 55792
(218) 749-4191

Northwest Minnesota
Initiative Fund
722 Paul Bunyan Dr., NW
Bemidji, MN 56601
(218) 759-2057

Women Venture
Midtown Commons
2324 University Ave.
St. Paul, MN 55104
(612) 646-3808

Delta Foundation
819 Main St.
Greenville, MS 38701
(601) 335-5291

Friends of Children of
    Mississippi,
    Head Start
Self-Employment Investment
    Demonstration
650 East Peace Street
Canton, MS 39046
(601) 859-5553

Green Hills Rural Development
    Revolving Loan Fund
909 Main St.
Trenton, MO 64683
(816) 359-5086
(816) 359-5086

Neighborhood Housing
    Service of Jackson
1066 Pecan Park Cir.
Jackson, MS 39209
(601) 355-5012

Billings Area
    Business Incubator
SBA & Montana Small
    Business Development
    Center
Capital Opportunities
    Loan Center
U.S. Department of Defense
    Procurement Tech Assistance
    Center
P.O. Box 7213
Billings, MT 59103
(406) 245-9989

Human Resource Development
   Council/
Capital Opportunities
321 E. Main
Posseman, MT 59715
(406) 587-4486

Women's Opportunity and
   Resource Development
Women's Economic
   Development Group
127 North Higgins,
3rd Floor
Missoula, MT 59802
(406) 543-3550

Center for Rural Affairs
Rural Enterprise Assistance
   Project
P.O. Box 405
Walthill, NE 68067
(402) 846-5428

Institute for Cooperative
   Community Development
2500 N. River Rd.
Manchester, NH 03106
(603) 644-3101

Working Capital
2500 North River Rd.
Manchester, NH 03106
(603) 644-3124;
MA (617) 547-9109

New Jersey Community
   Loan Fund
126 North Montgomery St.
Trenton, NJ 08608
(609) 989-7766

Ganados Del Valle
P.O. Box 118
Los Ojos, NM 87551
(505) 588-7896/
(505) 588-7231

Women's Economic
Self-Sufficiency Team
(WESST Corp.)
414 Silver SW
Albuquerque, NM 87102
(505) 848-4760

Adironadack Economic
   Development Corp.
30 Main St.
Saranac Lake, NY 12983
(518) 891-5523

Alternatives Federal Credit Union
301 West State St.
Ithaca, NY 14850
(607) 273-4666

Hudson Development Corp.
444 Warren St.
Hudson, NY 12534
(518) 828-3373

National Federation of
   Community Dev. Credit Union
Business Lending Program
59 John St., 8th Floor
New York, NY 10038
(212) 513-7191

Opportunity Resource Institute
Minority and Women Revolving
   Loan Trust Fund Program
863 Prospect Ave.
Bronx, NY 10459
(718) 328-1356

Rural Opportunities Inc.
339 East Ave., Ste. 401
Rochester, NY 14624
(716) 546-7180

Center for Community Self-Help
Self-Help Credit Union
409 East Chapel Hill St.
Durham, NC 27701
(919) 683-3016

Mountain Microenterprise
   Fund
29 1/2 Page Ave.
Asheville, NC 28801
(704) 253-2834

The North Carolina Rural
   Economic
   Development Center
4 N. Blount St.
Raleigh, NC 27601

Self-Help Ventures Fund
Box 3619
Durham, NC 27702
(919) 683-3016

Athens Small Business
Center, Inc.
900 E. State St.
Athens, OH 45701

Women's Economic Assistance
   Ventures
100 Corry Street
Yellow Springs, OH 45387
(513) 767-2667

Hamilton County
   Development Co., Inc.
1776 Mentor Ave.
Cincinnati, OH 45212

Women's Economic Assistance
   Ventures
105 West North College Street
P.O. Box 512
Yellow Springs, OH 45387
(603) 767-2667

Women's Entrepreneurial
   Growth Organization
P.O. Box 544
Akron, OH 44309
(216) 535-9346

Cherokee Community Loan Fund
218 South Musokee
Tahlequah, OK 74464
(918) 456-0765

Economic Opportunity
   & Training Center
Self-Employment Training
Jane Building, Ste. 3D
116 North Washington Ave.
Scranton, PA 18503

Elmwood Neighborhood
Housing Services
9 Atlantic Ave.
Providence, RI 02907
(401) 461-4111

The Charleston Citywide Local
   Development Corp.
496 King St.
Charleston, SC 29403
(803) 724-3796

The Lakota Fund
Circle Banking Project
P.O. Box 340
Kyle, SD 57752
(605) 455-2500

Northeast South Dakota
   Energy Conservation Corp.
414 E. Third Ave.
Sisseton, SD 57262
(605) 698-7654

Southern Dallas
   Development Corp.
1201 Griffen St. W.
Dallas, TX 75215
(214) 428-7332

First National Development
   Institute
Navajo/Shiprock Chapter
Lakota Fund
Cherokee Circle Bank
69 Kelley Rd.
Falmouth, VA 22405
(703) 371-5615

Central Vermont Community
    Action Council
15 Ayers St.
Barre, VT 05641
(802) 479-1053

City of Burlington Community
    and Economic Development
    Office
Burlington Revolving
    Loan Program
Room 32, City Hall
Burlington, VT 05401
(802) 865-7144

Northern Community
    Investment Corp.
P.O. Box 904
St. Johnsbury, VT 05819
(802) 748-5101

Vermont Office of
    Economic Opportunity
Vermont Job Start
103 South Main St.
Waterbury, VT 05671-1801
(802) 241-2450

First Nations Development
    Institute
69 Kelly Road
Falmouth, VA 22405
(703) 371-5615

Greater Spokane Business
    Development Association
Spokane Area Small Business
    Loan Program
City Hall, Room 250
W. 808 Spokane Falls Blvd.
Spokane, WA 99201
(509) 625-6325

Private Industry Council
    of Snohomish County
DBA Down Home Washington
    and Inter City Entrepreneurial
    Training Program
917 134th St. SW
Everett, WA 98204
(206) 743-9669

U.S. Department of Labor/
Unemployment Demonstration
    Work Group
Unemployment Ins.
Self-employment Demonstration
Washington SEED Project and
    Massachusetts Enterprise
    Project
200 Constitution Ave., N.W.
Room S-4231
Washington, DC 20210
(202) 535-0208

Advocap, Inc.
19 W. First St.
Fond du Lac, WI 54935
(414) 922-7760

CAP Services, Inc.
The Self-Employment Project
5499 Highway 10, East
Stevens Point, WI 54481
(715) 345-5208

Impact Seven
100 Digital Dr.
Clear Lake, WI 54005
(715) 263-2532

Menominee Indian
    Tribe of Wisconsin
Menominee Revolving Loan Fund
P.O. Box 397
Keshena, WI
(715) 799-5141

Northwest Side Community
    Development Corp.
5150 N. 32nd St.
Milwaukee, WI 53209
(414) 438-8310

Women's Business Initiative
120 N. Broadway, Ste.G9
Milwaukee, WI 53202
(414) 277-7004

Northern Arapahoe Tribal
    Credit Program
Credit Committee
P.O. Box 889
Fort Washakie, WY
(307) 332-7744/3059

9
Smart Technology: The Effective Tool in a One-Person Business

■ As an entrepreneur, it's possible to start a business and succeed with only two office equipments: a typewriter and a telephone. However, it will be an uphill battle. To be a real success as a one-person business owner, you must use today's smart technology.

In other words, your home office must be wired for telecommunications and computer functions.

Today's advanced technology includes a computer, a modem, a fax machine, a fax/modem, a voice mail machine (and/or any other answering machines) and telephones.

With all these pieces of equipment, you can get in touch with your customers, contacts, and distributors in New York, Paris, London, or Manila.

I. Computers

The computer is one of the most important equipments you'll need. Since technology is improved at a very fast phase, think carefully about what kind of computer you'll buy and how powerful it should be. (See Chapter 10, *Choosing the Right Computer*, page 79.)

II. Telephone Lines

You'll use your telephone lines in many ways in your business.

Voice and Fax Lines

You'll need at least two business telephone lines if you want to take advantage of smart technology. Of course, a separate residential telephone is also needed so that your business phone bills will be separated from your family telephone bills. Some people want three telephone lines installed: two for voice communications and one for the fax machine and modem.

Two Lines. Usually, when you have two telephone lines, one line will be for all voice communications and the other line will be for a stand-alone fax machine, which can also be used for modem transmissions. A stand-alone fax machine is very important because, even while you're using the other line, the fax machine can receive messages 24 hours a day. (Yes, even late at night, I've received purchase orders and messages from dealers and customers.)

The trouble with having only two lines is that while you're using the first line (and the other line is hooked to the stand-alone fax machine), no calls can come in. A simple remedy is to have "call waiting" on your first line. That is, while you're talking on the telephone, you can at least acknowledge the call and receive the message.

Three Lines. Some entrepreneurs prefer three telephone lines: two for voice communications and one for the fax machine and modem.

Even if you have two lines for voice communications, the caller oftentimes calls the first line. So when you're using it and there's another incoming call, the caller can't come through and will receive busy signals. One remedy is to have the second line hooked up as a "hunter" by your telephone company. In that way, calls coming in on a busy *line one* hunt for and "roll over" to *line two* automatically.

Another step you should take if you want two "incoming call" lines (and you have only two lines; one for voice communications and the other for fax or modem) is to acquire a fax machine that offers automatic switching between fax and voice communications.

Answering Machines

As a one-person business owner, you'll need an answering machine. It is the most common telephone peripheral and acts your "secretary." Usually, the message of an answering machine is something like this: "You have reached _____(name of your company). We can't come to the telephone right now, but if you'll leave your name, telephone number, and message, we'll get back to you as soon as possible. Thank you." (If the machine has the time and date feature, the answering machine records the time and day of each message, such as: "Thursday, 9 p.m. End of messages."

Answering Machine Types. There are two kinds of answering machines: a stand-alone machine and a machine integrated into the telephone itself.

The advantage of a stand-alone answering machine is that you can move it to another line, should you wish to do so. (If you're in the office and there's a call, you can answer the telephone before the answering machine picks it up.) On the other hand, if your desk space is limited, you can purchase the smaller, integrated answering machine-telephone combination.

Answering Machine Features. Today's answering machines have different features, such as call screening, toll saver, display message, and ring selection.

Also, you can choose a machine that can let you turn it on and off, change announcements, or play, save, and erase messages, even from a remote location.

Voice-Mail

A voice-mail service from your local telephone company is preferable to "call waiting." If your telephones are busy, the caller receives a recorded message and is asked to leave a message in one of several "mailboxes."

You can retrieve the messages by punching in some codes.

Voice mail, a smart message system, provides an answering machine with a brain. As a computer-linked system, voice mail is used for receiving, sending, storing, and retrieving telephone messages.

Mail Boxes. If you're out of the office, you can call in to the voice-mail system to retrieve any messages in the "mail boxes."

For instance, when a customer asks for information about a product, the voice mail can direct the caller to press a certain number and receive pre-recorded information about the product with regard to price, availability, etc., or the caller can leave a message.

How It Works. Usually, a voice-mail system operates this way:

"You've reached (company name). If you wish to talk with a person, press 1; to receive information about our products, press 2; to talk to the manager, press 3; to leave a message, press 4; etc.

Voice-mail systems attached to a telephone switchboard that connects all phones in a company or another principal unit with outside lines are the most expensive systems.

AT&T Mini-Voice Mail. An example of an answering machine that can serve as a voice mail instrument is AT&T's Digital Answering System Speakerphone 1545.

Among the feature are:

■ *Handset Playback and Record.* It allows privacy because you can use the telephone handset to listen to the messages, as well as to record the outgoing announcement.

■ *Time/Day Stamp.* It announces the time and day of each message during playback.

■ *Multiple Outgoing Announcements.* It provides options for primary outgoing announcements. It allows the use of a pre-recorded announcement or records personalized greetings, including an announce-only message. It also allows the flexibility of changing the announcement quickly and easily at the system or by remote control.

■ *Two-Way Call Recording.* It records both sides of a telephone conversation.

■ *Call Intercept.* It stops outgoing announcement when any phone is picked up on that line, allowing that person to take the call.

This AT&T's tapeless digital technology system really ensures consistent recording quality. It is an ideal answering system for a one-person business.

AT & T Digital Answering System Speakerphone 1545

It has four individual voice mailboxes: 1, 2, 3, and 4. It allows callers to leave separate messages for up to four people. Each of the voice mailboxes allows for a personal outgoing announcements. At least three of the mailboxes can also be used for announcements (such as product or ordering information) and other purposes.

You can use the first mailbox for your so-called primary announcement and other mail boxes for other announcement. Any caller can leave a message in each of the four mail boxes unless, of course, one or two of them are used for announcement only.

For instance, in mailbox 1 you may record your primary announcement, such as:

"Hello. This is Import International Products. No one is available to take your call right now. If you're calling from a touch-tone phone and would like information about our products, press 2; to order our products as a distributor or as a dealer, press 3; to order products as a retail customer, press 4; and to leave a message with your name and phone number, please wait for the beep. Thank you."

If you don't answer the phone after three or four rings (depending on your choice of number of rings), the above announcement will be heard by the caller. So if you're out of the office, the callers may choose to press any of the mailboxes, depending on their purpose for calling you.

As you can see, with this machine, you can provide information about your products or services, and any of the mailboxes can record all orders

from your distributors, wholesalers, dealers, and retail customers.

(I bought this AT&T answering machine for $199.96 from an AT&T dealer in August 1993.)

If you wish information about this device, write to:

AT&T Consumer Products
5 Woodhollow Road
Parsippahy, NJ 07054

PC-Based Mail Voice. The less expensive systems are PC-based. They are priced from a few hundred dollars to a couple of thousand dollars. One of the least expensive ones that can be used by a one-person business is The Complete Answering Machine.

For information, write or call:

The Complete PC
983 Concourse Dr.
San Jose, CA 905131,
(408) 434-0145, (800) 229-1753.

This sophisticated system is a board that plugs into a personal computer. It's simple to operate and doesn't require a service technician.

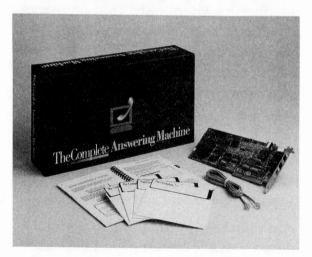

The Complete Answering Machine

Features. Some of the advantages of The Complete Answering Machine follow:

■ Presents a professional image and improves customer service with high-quality voice mail.

■ Offers product or service information to your customers.

■ Records customized greetings and leaves messages for important callers.

■ Keeps messages private and organized with 999 password-protected mailboxes.

■ Forwards messages to another location.

■ Gives message retrieval by remote control by using a touch-tone phone.

■ Does all this and more while your PC is running other applications.

Of course, there are other models of voice mail systems that you can choose.

In spite of the advantages of voice mail, there are, however, many tales about frustrations with some of these automated telephone services. Here's a story that was published in a local newspaper. The message was told to the newspaper's (what else?) voice-mail system.

"My worst experience was trying to order a part," the caller told the newspaper machine.

"I had to make a selection, listen to a recording, make another selection, listen to another recording and then spell out my name by numbers and give the last four digits of my phone number. I thought I was doing pretty good, but then nothing happened. I waited a while and then a phone started to ring, and I was still waiting and then a recording came on and a voice said, 'Sorry, your part is not in stock.'

"And then I waited for someone to come on the line and she said, 'Let me see, I'll have to transfer you,' and she punched in something else and the phone rang. It was a funeral home. I thought, 'I'm dead.'"

III. Cellular Phones

More than 70 years ago, police began to use two-way radios. In the 1940s, two-way radio technology became available in the form of the first private car phones. But it was only in the 1980s, with the rising of computer technology, that the cellular phones began to be widely used.

Types of Cellular Phones

Nowadays, the three types of cellular phones are *mobile, transportable,* and *portable.*

The Mobile Cellular Phone. The mobile cellular phone consists of three parts: *electronics, antenna,* and *handset.* The electronic system, contained in a box, is usually mounted in the car's trunk, while the antenna is glass-mounted to the back window or is roof-mounted. The handset is typically located between the front passenger seats.

The Transportable Cellular Phone. Many of the features of the mobile phone are found in the transportable phone. The only difference is that this type of cellular phone is moved from place to place. Contained in a single carrying case, the transportable phone consists of a 3-watt transceiver, rechargeable batteries, and an antenna. Sometimes, the transportable phone is simply called the "bag phone" because it is contained in a bag.

The following few basic features are found in almost all mobile and transportable phones:

1. An LCD or LED display that indicates the phone number you're calling, the transmission-signal strength, the elapsed time of the call in progress, and other information.

2. An illuminated dialing keypad and the display for night use.

3. A volume control on the earpiece volume.

4. A mute button, multiple call-timers, a redial function, a scratch-pad memory, and an electronic lock with password protection (to avoid any unauthorized use).

The Portable Cellular Phone. Today's portable cellular phones weigh as little as 6 to 14 ounces, including the battery. However, a few older models are heavier.

The transceiver power of the portable cellular phone is reduced from 3 watts to as little as.6 watts. In a sense, a portable's battery power often lasts longer than the older transportable type. However, the drawback is that you won't have the range of a full-time watt mobile phone. There are instances that you may be disconnected. At other times, you may suffer from excessive static. However, a portable phone may be of good use

in areas with flat surroundings, such as cities with closely spaced "cells."

However, many of the same features in the mobile cellular phone are also found in the portable phone, except radio mute, horn alert, one-touch dialing, electronic lock, and alphanumeric memory.

An example of portable cellular phones is the AT&T Portable Cellular Telephone 3760.

AT&T Portable Celullar Telephone 3760

How Cellular Works

The cellular divides a city into small areas called "cells." In miniature, each cell is a little bit like one of the old two-radio systems. It has its own low-powered transmitting and receiving equipment. This system, simply known as "cells site equipment," serves a particular area. If you are a subscriber and you move from cell to cell, you are electronically transferred from one lot of cell site equipment to another.

Carriers

If you want to use a cellular phone, you need to obtain the services of a carrier. Metropolitan areas are usually assigned to two carriers: a wireline carrier, which is affiliated with the local telephone company; and a non-wireline carrier, which is not affiliated with the local telephone company. The non-wireline carrier may or may not be associated with a long-distance telephone company or with an out-of-state local phone company.

Prices for cellular service vary from area to area. Usually, the fee is from $15 to $60 per month for basic service. Each local call may cost you an additional 20 to 80 cents per minute. You'll be charged extra for long-distance calls.

IV. Beepers

Beepers are small, portable electronic devices used to contact people for messages. Once the exclusive use of doctors, more and more people, especially entrepreneurs, now use beepers. They are very important communications tools, particularly for service-oriented entrepreneurs.

When there's a message for the owner, the beeper beeps. That's why it's called a *beeper*. It is also known as a *pager*. Usually worn around the waist, the beeper relays messages. For instance, the beeper may relay messages, such as "We'll meet at the same place, same time tomorrow," or "Come home and get me!" or "I love you always, darling!"

How the Beeper Works

You can lease or buy a beeper from a local or national paging company or from any other outlet. You can probably find paging companies listed in your local telephone book's Yellow Pages.

Wherever you buy your beeper, you need to subscribe to a paging company to activate the device. Paging companies charge a monthly fee, which varies, depending on the location, coverage, or service type. Most services charge fees from $15 to $25 per month for a standard model and local service. (These charges, are of course, subject to change.) If you buy the beeper, the monthly service charge drops.

Some people need only a local service. However, others may need a regional or a nationwide service. For instance, for a regional service (usually within a U.S. time zone), the charge is about $25 per month if you own the beeper, approximately $45 if you lease.

Types of Beepers

Beepers are of different kinds. The following paragraphs describe the basic types.

Numerical or Digital Display This is the most popular type of beeper. Displaying a number of up to 20 digits on a small screen, this model emits a tone or a silent vibration. It doesn't say, "If you need to talk to a computer, press 1 or if you need to go to sleep, go home." It merely indicates a phone number or a private code (for instance, the digit "4" which may mean "The deal is approved!"

Alphanumeric Display. This is the most advanced type of beeper. Displaying up to 6,400 characters (both numbers and letters), the owner may receive a full message without a telephone.

Tone and Voice. When you receive a message on this type of beeper, you simply push a button and you hear a message, such as, "Come and see me!" The message plays only once; then it's gone with the wind. So better buy a model with a "memory" if you want a message to be repeated.

Tone Only. This is the simplest type of beeper. Tone only beepers are used mostly with voice mail that answers calls with your own voice. These beepers simply page you to let you know that you have a message.

V. Modems

Modems enable computers to communicate with other computers and online databases.

A computer is a digital device. By turning on or off a series of electronic switches, it can accomplish many functions. On the other hand, the telephone system is an analog device with the ability to transmit different sounds and tones of the human voice.

A bridge between digital and analog signals, a modem can convert on-and-off digital data into an analog signal by modulating the frequency of an electronic wave. This process is similar to that used by FM radio stations.

Telecommunications Software

Connected to your computer and a a telephone line, you can use your modem to transmit and receive data. Needless to say, a modem provides a faster and more efficient means of telecommunications. However, you must also have communications software to be able to use your modem.

Speeds

Speeds of modems are measured in bauds. However, the word *baud* is now an obsolete word. It has been replaced by the word *bit*. The most-common models have the 1200 and the 2400 bps (bits per second). These two types of modems are sufficient for electronic mail and ordinary transfer of files. However, if you need more speed, you may buy the 9600- or the 14400-bps modem. Some experts recommend a 14400-bps modem rather than a 9600-bps modem. In short, the higher the bit, the quicker data is transmitted, saving money in telephone bills. (Who knows, by the time you read this, there may be a new, faster modem!)

VI. Fax/Modems

You may also consider buying a fax/modem. Even if you already have a stand-alone fax machine, you can send faxes straight from your computer files by using a fax/modem.

In order to buy this equipment, your computer must have a fax/modem board. This board fits into a slot in your computer's central processing unit (CPU)and lets you transmit data from your computer monitor to another computer or to a fax machine. Of course, you'll also be able to receive data. However, you can only send data that is already entered into your computer. Some fax/modems are send-only models and cannot receive faxes.

VII. Fax Machines

It is wise to have a stand-alone fax machine even if you have a fax/modem. Why? Because with a fax/modem, you have to leave your computer on day and night to receive faxes even when you're not in the office. Also, with a fax/modem, you may be bothered by fax transmissions while you're working with your computer.

In 1942, a Scottish inventor discovered that he could send visual symbols over telegraph lines by using a swinging pendulum and treated paper. Thus, the facsimile machine was born!

Three Basic Parts

Today's fax machines have three basic parts: *a scanner, a printer,* and a *fax telephone-dialing-and-answering system.*

When you send a document, the scanner reads the page, one horizontal line at a time. The standard resolution is 100 horizontal lines per inch (hlpi) by approximately 200 dots per inch (dpi). Every modern fax machine offers a choice between two resolutions: standard resolution, at 100 hlpi; and fine resolution, at 200 hlpi. However, certain Hewlett-Packard models have a unique 300-dpi, 300-hlpi resolution. Moreover, advance fax machines usually offer a halftone option that improves the images of photographs.

Three-in-One Machine

Most fax machines have a telephone hand set. So you can also use the telephone for outgoing calls instead of the regular business telephone—to give way to incoming calls. You can also use it as a copier for single-fed sheets. You can copy only individual sheets of paper fed through the fax scanner. You can't copy pages from a book or a magazine without tearing the pages. In short, a fax machine is a three-in-one device: fax, telephone, and copier.

How a Fax Machine Works

A fax machine scans documents, drawings, or pictures and converts them into an electronic format that can be sent over ordinary telephone lines. In turn, the receiving fax machine converts the electronic information back into a document.

Thermal versus Plain Paper Fax

There are two types of faxes: the *thermal paper-fed machine* and the *plain paper-fed machine.* Thermal fax paper comes in rolls. Most of the thermal paper-fed faxes have automatic paper cutters, but some older models still require you to tear off the paper. Thermal paper is slippery and tends to curl up. It also fades and is not ideal to incorporate faxes into reports or presentations. While it is convenient to use plain paper, plain-paper faxes cost more than thermal models.

Choosing between thermal and plain-paper faxes depends on how much faxing you will be doing, and how much money you are willing to spend.

There are many models of fax machines. So choose the right one for your business.

Broadcasting

You can send one fax to a list of numbers by using custom mail-merge faxing software. This is called "broadcasting," which is similar to doing a mass mailing. Broadcasting enables you to send hundreds of faxes to clients, colleagues, or contacts within hours or even minutes. This way, you can send your message faster. Imagine, once the lists and messages are on file, you just push a button and the machine takes over the job! This feature, however, is usually available only on the more expensive machines.

But beware! Be sure that the recipient—a person or a company—wishes to receive your faxes. Since December 20, 1992, it has been illegal to send unsolicited ("junk") mail faxes that advertise a product or a service. The FCC's Telephone Consumer Protection Act (TCPA) provides that a person or an entity may file suit to stop anyone from faxing unsolicited material or may file suit for actual monetary loss from violations or receive $500 or more in damages for each violation (whichever is greater). For more information on this act, call the FCC at (202) 632-7554.

Polling

Polling, which is the opposite of broadcasting, is the fax machine's ability to call a sequence of numbers to receive transmission from various places. With this polling feature, you can perform "delayed polling"—which enables you to set the machine to poll at a specific time (at late night, for example, when phone rates are at their lowest). This is ideal for entrepreneurs, such as consultants, who have clients or customers throughout the country. Even low-cost machines have a polling feature.

VIII. Photocopiers

A photocopier is also an important tool in a one-person business. However, if you'll only do a little copying in your business, you can postpone buying this machine to a later stage of your business. You may use a copier in your local library or copying center for all your copying needs.

But if you're a writer or a researcher, for instance, you should try to buy a copying machine. You'll not only save time but also save money in the long run.

Photocopier Types

There are many types of copiers manufactured by Sharp, Ricoh, Canon, Kodak, Sanyo, and others. But among the commonly used copiers are those manufactured by Canon, known for having the no-mess, single-cartridge system that's familiar to laser printer users.

Prices

Prices of copiers vary. They depend on the copier's functions: what they can do. The cheapest, of course, are those small photocopying machines that are incapable of reductions or enlargements or those that are capable of copying only 8 1/2 x 11 documents. The cheapest may cost a few hundred dollars, while the sophisticated copiers may cost over a thousand dollars.

So shop around for a copier to meet your needs. Also, consider buying only from a company that can service its equipment. The machine needs more careful maintenance than other machines—like the printer.

Your decision to purchase a copier depends on your needs and your budget!

IX. The Bottom Line

To be a successful one-person business owner, your office must be wired for telecommunications and computer functions. You must have today's advanced technology. That may include a computer, a modem, a fax machine, a fax/modem, a voice mail machine (and/or other answering machine) and telephones.

If you can't afford a voice-mail system attached to a telephone switchboard, at least purchase a voice mail machine with several mail boxes for primary and different announcements for your business. There are several on the market. Choose one that fits your needs.

Another Type of Equipment

10

Choosing the Right Computer

■ Choosing the right computer for your business is critical to your success. For that reason, this chapter, written simply in detail, is devoted to the discussion of computers and their peripherals and how they work.

I. Operating Software

A PC (personal computer) must have an operating system—the software that lets the PC use other programs. Although most computers based on microprocessors built by Intel use MS-DOS (Microsoft Disk Operating System), there are alternative operating systems, such as the OS/2 and the UNIX. Yet another operating system is used by Apple's Macintosh computers.

The operating system does not work by itself; it depends not only on the assistance of other programs, but also on meshing smoothly with the BIOS (basic input/output system).

Some parts of the operating system are loaded from disk; then they are added to the BIOS to be joined by device drivers. All of them do routine hardware functions. In other words,

the BIOS, the device drivers, and the operating system perform many functions together.

An operational program includes the system that "reads" and "writes" information. It is a program that determines which application programs will work in your system.

In view of this, the first thing to decide when buying a PC is to know which operating system will be ideal for your computer.

The two well-known major operating systems are the MS-DOS or the IBM PC-DOS and the Apple Mcintosh. (So your choice will be either a DOS-operated IBM or IBM-Compatible or an Apple Macintosh.)

MS-DOS or PC-DOS

MS-DOS is used by IBM-compatible computers, while PC-DOS is used only by IBM. Either of the two is just called DOS. Much business software is designed for DOS. So if you buy a computer that is DOS based, you'll have a wide selection of software from which to choose.

Macintosh Operating System

The Macintosh operating environment, according to some users, is easier and more enjoyable to use. Apple computers are used by businesses because of their proficiency in desktop publishing, particularly in graphics creation. Of course, the Macintosh system needs its own software—software that cannot be used by IBM-compatible machines. The use of a mouse is standard for Macintosh users. (A mouse is a device that points an arrow to a symbol or a word on the screen.) When the mouse button is clicked, the computer follows its command. The use of the mouse minimizes keystrokes in many operations.

In choosing between DOS and Macintosh systems, be reminded that IBM compatibles are "character based" and Macintosh is "graphics based." That is, IBM compatibles are good with words and numbers, while Macintosh computers are great with pictures and graphics. Needless to say, determine first what software you will use, then you can decide on what hardware to buy. Your choice depends on your needs.

Windows

While a Microsoft Windows program is not strictly an *operating system*, it may be considered as an *operating software program* used for DOS computers.

Sometime ago, when I told my son, who is a computer engineer, that I didn't like to use Windows, he said, "Daddy, Windows is the industry standard for the 1990s." In view of this, he installed a Windows program on my computer. Before, I hated it! Now, I love it!

Microsoft Windows is a software program that provides a graphical operating environment. This is known

as a "graphical user interface" or a "GUI." It doesn't replace either the DOS or the applications programs. In fact, it supplements them by sitting Windows between the DOS operating system and the applications programs. (Application programs are discussed later in this chapter.) Windows is a screen within a screen. You can move from one screen to another by clicking on different windows. Sometimes, you may have several windows open at one time, with each of them containing data from different parts of a program or even from different programs. In other words, with Windows, you can easily copy data from one open program to another.

With Windows, you also use the mouse. Using Windows with MS-DOS is much like using a Macintosh computer.

Why was Windows developed for MS-DOS computers? Because windows-based graphical operation was a hit on the Macintosh. Thus, Seattle-based software giant Microsoft introduced the Windows for MS-DOS computers. Since then, Microsoft Windows has become a bestseller.

When using a DOS-based computer, you cannot just use DOS software for Windows. To use Windows, you must use the Windows versions of the software programs. For instance, if you now use *Aldus Pagemaker*, you can buy that program marked "Microsoft Windows Compatible."

However, Windows can't be used for all DOS-operated computers. A software program sometimes preinstalled on new computers it should be used only on PCs with at least a 386 processor and 2 MB (megabytes) of RAM. A color monitor is also preferable.

II. Other Systems

There are two alternative operating systems besides the DOS and the Macintosh system. They are the OS/2 and UNIX.

OS/2

A complete operating system, the OS/2 was originally developed jointly by Microsoft and IBM. However, IBM later backed out of the deal. While Windows is the industry standard of the 1990s, IBM claims the OS/2 is the standard of tomorrow. OS/2 provides a screen environment similar to Windows, but the product, in some ways, is more sophisticated underneath. It has, for instance, superior multi-tasking abilities. You can load more programs without slowing down the machine, although other applications are still open.

IBM claimed that it had finally perfected OS/2.1 for Windows in 1993. This operating system will let you run DOS, Windows, and OS/2.1 software almost flawlessly.

The OS/2.1 system can run more than one program at a time. IBM claims that you can multitask DOS and Windows with more speed and reliability than ever before.

UNIX

The UNIX operating system is intended only for a niche market. It is used only by companies engaged in specialized fields, such as engineering and scientific applications and some large businesses.

III. Applications Programs

Before you buy a computer system, you must decide first which applications programs you will use. An applications program is a software package that handles a particular task, such as word processing, databases, spreadsheets, fulfillment, communications, graphics, project management, and integrated activities.

Word-Processing Software

A word-processing program is used for writing letters, reports, or manuscripts. Together with a mail-merging feature, it can be used to address mailing lists. It can be used to edit text and to check spelling, grammar, and punctuation.

Database Software

A database program organizes data on customers, suppliers, products purchased, inventory, and more.

Spreadsheet Software

A spreadsheet program is primarily used for accounting. The best known spreadsheet program is Lotus 1-2-3. But this program is complicated and difficult to learn.With a spreadsheet program, you can prepare a single-entry accounting system—doing mathematical calculations. With it, you can enter accounting records and do financial projections.

Fulfillment Software

A fulfillment program is used for entering orders, shipments, and receipts of goods. As an invoice is prepared, the inventory automatically adjusts its figures. Also, with this program, statements, consignments, and other reports are produced. Since this program has a database, it can also make labels for particular customers, based on the codes used for retrieval.

Communications Software

A communications program is used for interfacing with other computers and for gaining access to database information services via modem through telephone lines. In other words, it is used for sending to or receiving files from other computers.

Graphics Software

A graphics program is used for turning your computer monitor into an easel or a drafting table. With it, you can create charts, maps, graphs, illustrations, and other works of art.

Project Management Software

A project management program is used for monitoring current projects and determining their progress, including schedules and production.

Integrated Software

An integrated program is a combination of two or more applications, such as database, accounting, and word processing.

IV. Central Processing Unit

The components of the computer are the system unit, known as the central processing unit (CPU), the keyboard, and the monitor, which is a cathode-ray tube (CRT).

Inside the case of the system unit are the microprocessor (or simply processor), the random access memory (RAM), the read-only memory (ROM), the disk drives, and other components.

Processor

The heart of the system is the processor. It is used in the case where the RAM and ROM storage drives are housed.

If you wish to buy an industry-standard computer to run DOS/Windows software, you must have either of the two main processor families: 386 series or 486 series. Usually, letters and numbers such as SX, DX, and DX2 are added to the numbers 386 or 486. The SX is considered as the entry-level product and the DX as the later model.

The era of 386 processors, however, is coming to an end because the 486 series is rapidly becoming the main industry standard. The 286 processor, which was prominent only several years ago, is now considered obsolete because it is not powerful enough to handle today's new software programs. Besides, no company is making the 286-based computers anymore.

(I bought my 386 computer system a year ago. In retrospect, I should have bought the 486 model.)

Two of the well-known manufacturers of computer processors are Intel Corporation and American Micro Devices (AMD).

Intel's new computer processor has arrived. It decided to drop numbers in favor of names in naming its products.

Hence, they called the latest processor, Pentium, instead of 586. Needless to say, this is more powerful than the others. Intel has claimed the Pentium, available at either 60 or 66 MHz, runs about five and a half times faster than a 25-MHz 486SX. It has a built-in math coprocessor which speeds up complex graphics and other numerical-computation operations.

Processors are not created equal. Each processor has a speed known as *clock speed,* which is measured in megahertz (MHz).

In other words, the higher the megahertz, the faster the computer will run. The 386 processors run from 20MHz to 40MHz. The 486 processors have speeds from 20MHz to 66MHz and beyond. Needless to say, clock speeds continue to rise, whichever series it is.

Besides the "original" processor, there's a co-processor that you may install on your computer, if you need very heavy-duty number-crunching. This is an auxiliary processor that speeds up mathematical calculations.

If you're buying a 486-based desktop computer, the choices will be among the 486SX, the 486DX, and the 486DX2. It is understood that the 486DX is more powerful than the 486SX, and the 486DX2 is more powerful than the 486DX. So the choice is yours.

Intel also introduced an OverDrive processor in 1992.

Memory (RAM and ROM)

Memory in the random-access memory (RAM) is used for different purposes.

The first kilobyte—1,024 bytes—holds the *interrupt vectors* set by both the BIOS (basic input/output system) and the DOS. The vectors point to locations of program routes in other parts of the memory locations. It is there where operations normally go when various hardware components transmit a special signal called an *interrupt.*

The next 256 or more bytes contain BIOS data called *flags.* These flags are used to indicate the state of various conditions of the internal system. Also in this area is a 16-byte *keyboard buffer.*

The rest of RAM, up to 640K, consists of the ordinary memory. This is the place where COMMAND.COM, device drivers, memory-resident programs, and application software are usually loaded. Part of this is reserved for BIOS use by various types of display adapters, network cards, and hard-drive controllers.

You can enter or delete data in the RAM, but not in the read-only memory (ROM). In other words, data stored in RAM is temporary, while that on the ROM is permanent. ROM is where operational information is stored. When information is in the RAM and you don't save it on a proper disk (floppy or hard disk) it will be lost when you turn off the system or if there is a power outage.

Nowadays, the absolute workable minimum (especially if you're using Windows) is two megabytes (2MB) of RAM, roughly equivalent to two million characters. To take advantage of Windows, you should have at least 4MB or up to 8MB, depending upon the applications program require-ment. For instance, PageMaker requires at least 2MB of RAM, while other programs may require more.

Of course, you can add extra mem-ory to the main system board (also known as the motherboard) contain-ing the processor and the standard memory. But you can also add mem-ory into one or two of the vacant expansion slots. For memory upgrades that are easier to install, look at machines that accept SIMMs (single in-line memory modules). SIMMs have different speed ratings. The ratings are typically between 70 and 100 nanoseconds (one billionth of a second). Just remember, the lower the figure, the faster the speed.)

RAM Cache. All computers have RAM chips. However, these chips have different speeds. The faster the RAM chips, the quicker data is transmitted. But the faster the chip, the more expensive it is. For this reason, some manufacturers make slower memory chips for the bulk of a PC's memory. But they use a few faster RAM chips on the motherboard as an external RAM cache. The cache, usually con-sisting from 8 to 256 kilobytes of memory, beefs up performance by using these high-speed memory chips—known as *SRAM chips.* The memory holds data that the cache controller predicts the CPU is going to require next. Without the cache, the processor may sit idle for several clock cycles while it awaits the requested data to be passed to it. (A clock cycle is the shortest time during which any operation takes place in a computer.) The 486DX and DX2 computers come

with an 8K *internal* cache as stan-dard. Many 486DX/DX2-based PCs also have additional or *external caches.*

Expansion Slots. Every personal computer needs expansion slots, which are plug-in connectors. These connectors allow you to insert addi-tional circuit boards that attach to the rest of the computer through special circuitry called the *bus.* A circuit board, called an *adapter* or an *expan-sion card,* is usually inserted into the plug-in connectors for various pur-poses. For example, the adapter or the expansion card can increase the reso-lution or the number of colors used by the monitor. It can also transform the computer into a machine for recording and playing music and can operate drives, printers, tape backups, and other peripherals.

Disk Drives

The most common form of perma-nent storage is magnetic disks—both floppy and hard, which almost all PCS have. This section describes floppy disks, hard disk drives, magnetic tape drives, and CD-ROM drives.

Floppy Disks. Floppy disks are of two sizes: 5.25" and 3.5". The 5.25" disk is the real floppy; it's bendable. The 3.5" is not actually floppy as you can't bend it. The 3.5" disk usually holds 1.44MB of memory. It is wise to buy a computer with a 5.25" drive and a 3.5" drive.

Hard Disk Drives. If you will not use Windows, then probably a 40-MB hard disk drive is enough. On the other hand, you should have about

80MB on the hard drive if you'll use only entry-level Windows applications. Better still is a 120-MB or a 170-MB hard drive, depending on the applications you'll use. An external hard disk can also be installed if you wish.

Magnetic Tape Drives. Magnetic storage is also used in the form of tape drives. Tape drives usually provide lost-cost storage, but they are so slow that they are used only as a backup medium. They are necessary because you need a backup of your files. For instance, if your hard disk containing hundreds of megabytes crashes, that's a tremendous disaster! You'll lose data that you have stored for a year or even years! (Of course, if your data is not yet tremendous, then you can save it on floppy disks. But that's only temporary.)

There are two kinds of tape backup drives: the quarter-inch cartridge and the digital audio-tape.

1. *Quarter-Inch Cartridge (QIC) Backup Drive.* Typically, the format of a QIC tape contains from 20 to 32 parallel tracks. When the tape reaches either end of a spool, the tape's movement reverses. Then the flow of data loops back in a spiral fashion to the next outside track. Each of the tracks is divided into blocks of 512 or 1,024 bytes with segments generally containing 32 blocks. Normally, backup software reserves space for a directory of backup files.

2. *Digital Audio-Tape (DAT) Backup Drive.* The DAT's drive has a read/write head that allows it to backup huge amounts of data onto a small tape cartridge approximately the size of a matchbox. Ninety degrees apart, the rotating cylinder contains four heads. Two of the heads write heads A and B; they also write backup data. Two corresponding read heads, in turn, verify the data. Tilting slightly in order to rotate at an angle to the tape, the cylinder spins 2,000 times a minute. As the cylinder spins, the tape passes in front of it in the opposite direction. It spins at 1/3 inch per second.

CD-ROM Drive. A new form of storage for some PC users who store enormous amount of data is the so-called CD-ROM. A CD-ROM drive can pack up to 500 megabytes of data on a disk. It is similar to the compact disk that plays music. CD-ROMs are cheap to produce. However, they are read-only-memory; you cannot use the disk to store your own data that you can revise or delete.

In other words, you can store massive data on the disk—data that won't need frequent updating. You can find CD-ROM disks of clip art, photographs, dictionaries, etc. An extra bonus is that most CD-ROM drives can play ordinary CD music. The CD-ROM drive is controlled by software in your PC that transmits instructions to controller circuitry. The circuitry may be on the computer's motherboard or on a separate board installed in an expansion slot.

Serial and Parallel Ports

There are two relay stations on your computer. They are the *serial* and *parallel ports*. They are discussed here.

Serial Port. The jack-of-all-trades among computer components, the serial port serves as the simple relay station with one line to send data, another line to receive data, and a few other lines to monitor and regulate data sent over the other two lines. Both 9-pin and 25-pin connectors are used as serial ports. Commonly referred to as an RS-232 port, it is most commonly used with a mouse or a modem.

Parallel Port. The parallel port, also called the *centronics port,* is faster than the serial port. Since graphics and scalable fonts are usually common in printed documents, the parallel port is the only practical choice. While a *serial port* sends data one bit at a time over a single one-way wire, a *parallel port* transmits several bits of data across eight parallel wires at the same time. In other words, while a serial connection can send a single *bit,* a parallel port can transmit an entire *byte.* (A bit is represented by every burst of electricity that is sent off by software when transistors connected to a data line in a RAM chip are turned on. Each burst is represented by a bit, either a 1 or a 0, in the native language of processors. On the other hand, the combination of 1s and 0s from eight data lines forms a byte of data.)

In addition, parallel ports are used for transporting files between two computers. They can also work with peripherals, such as drives and sound generators.

IV. Monitors

A monitor may or may not be included when you buy a computer. Before buying a monitor separately, be sure that there's a video adapter installed in your computer that acts as a link between the central processing unit and the screen. Of course, most computers come with a video adapter built into the main system board.

There are two kinds of monitors: the color monitor and the monochrome monitor (which is usually green or amber and black or white). In order for your screen to display color, the system must have a color card. To display information in graphics, you need a graphics card in the system. Software uses color not only to make itself beautiful, but to convey more information. Decide if you want a color or monochrome monitor.

If you'll use graphics, whether in color or black and white, you'll need a color display that can display at least 256 colors instead of the 4 colors of yesteryear. While the 256-color monitor is commonplace, there are some monitors that provide thousands of colors. So instead of the CGA's (color graphics adapter) monitor with an Etch-a-Sketch-type resolution, you should get the (VGA) variable-graphics-array display adapter because the VGA monitor has become the industry standard for graphics. Graphics involves not only pictures or illustrations, but also different sizes and styles of types on documents. The CGA provides resolutions of only 200 lines high by 640 pixels wide, while the most improved VGA provides resolutions of 768 lines by 1,024 pixels wide. (A *pixel*, short for picture element, is considered as the smallest logical unit that can be used to make an image on the screen.) A single pixel is generally created by several adjoining points of light. The fewer the dots of light, the higher a display's resolution. VGA offers different levels of resolution of the image.

For the purpose of discussion, a standard VGA displays a resolution of 480 x 640. The so-called Super VGA has a resolution of 600 x 800. However, at this writing, the ideal resolution is 768 x 1,024. (There are some monitors that are capable of 768 x 1280 resolution. But it must be noted that the higher the resolution, the higher the price. The old video standards (CGA, EGA, and Hercules) are now considered obsolete.

V. Keyboards

Keyboards are of two kinds: the capacitive keyboard and the hard-contact keyboard.

Capacitive Keyboard. When you press the key cap in a capacitive keyboard, a spring inside causes a plastic and metal plunger to move nearer to two pads with areas plated with tin, nickel, and copper. (The pads are attached to the keyboard's printed circuit board.) The amount of charge on the two pads is lowered when the metal plunger passes between the pads. Then the difference in the charge causes a small current to flow through the circuitry. (The circuitry is attached to the pads.)

If you release the key cap, the spring expands. Then the key cap returns to its original height, causing the plunger to move away from the pads. This then causes the current flowing through the circuits leading to the pads to return to its original level.

Hard-Contact Keyboard. When you press the key cap in a hard-contact keyboard, a foam rubber dome collapses. The collapsed dome then presses against a sheet of plastic. (On the bottom of this plastic is a metallic area attached to the rest of the keyboard's circuit board.) This metallic area then contacts a similar surface on another plastic sheet. This causes current to flow through the printed circuits connected to each of the pads.

As soon as you release the key cap, the rubber dome goes back to its original shape and position. As a result, the pressure on the plastic sheet is released. Then the plastic returns to its original position; it breaks the electrical circuit and cuffs off the flow of current.

Keyboards come in two styles: the old-style (standard) keyboard and the enhanced keyboard. The old-style keyboard has function keys placed on the left-hand side of the keyboard next to the letter keys, while the enhanced keyboard has function keys above the regular typing keys. Some people prefer to use the old-style keyboard, while others the enhanced keyboard.

VI. Peripherals

Peripherals are pieces of equipment that are used with a computer to increase its functional range. They may include one or more printers, a mouse or a trackball, a modem, a plotter, and a scanner.

Printers

Printers are of four kinds: dot matrix, daisy wheel, inkjet, and the laser.

Dot-Matrix Printer. The dot-matrix printer operates by striking a sheet of paper with a set of tiny rods or pins. The pins form letters and numbers and create graphics. The more pins, the finer the print quality. For a letter-quality printing, you need a printer with 24 pins. The dot-matrix printer is a necessity for tasks that require printing multilayer forms. The 24-pin dot-matrix printers increase both the printer speed and the quality of type.

Daisy Wheel Printer. The daisy-wheel printer produces crisp, clean, and letter quality printing like a typewriter. Letters, numbers, punctuation marks, etc., are contained on interchangeable daisy wheels. These daisy wheels rotate, as keys are hit, to strike the paper. The two disadvantages of this printer are its slowness and its inability to create graphics like a dot-matrix printer.

Inkjet Printer. The inkjet printer resembles the dot-matrix printer. Both have print heads that move across the page, making an entire line of text with each pass. They are in the same speed class as impact printers (daisy-wheel printers), but they leave smaller dots than do impact printers. The inkjet printer is a perfect compromise between dot-matrix and daisy wheel printers with regard to speed,

cost, and quality. It spits little drops of ink onto paper.

The inkjet printer is especially good for creating graphics and printing first-draft copies. It operates by spraying ink onto the paper to form symbols, letters, and numbers. Although faster and quieter than both dot-matrix and daisy-wheel printers, the lower-priced models usually lack the clarity to produce letter-quality printing. However, the higher-priced models can produce letter-quality printing.

Laser Printer. At the heart of the laser printer is the print engine. This engine transfers a black powder onto the page much like a photocopier. The state-of-the-art printing technology includes laser imaging and precise paper movement. All its movements are controlled by the microprocessor. The printer actions involve five different operations: (1) the interpretation of the signals coming from a computer; (2) the translation of those signals into instructions that control the movement of a laser beam; (3) the control of the paper movement; (4) the sensitization of the paper so that it will accept the black toner that makes up the image; and (5) the fusing of that image onto the paper.

Having improved tremendously for the past years, the laser printer offers quality and versatile printing. Particularly an ideal tool for graphic designers and desktop publishers, the laser printer generally prints 300 dots per inch (dpi) versus the 1400 dots per inch used by service bureaus. However, Hewlett-Packard has come out with an HP LaserJet 4 that prints both 300 dpi and 600 dpi. In 1992, these printers were rather costly; however, those prices have decreased since then.

Much like a computer system, the laser printer also has a built-in memory, or RAM. To produce good graphics, the laser printer should have from 2 to 4 MB of RAM. In other words, the more quality graphics you need, the more memory your laser printer should have.

Fonts for laser printers come in several different forms. Some fonts are actual cartridges of typefaces (considered as hardware) that plug into the printer's cartridge slot. Others are on disk, called soft fonts (considered as software).

Mouse and Track Ball

Computers use two types of pointing devices: mouse and track ball.

Mouse. The mouse is a pointing device that a computer user can operate with his or her hand to make movements on the monitor screen. It is another input device that affords easier use of a computer, particularly for both word processing and desktop publishing. The mouse does not replace the keyboard; rather, it supplements it. By moving and pointing to on-screen subjects, it sometimes place the capital "I" like symbol of the mouse in order for the user to insert words or sentences. As a neophyte mouse user, you'll find it slow and awkward to use at first. However, the more you practice, you'll find it faster and more enjoyable to use. A mouse points with an arrow to whatever function you need. When you click its button, it directs the computer to follow your instruction. With a click of the mouse button, you can move the cursor to wherever you want it to be.

In a nutshell, the mouse is the most popular pointing device for the newest breed of operating environments—graphic user interfaces represented by Macintosh, Windows, and OS/2.

Track Ball. The track ball may be considered as a cousin of the mouse. Consisting of a ball mounted to a frame, the track ball activates the cursor. By spinning the ball, you can make drawings or create pictures on the computer monitor.

Modem

A modem, connected to a computer, is a piece of equipment used to transmit and receive data. (See Chapter 9, *Smart Technology: The Effective Tool in a One-Person Business,* page 67.)

Plotter

Especially designed to produce graphics, the plotter is used to produce high-quality architectural plans or technical diagrams. With a plotter that offers a rainbow of colors to choose from, you can print on different sizes and types of surfaces, such as films, glossy paper, or overhead transparencies.

Scanner

A scanner converts printed matter (whether text, drawings, or photographs) into an electronic code that is transmitted directly into your computer. Most commonly used by desktop publishers, the scanner can scan a page in only seconds. Thus, it is used for word processing, layout, and/or paste-up.

In other words, you can scan a picture or an illustration and enter it into the computer, instead of directly doing the paste-up on the hard copy. Scanner prices vary, depending on their reproduction capabilities. Color models are more expensive than black and white models. Also, the higher resolution they have, the higher the price.

The three types of scanners are the sheet-fed, flatbed, and hand-held.

Sheet-Fed Scanner. In a sheet-fed scanner, mechanical rollers move the paper past the scan head. With this scanner, the image is captured more accurately. But scanning is limited to single, ordinary-sized sheets.

Flatbed Scanner. In a flatbed scanner, the page is stationary behind a glass window. It is the head that moves past the page, much like a photocopier. The scanner has a series of mirrors that reflect the image to a bank of sensors. However, because there's no perfect mirror, the image sometimes undergoes degradation each time it is reflected. The advantage of a sheet-fed scanner is that it can scan oversized or thick documents.

Hand-held Scanner. The hand-held scanner can scan pages in books. The scanning head, is not as wide as that in either a sheet-fed scanner or a flatbed scanner. The accurateness of an image produced depends on the steadiness of your hand in holding and moving it. It is less expensive than the first two scanners.

VII. Portable Computers

The personal computer has re-invented itself in the 1990s. PCs are becoming smaller and smaller. It's because more and more entrepreneurs and computer users are hitting the road. These computers are called portables because they seem to be everywhere these days: on airliner's coach-class tray-tables and in cars used by traveling entrepreneurs. These portables run on batteries. Most portables have backlighted liquid-crystal display (LCD) monitors that can show up to a half-page of text and are usually compatible with high-quality VGA graphics.

The six types of portables are laptops, notebooks, subnotebooks, palmtops, organizers, and the new personal digital assistants (PDAs). They are, however, generally known as *notebooks*. Basic MS-DOS portables use a 386-based microprocessor; the better models even use a version of the faster 486 chip. Notebooks usually include between 1 and 4 megabytes of memory, which are typically expandable. Some laptops can hold more.

Laptop Computers

The laptops are the larger version of the notebooks. Some are as large as a briefcase and have more processing power and expanded capabilities than other portables. Laptops offer full-size detachable keyboards and weigh as much as 20 pounds. A few of them are so powerful that they can only operate when plugged into an electrical outlet. One model even has a whopping 400-megabyte capacity.

Notebook Computers

The typical notebook computer weights 4 to 7 pounds. It comes with a color screen and more hard-disk space. *PC Laptop* magazine named Compaq's color LTE Lite/25C as one of its 1993 notebooks of the year.

Subnotebook Computers

The subnotebooks arrived in 1992. Weighing less than 4 pounds, the subnotebooks use credit-card-size flash memory cards instead of the bulky floppy-disk drives. They don't use heavy batteries because this new breed of portable comes with low-drain processors and low-voltage circuits that require less energy.

The hot subnotebook in 1993 was the Dell 320SLi, which was called by *PC Magazine* as a "near notebook." With a 386-chip machine, it has 2 megabytes of RAM, a 9.5-inch display, and a 60-megabyte hard drive. It weighs 3.6 pounds.

Palmtop Computers

Palmtops are great for crunching numbers and for communications. However, because of their tiny screens and keyboards, they can't be used for full-time work. One of the known palmtops is Hewlett-Packard's best-selling 95LX. Running on plain old alkaline batteries, the 95LX is just 11 ounces, measuring 6.3 inches x 3.4 inches x 1 inch. It has all kinds of built-in software (such as the Lotus 1-2-3) and a slot for memory cards.

Business Organizer Computers

For making appointments and phone calls, poking a calculator, or scribbling notes, you may buy a pocket organizer.

Among the most popular organizers in 1993 were Sharp's Wizard and Casio's B.O.S.S. (Business Organizer Scheduling System).

Personal Digital Assistant Computers

The personal digital assistants are the combinations of a pen-based notebook computer, an organizer, and a fax machine.

An example of this product is Apple Computer's *Newton*, which is a pen-based, hand-held device that has no keyboard or keypad. You scribble a note on the screen, and this device converts the note into typewritten text and sends it out as a fax.

VIII. The Brain and the Computer

To be a smart entrepreneur, you should use much of your brain, instead of your muscles. We should study how the brain works because it is the instrument that humans use to think, plan, and take actions.

In these days of advanced technology, comparisons are always being made between the human brain and the computer. They are alike—in fact, it's said that the computer is patterned after the human brain. Your brain senses what you see, hear, or touch, thinks about it, and stores it.

When you put information into your biocomputer, it is called *input*; when you retrieve information, it is called *output*. It's like depositing and withdrawing money at the bank, but without a deposit you cannot make any withdrawal. The same is true with the computer. The human brain, however, has feelings. The computer doesn't; it cannot fall in and out of love.

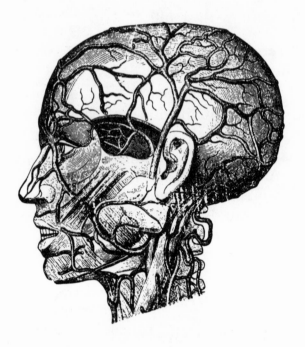

The Human Computer

The brain, the computer of the human body, consists of approximately three pints of moist, greyish-yellow matter and is an amazing, complex mechanism. Though it controls all human activities, it weighs only about three pounds, or half as much as a new born baby.

According to scientists, the brain contains from one hundred billion to one trillion nerve cells; it floats in a liquid that acts as its shock absorber. Serving as the "switchboard" of the whole nervous system, it consists of the *gray matter* (the outer cortex of nerve cells). It is divided into different compartments where electrical and chemical activities take place, controlled by its self-made codes.

Physical Features of the Brain

The brain is divided into three parts: the *forebrain* or the *front brain*, the *midbrain* or the *middle brain*, and the *hindbrain* or *rear brain*.

The Forebrain. This section consists mostly of the cerebrum, formed by two large hemispheres. In the *cerebrum*, your memory and intelligence thrive; this is where you think, remember, and decide. The *thalamus* is situated in the middle of the brain, above the brain stem; it sends information from ears, nose, eyes, skin, and tongue to the different parts of the body. The *hypothalamus*, located below the thalamus, acts as the relay manager of the nervous system; it is also involved in emotions.

The thalamus, covered by four neuron clusters known as *basal ganglia,* helps control the body's movements. The *limbic system,* another part of the cerebrum, is overlapped by the basal ganglia; it largely controls emotions and actions and also takes part in learning and the operation of the short-term memory. The *archicortex* (original bark), and the *paleocortex* (new bark) cover most of the forebrain.

Each hemisphere in the cerebrum is divided into the *frontal, occipital, temporal,* and *parietal lobes*. These hemispheres are known as the *left brain* and the *right brain*. If you are left-handed, your right brain tends to be dominant; if you're right-handed, your left brain tends to be dominant; some people have mixed dominance.

According to scientists, the left brain governs logical, mathematical, verbal, and written language skills. The right brain controls imagination, spatial and color sensitivity, and emotions. These are generalities; however.

The Midbrain. This portion is situated between the forebrain and the hindbrain on top of a network of nerve threads and a nuclei called the *brain stem*, which connects the brain to the spinal cord. The midbrain is the relay station for sensory impulses.

The Hindbrain. This portion forms part of the *pons* and the *medulla*, the brain stem's two lowest communications network stations. These two structures transmit vital messages to and from the spinal cord. Another part, the *cerebellum*, is the largest structure in the hindbrain and the second largest region of the whole brain; it coordinates the body's complex movements.

As you can see, the brain is loaded. It has all the standard equipment, plus all the options. It has power, acceleration, and speed; its capacity is limitless. I've been loading my brain with data since I was born, but I cannot fill it. I can't empty it, either. Amazing!

The Brain-Mind Connection

What is the difference between the brain and the mind? The brain is matter: it can be weighed, dissected, and examined. But how about the mind? Is it spirit? energy? No one knows. It's not flesh; it's not bone; it's a mystery!

Scientists can't give the exact location of the mind—I can't, either. They are trying to explain that the brain and the mind operate by separate sets of laws; the former by physical laws, the latter by laws still unknown. They speculate that our thoughts, feelings, and dreams are produced by chemical and electrical impulses in the networks of nerve cells.

The human brain and the computer both contain wirings: the human brain is wired by intricately laid-out nerve fibers; the computer is wired by metal threads. They are both word processors, and both have two kinds of memory: *short term* and *long term.* Your brain's short-term memory keeps track of immediate concerns; for instance, remembering your date at seven that evening or where you put your eyeglasses. Long-term memory stores memories of playing hide-and-seek with the girl or the boy who became your playmate in adulthood.

The computer also has short-term and long-term memory, called RAM and ROM. Ram stands for random access memory; the central processing unit (CPU), the brains of the computer, can add to or take from this memory at any time. When a CPU adds information to memory, the process is called writing; when information is taken out, it is called *reading.*

ROM stands for read-only memory. Although the CPU has access to ROM, ROM cannot be changed: it was "born" there with the computer because the manufacturer placed it there. According to an expert on computers, ROM is like a phonograph record because the information is stored permanently, as in long-term memory, while RAM is like a cassette tape on which you can add, delete, or retrieve information, as in short-term memory.

Input and Output. When you put information into your brain or into your computer, the information is called *input;* when you retrieve information, it is called *output.*

A human being writes the computer's program, but the brain writes its own program. The computer is controlled by "on" and "of" signals, but the brain is always "on"—unless the owner is dead.

How Does the Brain Work?

Types of Cells. According to scientists, the brain is governed by two types of cells: *glial* or *neuroglial* cells and nerve cells called *neurons.* The former do much of the basic biochemical work, while the latter perform the brain's main work of processing impulses from sense organs.

Neuroglial Cells. The neuroglial cells help and nourish the neurons. They keep the neurons separated by "gluing" them so that the messages in one neuron do not interfere with those in another. They are the brain's welders.

The Neurons. Each neuron has three main parts: the *cell body,* the *axon,* and the *dendrite.* The cell body is a central nucleus composed of a sticky fluid containing microscopic structures; the axon is a slim "tree trunk" that transmits signals between the body and other cells and between other parts of the body and the brain through stations known as *synapses.* The dendrite is a short fiber cable that relays signals to its own cell body. Each neuron receives and transmits information signals through thousands of tiny nerve wires that join it with other neurons in the nervous system. The neurons are divided into different groups, such as with its own neurotransmitter.

Neutrotransmitters are brain chemicals that control the flow of messages through synapses over which the messages jump from the axons to waiting dendrites. These are called "handshakes" between neurons. Millions of handshakes make up a single response, thought, or memory. This activity takes place in the cortex, the outer layer of the brain. Here the neurons process the complex stream of information flowing from the sense organs. After being processed, these electrical and chemical messages are relayed by neurons to deeper layers of the cortex, to other brain structures, and to other parts of the body.

Floyd Bloom, a neuroanatomist at the Scripps Clinic in La Jolla, California, believes that perception, memory, and self-awareness becomes scrambled when brain chemistry goes awry. Once when I was printing out the manuscript of one of my books, the printer produced strings of letters like xuelghcwptndkaaaqklc. Probably the electrical activity between the computer, the software, and the printer got scrambled. The computer; like the mind, goes crazy too.

How Information Is Processed

According to one theory, input from the senses to the brain first enters the short-term memory, where information is stored as coded sounds of words. New items entering the short-term memory drive out the old ones, as if saying "Get out of here!" When items are repeated again and again in a process called *rehearsal,* their stay is prolonged, and the rehearsed and remembered items move to the long-term memory bank.

Kinds of Long-Term Memory. Scientists divide long term memory into *stimulus-response memory, event memory,* and *abstract memory.* Stimulus-response memory makes you salivate when you hear someone say "Let's eat now!" Event memory may help you remember your childhood, even if you're already in your eighties. Abstract memory has a huge capacity; it stores general knowledge and the meanings of objects and events. It is located in the neocortex, the brain's outer gray layer. Some scientists believe that memory formation involves creating chains of molecules called *peptides*—possibly one for each memory created.

Data Retrieval System. If you're using a computer and want to store names and addresses, you use codes for input and output. For instance, you may create codes with the first three letters of the last name and the last two numbers of the addresses, and then save them. To retrieve the same data, you key in the same letters and numbers.

You do the same thing with the brain. You code your ideas by forming codes or key words., and then your brain stores them. I call this process *coding.* You retrieve this information from your long-term memory by using the same codes or key words to help you find and obtain the data. I call this process *decoding.*

How Data is Stored

The brain automatically saves information after a number of repetitions. You don't have to save it by hitting the special control keys as you do on the computer. When I want to place data in my brain, for instance, about my marketing plans, I don't say "save": the information is saved automatically by my body's computer. The trouble is that I can't delete any information. The more I try to delete, the more I save. In spite of that, I like my brain; it doesn't say, "Disk is full!"

Now that you know how the brain works, we may go back to the discussion of computers used in business.

Use these two types of computers and you'll succeed in business!

IX. Where to Buy PCs and Notebooks

Mail Order Vendors

There are a number of mail order direct sales manufacturers. These are companies that obtain different parts of a computer from a number of manufacturers. For instance, they get monitors, hard disks, and keyboards from various firms. They put a name or a trademark on the computer and advertise heavily in computer magazines, such as *PC Magazine*. In other words, they set up a computer system of their own.

Because they have no dealers nationwide, these companies often offer a 30-day money-back guarantee; that is, you can return the computer within 30 days if you don't like it. These vendors offer 1-year warranties that include on-site-service on desktops and towers. In addition, they provide toll-free technical support. They take orders on the telephone, asking for your credit card information. They ship orders within several days via Federal Express or United Parcel Service.

The majority of these firms are small companies. However, some of them have expanded into large companies, such as Gateway and Dell. (I bought one computer system from Gateway and another from a small company.)

What is good about buying by mail order from these companies is that their prices are lower than those offered by local dealers or stores. The drawback, however, is that you have to assemble the computer system yourself. If you don't know how, have a friend or an expert to assemble it.

(Don't confuse these companies with mail order dealers who don't manufacture computers. For instance, mail order dealers who don't manufacture their own just sell brand name computers, such as IBM PC, Compaq, etc.).

Dealers of Brand Manufacturers

Brand manufacturers are those manufacturers that usually sell through dealers. Such companies are IBM, Apple, NEC, Compaq, Packard Bell, and Leading Edge. Dealers of these companies have improved their services and technical support. If you want to see your computer before you buy it, then you can visit any of these dealers. But you have to expect a higher price. And, depending on the store, you may not be able to return the computer if you decide within a specified period of time that you don't want it.

IX. Desktop Computer and Notebook Vendors

Here is a directory of desktop computer and notebook vendors:

Acer American Corporation
401 Charcot Ave.
San Jose, CA 95131
(800) 637-7000

Apple Computer Inc.
20525 Mariani Ave.
Cupertino, cA 95014
(800) 446-3000

AST Research
P.O. Box 57005
Irvine, CA 92619-7005
(800) 876-4278

Advanced Logic Research
9401 Jerinimo
Irvine, CA 92718
(800) 444-4257

Austin Computer Systems
10300 Metric Blvd.
Austin, TX 78758
(800) 752-1577

Canon Computer Systems, Inc.
123 East Paularino Ave.
P.O. Box 5048
Costa Mesa, CA 92628-5048
(800) 848-4123

Compaq Computer Corporation
P.O. Box 692000
Houston, TX 77269-2000
(800) 345-1518

CompuAdd Computer Corporation
12303 Technology Blvd.
Austin, tX 78727
(800) 627-1967

Compudyne, Inc.
1515A Surveyor
Addison, TX 75244
(800) 932-2667

Dell Computer Corporation
9505 Arboretum Blvd.
Austin, TX 78759-7229
(800) 426-5150

Digital Equipment Corp.
P.O. Box 4076
Woburn, MA 01888-9693
(800) 332-4409

Gateway 2000 Inc.
610 Gateway Dr.
N. Sioux City, ID 57049

IBM Corporation
Old Orchard Rd.
Armonk, NY 10504
(800) 426-2468

Leading Edge
117 Flanders Rd.
Westborough, MA 01581-5020
(508) 836-4800

NEC Technologies Inc.
1414 Massachusetts Ave.
Boxborough, MA 01719
(800) 374-8000

Nortegate Computer Systems, Inc.
7075 Flying Cloud Dr.
Eden Prairie, MN 55344
(800) 453-0081

Packard Bell, Inc.
9425 Canoga Ave.
Chatsworth, CA 91311
(800) 773-5858

Sharp Electronics Corp.
Sharp Plaza
Mahwah, NJ 07430-2135
(201) 529-8200

Tandy Radio Shack
Tandy Corporation
One Tandy Center
Fort Worth, TX 76102
(817) 390-3011

Texas Instruments, Inc.
Information Technology Group
P.O. Box 202230, ITG-009
Austin, TX 78720-2230
(800) 527-3500

Toshiba America Information
Systems, Inc.
Computer Systems Division
P.O. Box 19724
Irvine, CA 92713-9724
(800) 457-7777

Zenith Data Systems, Inc.
2150 East Lake Cook Rd.
Buffalo Grove, IL 60089
(800) 582-0524
(800) 553-0331

Zeos International Ltd.
530 5th Ave. N.W.
St. Paul, MN 55112
(800) 423-5891

X. Warehouse Stores

Warehouse stores are considered as giant stores wherein you can buy computers, printers, and other computer peripherals and accessories, much like in buying groceries. Such stores are CompUSA, Sam's Warehouse, and Price Club. A mail order manufacturer, Compudyne, also sells through CompUSA.

Super Channel Dealers

These are giant mail order dealers that are authorized by leading PC manufacturers.

Examples of such companies are listed on the next page.

PC Connection
1-800-800-0004
(Compaq)

Insight Computer Systems
1- 800-998-8036
(Compaq, Toshiba, own brand)

PCs Compleat
1-800-669-4727
 (AST, Compaq, Leading Edge,
Texas Instruments, Toshiba)

USA/Flex
1-800-477-8323
(Compaq, Toshiba, own brand)

Office Supplies Warehouse Stores

Business-oriented stores also sell computers and peripherals, and accessories. They include Office Max, Office Depot, BizMart, and Staples. Although their main goods are office products and supplies, they sell copiers, small telephone systems, computers, modems, and printers.

Major Department Stores

Department stores, such as Sears and Montgomery Ward also sell computers.

Decision! Decision!

It's your decision, of course, where to buy your computer. If you want to buy by mail to obtain a powerful computer with less money, then select a well-known mail order computer manufacturer. Better still, you can look for a reliable smaller company that offers a lower priced PC. To find such a company, ask a friend or anyone who has bought a computer by mail order and is satisfied with it. Whether your choice is an IBM compatible or a Macintosh, it all depends on your preference.

XI. The Bottom Line

Buy the computer that is right for your business needs. As long as you're buying a computer from a reputable manufacturing company, it doesn't matter whether you buy it from a local dealer or from a mail order marketer.

Selling Products: An Ideal One-Person Business

11

■ As a single-person business owner, you can reach your entrepreneurial destiny by selling products or services.

I. Kinds of Product Needs

Whether you live in Florida, in Pennsylvania, or in Columbia, you use products in your daily life. For instance, you need shoes for walking, a watch for knowing the time, or a car for going to places where you what to be.

Products are manufactured and sold so that man may have an enjoyable and comfortable life.

Product needs are of two kinds: necessities and luxuries.

Necessities

Necessities are used by most of us. They include clothes, toothbrushes, kitchen utensils, etc. You need these simple products to make life easier and more enjoyable. You don't need to be rich to buy these products for your daily use.

Luxuries

Luxuries include high-cost jewelry, private swimming pools, yachts, and some small planes. Luxuries are things that you live without. But to some people, luxuries are necessities. For instance, to Ross Perot, a private plane is not a luxury because he has the money to buy it. He may need it to make his travel time shorter, thus saving time in managing his business empire. To actress Sharon Stone, a collection of high-priced clothes and pieces of jewelry is a necessity, not a luxury.

So you see, while some products may be luxuries to some people, they may be not be luxuries to others.

As the saying goes, "Find a need and fill it." Based on this theory, many an entrepreneur has become wealthy—providing products to the general market or to a niche market.

II. Right Products

In selecting a product or products for sale to your market, you must answer several questions: Do people have a need for your products? Is there a market for them? How would you reach your market?

Competition

Study the competition. See if many companies are already selling the products. Study how you will approach the market.

Distributors, Wholesalers, and Retailers

Research how you can find wholesalers and retailers that can resell the products. As a one-person business owner, you need the services of these marketers to cover a large segment of the market.

III. Sources of Products

You can have products for your market in two ways: 1) You can manufacture your own products or have them manufactured for you by other people or companies, or 2) you can purchase them from other manufacturers or distributors for resale.

Manufacturing

Manufacturing involves the turning of raw materials or semiprocessed goods and components (parts) into finished products.

When you make dolls or knitted wear at home and sell them to customers, you're engaged in manufacturing.

Manufacturing the Products Yourself. There are many advantages if you make your own products.

The name of the game is *mass production.* You can have the products mass-produced. You'll be the prime source of the products. You can have distributors or wholesalers distributing to retailers and other outlets.

This Man Wants to Be a Millionaire!

If you manufacture goods at home, you may need to produce goods with the following characteristics or needs:

■ Simple products
■ Simple or no machinery needed
■ Minimum production steps
■ Low-cost materials
■ Mass production possible

Let Other People or Businesses Manufacture Them. If the supply demands it, have your product or products made by other people or other companies who have the necessary equipment and personnel to manufacture them. In other words, subcontract the manufacturing of your products. Usually, it's best to pay the producer per piece or per unit.

When you bring a manuscript, for instance, to a book printer, you and the latter become the manufacturers. You, being the writer and publisher, write, typeset, and layout the book through your desktop publishing software and the printer then produces it into a book. Thus, mass production takes over. With enough money, you can have a print run of 10,000 or 50,000 copies, depending on the demand for it. Also, if you engage in newsletter publishing, (See Chapter 19, *How to Publish a Newsletter,* page 203), you can use the services of a commercial printer to print it for your subscribers. This applies to whatever products you manufacture or other people or companies manufacture for you.

Merchandise for Resale

If you don't want to manufacture your own products or you don't know what products to produce, you can search for new or improved products from suppliers and wholesalers.

Import. You may wish to import products from abroad and resell them. (See Chapter 17, *Running a Home-Based Import-Export Business,* page 161.)

Buying from Manufacturers, Distributors, or Wholesalers. When you purchase merchandise at wholesale price from manufacturers or distributors for resale, then you are a buyer and seller of products.

To look for new products, read business magazines such as *Business Opportunities*, and newspapers such as *The Wall Street Journal.* You may also regularly read the business sections of your local newspaper. In particular, read the new-product columns of every magazine in your field of interest.

IV. Selection of Suppliers

The selection of your suppliers is one of the most important decisions in acquiring goods for resale.

Single Supplier

For instance, for many years, conventional business wisdom has warned that depending on a sole supplier could sink your business. This may happen when a fire or a natural disaster occurs that causes a breakdown in the supply line of your lone supplier.

However, with a single supplier, you may get the best overall package deal in terms of price, cooperative advertising, product warranties, and service arrangements.

Several Suppliers

If you, however, have several suppliers of goods, there will be more backups whenever one or two of your suppliers cease operations.

The disadvantage, however, is that you may not get the package deals that you may obtain from a single supplier.

A Small Supplier

The Way to Do It

Whether you want to have a sole supplier or a group of suppliers, you need to use a few common-sense purchasing rules. Here are some of them:

■ Always establish a smooth working business relationship with your supplier or suppliers. You can do it by having constant communications about deliveries, potential substitutions for materials or products (if the original products are not available), product improvements, etc.

■If you have one supplier, keep abreast of other alternative supply sources that may supply you with products in case your supplier is unable to do it. To expand your supplier pipeline, you can acquire information from your trade association directory as well as from other contacts to expand your supplier pipeline.

■ Investigate the supplier's financial condition.

■ Request customer references whether you're looking for a sole supplier or a group of suppliers. Call these references and ask about the supplier's performance regarding deliveries and availability of products.

Remember, a supplier can make or break your business.

V. Pricing Strategies

You are in business to make profits. Without profits, you'll go bankrupt. That's why you need to price for profits. Maximizing profits is the name of the game.

Manufacturer's Price Formula

If you are a manufacturer (whether you manufacture the product yourself or a manufacturer or a subcontractor makes it for you), here's the standard formula you may use:

Product and/or service cost + overhead + profit = wholesale price x 2 = retail price

As you can see, after you have determined the wholesale price, you multiply it by two. That is, the amount over wholesale price represents the *discount* you'll give to your national or regional distributor or wholesaler. Using this formula, you give a 50 percent discount to your distributor or wholesaler. A *discount* is a reduction from the regular selling price (list price) of a product, usually expressed in terms of a percentage of the selling price. (Usually, you should allow discounts of 50 to 60 percent.) Therefore, if you wish to give a 60-percent discount or it's the percentage that the distributor demands, add another 10 percent discount, multiplying the wholesale price by more than 2 to determine the retail price.

For instance, as a manufacturer you may give a 50-percent discount to your national distributor to the trade. (See Chapter 15, *Distributors: Your Lifelines to Profits & Growth,* page 135.)

Here's how it's done:

Citing the price of a particular product, say for instance $10.00, you give a discount of 50 percent to your distributor. Your distributor in turn may give different discounts to wholesalers and retailers.

Fifty percent of the selling price of $10.00 is $5.00 (your discount to your distributor). If you subtract $5.00 from $10.00, the answer is $5.00. That is, you have $5.00 left (from the retail price). If the costs of your printing and other variable costs such as promotion, amount to $2.00 (depending on the number of products manu-

factured), your contribution to overhead and profits is $3.00. (Overhead represents a small amount as a contribution to your yearly fixed costs, such as rent, license, and depreciation.)

To figure out how the above retail price was calculated, here's the formula used:

$2.00 + $3.00 = $5.00 (wholesale price) x 2 = $10.00 (retail price)

If you think the discount is not enough for your distributor or wholesaler, then you must increase the retail price to raise the percentage and reach your profit goal at the same time. It's because different industries have different percentages of discounts to distributors and wholesalers. For instance, in some industries, a 60-percent discount to national distributors is not uncommon; in some others, 50 percent. So if your industry demands a 60-percent discount to distributors, you must adjust your pricing.

If you want to give a 60-percent discount based on the above example, multiply the wholesale price by 2.5. Here's the formula:

$2.00 + $3.00 =$5.00 (wholesale price) x 2.5 = $12.50 (retail price)

Let's check the calculation: Sixty percent of $12.50 is $7.50. $12.50 minus $7.50 is $5.00 (wholesale price).

Here's another example, giving a 50-percent discount to distributor.

$2.50 (production costs) + $3.75 (contribution to fixed costs and profit)

= $6.25 (wholesale price) x 2 = $12.50 retail price.

If you wish to give a 60-percent discount, here's how it works:

2.50 + 3.75 = $6.25 (wholesale price) x 2.5 = $15.625 or just make it $15.63 or $15.65 (retail price).

Let's check the calculation: Sixty percent of $15.63 is $9.378 (just make it $9.38). $15.63 minus $9.38 = $6.25 (wholesale price).

You may use the above formula if you have a suggested retail price. Books, for instance, have only one price marked on the back cover of the book. If you have no suggested retail price, then the distributors and wholesalers just set their own retail prices by having a desired *markup* on cost (wholesale price) or by just multiplying the wholesale price by 2 or 3. (*Markup* is the difference between the selling price and the cost of the product purchased.)

Importer's Price Formula

If you are an importer of a product or products, you can use this formula:

Product and/or service cost + overhead + profit = wholesale price x 2 = retail price

(The product cost may include the freight and import costs. If you wish a larger discount, probably 60 percent, you may multiply the wholesale price by 2.5.)

Retailer's Price Formula

If you are a retailer or a mail order dealer acquiring products from suppliers, the formula may be like this:

Product and/or service cost (wholesale price) + overhead + profit = retail price

Many retailers apply this formula in setting their own retail price:

Wholesale price x 2 (or 3) = retail price

However, you cannot strictly use these mentioned formulas in all your pricing. Various factors can influence your setting of prices. Here are some of such factors:

1. *Price sensitivity.* This involves the "elasticity of demand" or sensitivity of buyers to price changes in terms of products purchased.

2. *Quality.* Usually, high quality products demand higher prices.

3. *Competition.* Competition may dictate the prices of goods. The more competition, the lower the prices. The lesser the competition, the higher the prices.

4. *Uniqueness.* If the product is unique, for instance, the only one of its kind, then the manufacturer may set a higher price. As competition comes in, the prices go down.

5. *Marketing objectives.* If you are just entering a new market, the price may be lower. If you just want a share of the market, the prices may be in comparison with the competition's or maybe a little bit higher.

6. *The business cost.* As a one-person entrepreneur with an office at home, you have lower overhead expenses. This may affect your pricing, setting it at a lower price.

7. *Volume.* Even if the profit per item is small, a product may be priced lower if a lot of items can be sold easily.

Bear in mind that different industries have different formulas for setting selling prices.

The bottom line is to set a reasonable price for your product that the market can afford to pay. At the same time, the price should give you a profit.

It is pure common sense that your profit will increase if you increase your volume of sales and reduce your overhead, production costs, and purchasing costs. You must at least have a minimum 10 percent profit in selling your products. If you can increase that to 20 percent or more, so much the better.

VI. Break-Even Point

The break-even point is the point at which income and expenses are equal. In other words, once you reach this point, your profits should start to mount. That is, provided you maintain the current trend of your expenditures and increase your sales volume.

The break-even point is a vital concept that is of importance to entrepreneurs because this analysis aids in determining how to price products. (That is, you must know how many units of your product you must sell in order to reach the break-even point, the level that is neither profit nor loss.)

Two types of costs must be understood in computing the break-even point: *fixed* and *variable*.

Fixed Cost

A fixed cost is one that remains almost the same, at least in the short run, regardless of operations or volume of sales. It includes rents, licenses, depreciation, etc. (The fixed cost is not directly related to the production of products or rendering of services.)

Variable Cost

A variable cost is one that changes in relation to output. This cost includes cost of product per unit (composed of materials, labor, and selling costs and commissions or discounts).

These figures are changeable, depending on volume manufactured or bought for resale.

Break-Even Price with a Given Target Number of Sales

In calculating a *break-even price* for a product, you need to know the approximate units that you can sell over a specific period of time, for instance, six months or a year. Then determine the fixed costs and the total variable cost for that same period. Then, apply this formula:

Fixed costs – total variable costs ÷ by number of units

For instance, your company has a fixed cost of $3,000 for a period of 6 months and you have a production cost (labor and material) of $3,000 for 1,000 units ($3.00 x 1,000 units) and a selling cost (commissions, discounts, etc.) of $4,500 ($4.50 x 1,000 units). Thus the variable costs will be $7,500. Three thousand ($3,000, fixed cost) plus $7,500 equals $10,500, the total costs. Ten thousand five hundred dollars ($10, 500) divided by 1,000 units equals $10.50 (break-even price).

So the formula with figures is:

$3,000 + $7,500 = $10,500 divided by 1,000 = $10.50 (break-even price)

Thus, the break-even price for 1,000 units is $10.50 per unit. So you have to price it over $10.50 for the desired profit.

Break-Even Units with a Target Price per Unit

The mathematical formula for computing *break-even point (BEP) in units* (to know how many units to sell to break even) is:

Retail price – variable cost per unit) ÷ by the fixed cost

Let's take the above product with a targeted price of $12.00, as an example. The fixed cost is the same, $3,000.

The formula with figures is:

$12.00 – $7.50 (variable cost per unit: $3.00 production cost and $4.50 selling cost per unit) = $4.50 (which is the margin or contribution to fixed cost)

= $3,000 (fixed cost) ÷ by $4.50 = 666 units

So 666 units should be sold to break even.

Break-Even Sales Volume

To know the *sales volume* the company needs to reach in order to attain the break-even point, simply multiply the number of units required to be sold by the selling price. In this particular case, multiply 666 units by $12.00. The answer is $7,992.00, which is the break-even point. From that point on, profits will be generated!

VII. Bottom Line

It's best to sell products because they can be mass-produced. Have products manufactured by you or by subcontractors. Products that are unique and useful sell well in the marketplace, whether sold in stores, through sales representatives, or via mail order.

Break-Even Sales Volume

Offering Services: Another Great One-Person Business 12

■ Today, more than ever before, services are booming!

In fact, the cutting of mid-managers, employees, and workers by large corporations and medium-sized companies has been a boon to service providers, including one-person operations. It's because reinvented companies have been delegating some jobs to outside sources.

Also, since most people are busy—working for someone else or running businesses of their own—offering services has become another great one-person business.

I. Service Businesses

"At-home" and "out-of-home" services can be offered or sold to individuals and businesses.

"At-Home" Services

Examples of those offering at home services include consultants, private teachers, tax preparers, writers, and newspaper and magazine clipping services. That is, these services can be provided while you are at home.

Usually, service-oriented businesses are offered locally to clients or customers. However, there are times that your service can be provided nationally or even internationally. For instance, if you're a psychic or a consultant advertising in classified ads of newspapers and magazines and using a 900 number, you can provide services nationwide.

As a trade consultant, you may provide services to clients from abroad who may want to export goods to this country.

"Out-of-Home" Services

Examples of those offering out-of-home services include insurance agents, interior decorators, photographers, general contractors, public speakers, sales representatives, and manufacturer's agents. In other words, these services can be provided to your clients out of home.

Of course, some services can be done both at home and out of home.

Your home service business may be based mostly on your craftman's skills or on your brain skills and/or your work experience.

Craftman's skills include technical work, such as auto or TV and radio repair, piano tuning, and watch repairing.

Shoe Repairing: A Service Business

Based on your brain skills, you may become a student tutor, a resume´ writer, or a publicist.

Acquiring Skills and Knowledge

Where do you acquire skills or knowledge? Based on your inborn talent, educational background, and work experience, you can become an expert service provider in a particular field.

If you do not have enough knowledge or information on the service that you may want to offer to clients, you may buy books in the special field you want to enter or enroll in a community college offering courses pertaining to the service you may wish to sell.

How to Package Yourself

Products are not only the ones to be packaged. As a service provider, you have to sell yourself and your services.

You must acquire special tools to practice your profession as a man or woman fixing things or giving advice or teaching. The necessary things for your business should be acquired, such as a desk, a file cabinet, a typewriter, a computer, a fax machine, a beeper, etc. (See Chapter 9, *Smart Technology: The Effective Tool in a One-Person Business*, page 67.)

In packaging yourself, you must dress properly according to your chosen type of work. If you're a plumber, there's no need to appear in coat and tie in your customer's home.

Business cards, letterheads, envelopes, brochures, etc. are necessary selling tools you may need to provide your services.

How to Get Customers

There are many ways you can do to seek customers.

Advertisement. You may reach customers by advertising in your local newspaper, especially in the classified ads section.

Referral. By giving quality work, you may have some customers referred by people you have serviced. Or you may request your friends or relatives to refer prospective customers to you. (See Chapter 24, *Effective & Smart Networking,* page 245.)

Call-Me Service

Call-Me Service. One person who uses the telephone for service (besides giving seminars) is Dr. Lillian Glass, a renowed author and communications specialist who has taught many people vocal fundamentals, savvy speak-

ing, and conversational etiquette. Such people were Sean Connery, Dustin Hoffman, Julio Iglesias, and deaf actress Marlee Matlin.

Whether you're in Maine or in the Virgin Islands, you can set an appointment with her and be serviced on personal speech, voice evaluation, etc. You must call her in her office in Beverly Hills, California, for your weekly sessions at a scheduled time.

900 Number. If you have a 900 number for clients to call you, you need not worry about billing. Ask your local telephone company on how you can set up a 900 number. This may bring you good business.

An example of a user of this service is a legal adviser. Let's name her Michelle Smith. Michelle gives legal advice anytime and anywhere she is; whether she's shopping in a mall, is on a picnic, or is playing golf. She is doing it with her portable cellular telephone. She advertises in her local paper for the service she provides. Her answers to questions are simple and direct to the point so that her customers won't pay too much on telephone bills.

Pricing Your Service

In determining the fee you should charge a client or a customer, you may ask the following questions: How much should I be paid per hour? How many hours do I need to work in a day?

For instance, as a freelance editor, you may charge $10.00 per hour or $1.00-$3.00 per page of a manuscript. Fees for editors vary; some of them are even higher. (You may see some editing fees in classified ads in *Writer's Digest* magazine.)

As another example, a photographer uses different price strategies. Usually, he goes mostly by the average prices set by the American Society of Magazine Photographers (ASMP). When he is on assignment, he sees the ASMP price ranges for assignment and sets his own fee in that range. On doing photography work, he charges a day rate.

Generally, there are the so-called standard rates in any particular field or industry. You can probably set your prices based on these prices or on what you think you should be paid for your expertise or on the client's ability to pay. You may also base your fees on your relation to the customer. When you're providing a service to your friend or a relative, that's a different story.

Selling Products

When you're offering services, you may also sell products to increase your income. For example, if you're a hairdresser, you may sell hair and skin products and other products, such Avon. While you're cutting a customer's hair, for instance, you may convince him or her to buy your hair products. But if you're coloring her hair, you don't want to sell her some easy-to-use hair-coloring products.

Subcontracting Your Services

Unlike in selling products, you can't use distributors and dealers as a one-person service provider. As one person, you can only do certain things at a certain period of time. Hence,

depending on your expertise, you may not be able to accumulate enough money that you set for yourself in a year's time if you do all the work by yourself. Of course, there are exceptions. If you're a successful consultant, for instance, you can name your price.

For other services, to earn for instance $100,000 a year, you may subcontract your services to as many people as possible.

As an example, if you're a deck contractor, you can accept several construction jobs at the same time if you have back-up contractors. You can work on a particular deck job, and you may subcontract the others to your fellow contractors. If you charge $7,000 for a certain deck, you may subcontract it at $5,000 or $6,000. Then $7,000 minus $5,000 or $6,000 equals your profit. Of course, you must be sure that your subcontractors can do real quality jobs, as you do. If not, you'll be in big trouble!

As an accountant, you may look for many accounts and then subcontract them to other reliable accountants.

Hiring Temporary Helps

Whatever your service business at home, whenever you have mountains of workload, you may hire temporary help. That is, you pay them per hour or per job.

II. Service Businesses

There are many service-oriented businesses. The following includes some service professions or service-oriented businesses that may be provided to individuals and businesses.

Accountant
Advertising Consultant
Apartment Locator
Back Issue Magazine Dealer
Beautician
Beauty Consultant
Bicycle Repair Service
Book and Magazine Binding
    Service
Bookkeeper
Business Information Service
Business Plan Preparation Service
Carpet and Drapery Cleaning
    Service
Chimney Sweeping Service
Collection Agency
Computer Consulting
Computer Literary Training
Computer Programmer
Cooking Classes
Counselor (Investments, etc.)
Courier
Credit and Collection Agency
Credit Repair Consultant
Desktop Publishing
Editing Service
Export-Import Management Agent
Financial Brokerage
Financial Planner
Finding Mates by Mail Service
Foreclosure Locator and Advisor
General Contractor
Graphics Designer
Hairdresser
Handwriting Analysis
Home Handyman
Home Inspection
Horoscope Reading
Image Consulting
Instruction Manual Writer
Interior Designer
Language Translator
Licensing Agent

Limousine Service
Mail Order Loan Finder
Match Making Service for Singles
Medical Claims Processing
Mobile Bookkeeping
Party Planner/Coordinator
Personal Advice by Mail/Phone
Personalized Children's Books
Personal Computer Maintenance
Personal Organizer
Photographer
Plant Service in Offices
Private Teacher
Property Tax Consulting
Publicist
Public Relations Agency
Public Speaker
Publication Clipping Service
Resume Preparation Service
Sales Representative/Agent
Seminar Promoting
Shopping Service for Busy People
Speed Reading Class Teacher
Stock Market Advisor
Student Tutoring
Studio Instructor (dance, etc.)
Tax Preparation Service
Telecommunications Consulting
Tradesman (plumber, etc.)
Translator
Telephone Salesperson
Travel Agency
Tutoring Service
Typing Service
Venetian Blinds Cleaning
Venture Capital Agent
Videotaping
Wake-up and Reminder Service
Wedding Photographer
Wedding Planner
Window Washing Service
Word Processing
Writer (Press releases, etc.)

They are only some service-oriented businesses that you may run at home or outside the home.

The service business that you may start and operate depends on your talent, educational and family backgrounds, work experience, and personal ambitions. Know your strengths and weaknesses, your skills and knowledge, and the things you most enjoy doing, and you'll find it easy to know what service-oriented business you should be in. As the saying goes, "find a need and fill it." (So the business service you may engage in may not be even listed in this book.)

As mentioned before, as a one-person business operator, you may subcontract some of your services to other experts or you may pay temporary workers per hour or per project in order to attain your projected periodic sales volumes. You must run your office simply but effectively, as discussed in different chapters of this book. Take advantage of advanced technology. For instance, as a service provider, you may be in dire need of a portable cellular phone or a beeper besides your office equipment so that you can be contacted by your customers anytime, wherever you are.

So start the business now and good luck to you!

III. Bottom Line

Select a business based on your education, experience, and ability. To be a successful one-person service provider, you need to have a partnership with allied businesses, subcontracting some of your services.

Go for It!

Savvy Marketing: How to Sell Your Products or Services   13

■ Before you offer a product or a service, you must first know if there is a market for it. The question you must answer is, "Who will buy it?" If you have enough buyers, then you have a business!

I. What is a Market?

A market is a particular segment of the population or business that needs your products or services and who has the money to buy them. The two major markets are the *general market* or *mass market* and the *niche market* or *single-target market*.

1. General market. The general market is a large part of the people who are in need of general products, such as cosmetics, health products, and appliances. Using mass marketing, it is expensive for an entrepreneur to reach this segment of the population, whether it is done through direct mail or ads in magazines or newspapers or on radio or television.

As an example of a product you may sell to the general market, you may manufacture a new kind of toothpaste—and you hope everybody buys it.

2. Niche Market. The general or mass market can be narrowed down to various groups or segments, which may be called *niche markets* that have special interests, needs, and characteristics. Niche marketing is less expensive because you target your products or services to a particular group of persons or businesses that may need them.

For instance, you may write and publish a book on how to maintain a Stealth and you can offer it to buyers of this Chrysler car.

Market Research

Before you manufacture your products or offer your services, you must make a marketing research, complete with a marketing plan.

Marketing habits do change. Today's products may no longer be saleable one or two years from now.

Here are some questions you may answer: What business am I in? Will my product or service sell? Who is my customer or client? (Male? Female? Rich? Poor? Teenaged? Middle-aged?) Is my product or service offered by many companies? Is it available in my local area? How can I reach my market? How much is my marketing budget? How are my products or services different from that of the competition?

Is my target market likely to expand? Suppose the economy worsens, will my product or service still sell? Suppose the economy improves, will my operations expand? How can I get a share of the market and compete as a one-person company? The questions can go on and on and on.

Market Testing

You can sell a product before you produce it. How? By market testing. You may test a market in various ways:

For instance, you can (1)go out and test the market yourself (2) do a mass mailing to a certain segment of the population with a business reply envelope in which to return the survey questionnaire, (3) place a classified ad in a magazine seeking inquiries or information on a certain product or service, (4) hire a marketing expert or a marketing research company to do the survey for you, (4) get free or nominally market-research assistance from a local Small Business Development Institute or Small Business Development Center (SBDC).

SBDC offices are staffed by professional business volunteers and usually are located in offices of the Service Corps of Retired Executives (SCORE), in chambers of commerce, or in community centers. Also, Small Business Institutes, affiliated with the Small Business Administration, are housed at colleges and universities and provide intensive management assistance by teams of qualified college students in business management. They are usually listed in local phone directories.

Testing the Market

II. Product Packaging

The packaging of your product is your best advertising tool. It can make the difference between a sale and an ignored item.

Materials

Whether you manufacture your own product or let a company produce it, you must decide how it will be packaged: plastic bags, cellophane bags, or boxes. Have a design that is simple, yet one that will convey the message you want to tell your prospective customers. A design, together with the total package, must attract attention as if saying, "Hey, come and buy me!" Remember that your product will compete with many others on shelves or in floor displays.

Package Designer

After you decide how you want your product packaged, search for a package designer. Ask for information from those in the know in your industry. Or look for a designer in the phone book's yellow pages. Search under the heading "Package Designers" or "Packaging Specialists." Or you may find a designer that advertises in your industry's magazine or newsletter. But remember, you must deal with professionals, not amateurs.

Sample Designs. Before you deal with any supplier of package design, ask for samples of designs that the designer has produced. In that way, you'll have an general idea about the supplier's style of product designs. Know beforehand what ideas the designer has about the packaging of your product.

Written Contract. It's wise to have a written contract between you and your package designer. For example, if you're dealing with a professional graphics designer who will prepare the cover of your book, specify what should be included in the design, the deadlines when the first sketch or rough should be submitted to you, and the date the final design is to be finished from the date the selected sketch is approved.

In short, don't settle for a single package idea; request the designer to come up with several alternative ideas in rough form. Then examine each of them when making your final decision. If you like some aspects of more than one concept, then work with the designer to have the good aspects of

two or more concepts combined in some way, into a single package design. Don't forget to include information on the product benefits or what the product can do, plus the price and the name of your company and/or the name of your distributor.

Also specify in the contract that the supplier should submit prototypes or mockups for feedback from your distributor or your prospective distributors. As an example, in the case of books, color mockups are distributed to sales representatives by a distributing company and then the books are sold to bookstores and wholesalers, even when the books won't be released until a few months later (See Chapter 12, *Offering Services: Another Great One-Person Business,* page 107.)

Of course, the terms of payment should be specified in the contract. Indicate the down payment and the schedule of payments of the balance. Most of the time, the cost of materials is extra; they are not included in the price quotation.

Display Materials

The product's package is not the only item to be considered. The display and point-of-sale materials are also included in the overall packaging of your product.

For instance, you may choose display materials that are counter displays, free-standing floor displays, or shelf displays. If possible, deal with a supplier that can provide you with both packaging and display materials. Then after the package is finished, have it (and the display material) photographed both in color and in black and white. The black-and-white photos are needed for press releases to various magazines and newspapers and the color photos are needed for inclusion in catalogs.

III. Distribution Channels

If you're a seller of a product that you manufacture or have manufactured by other companies, you may decide how it should be distributed and sold.

Master Distributor and Wholesalers

For instance, as a one-person company owner, you select a master distributor (other small distributors not covered by your contract with your master distributor) and wholesalers. (See Chapter 15, *Distributors: Your Lifelines to Profits and Growth,* page 135.) Of course, you may also promote and sell your products through your own mail order or through other mail order dealers who advertise and sell products by direct mail or by advertisements in newspapers and magazines.

You may attract distributors or wholesalers to sell your product by having a unique item, or by having a line of good products that can compete with other products in the market in quality, price, and dependability.

Department Stores and Convenience-Store Chains

If you have only one product and no distributors are interested in carrying it, or if you can't reach a favorable contract with another distributor, you may sell it yourself to chain stores.

Here's an example of a woman who did just that.

One day in August 1977, a unemployed woman, Sophia Collier, concocted in her kitchen a natural beverage drink that she called *Soho Soda.* She knew then and there that it was a unique product that could bring her big money.

Yet she had no money to hire anyone to distribute her product. She couldn't get a good contract with any distributor. Hence, she delivered bottles of soda herself from the back of her Jeep.

Collier defined her market and worked with small convenience-store chains. In other words, she carved her own niche in the gourmet soft-drink industry. As a result, her company, Collier's American Natural Beverage Company grew into a multimillion-dollar business and attracted takeover offers from companies such as Seagram Beverage Company, which eventually purchased Collier's company.

Sales Representatives and Manufacturers' Representatives/Agents

In every industry, there are sales representatives and manufacturers' representatives/agents. For instance, there are sales representatives or groups distributing educational books to teacher and school supply stores. You may choose to give discounts or commissions.

Catalog Sales

You may also send samples of your product to giant catalog houses that mail millions of catalogs every year for possible inclusion in their publications. You give these catalog houses from 50 percent to 70 percent discount on your product. So price your product in such as a way that you will have a reasonable profit.

There are also other mail-order dealers with catalogs of their own offering products by mail. You may contact them in business magazines, such as *Opportunities Magazine.* Place an ad in its classified section and you may be swamped with offers to sell your product. (See *Chapter 16, How to Start & Operate a Mail Order Business,* page 147.)

Door-to-Door Selling

You may sell your product door-to-door by hiring unemployed or high school students, giving them a discount of 50 percent (or more) on your product. So instead of paying by the hour, you pay them per piece of product sold.

IV. Promotional Methods

Promotion involves the marketing of your products and services to a general market or a niche market. Whether you sell your products through distributors and wholesalers and other dealers, or distribute or sell them on your own, you must create public awareness of your products: why they are different from other products and why people or businesses should buy them.

In promotion, you must develop a marketing campaign especially tailored for you. That is, you must base your promotion efforts on the following elements:

1. Your personality
2. Your budget
3. Your time

If you're an outgoing person and a good speaker, you probably should concentrate on seminars, speaking engagements, and public relations activities to promote your products or services.

On the other hand, if you're a conservative type of person and public speaking is not your forte, you must concentrate on direct-mailing and advertising activities.

Of course, all your efforts must be based on how much money you can afford to spend on advertising and how much time you need to do activities, such as seminars, speaking engagements, and public relations.

It will be of benefit to you if you can apply all the four major promotional or marketing methods. They are *word-of-mouth marketing, public relations, direct marketing,* and *advertising.*

Word-of-Mouth Marketing

Word-of-mouth marketing involves many facets of your business. For instance, the first thing to do for your business is to give it a name that will stick to minds of the public; that is, a name that will tell what business you are in and what products you sell. In other words, with a proper business name, you can create a good image for your products or services.

Networking. Word-of-mouth marketing also involves your dealing with other entrepreneurs in meetings where you network. (See Chapter 24, *Effective & Wise Networking,* page

245.) In those meetings, you may find some dealers for your products or they may refer you to other distributors and wholesalers. You, too, of course, may give them some tips on selling products or services. In other words, networking allows you to learn from each other.

To have successful word-of-mouth marketing, you must talk with many people as much as possible to tell them about your business and your products. These people may be your friends, relatives, and colleagues. In short, you talk to seek new contacts or to follow through on old contacts and to build good business relationships.

Word-of-Mouth Referrals. Word-of-mouth referrals may provide good business for you, whether you are engaged in a product-oriented or service-oriented business. Referrals, however, are especially important in most service-oriented businesses.

In a survey conducted by a business magazine, it was found out that most businesses surveyed received word-of-mouth referrals from business associates: 44 percent chose a lawyer by word of mouth; 45%, an accountant; 45 percent, an advertising agency, 42 percent, a business consultant, and 42 percent a marketing firm.

One of my books, *The Book of U.S. Postal Exams,* has become a very successful book for me through word-of-mouth referrals. (I seldom advertise this book.) Many postal applicants who bought my book scored 95 to 100 percent on their tests and landed post office jobs. They usually recommend this book to their friends and relatives

as the best postal exam review. Hence, the book has become a national best-seller.

So when customers buy your product, and are satisfied with it, they may recommend it to their relatives or friends.

The same is true with services. Clients or customers who are satisfied with your services may recommend you to other people.

Public Relations

Public relations involves free publicity in the media and holding seminars and giving speeches.

Free Publicity. You may get free publicity for your products or services by writing press releases and sending them to newspapers, magazines, radio, TV, and business and trade publications. If the products or services you're offering can benefit their readers or listeners, especially if they are new and unique products or services, publications may publish your press release and radio and TV stations may broadcast it. You may also be invited to be a guest of a radio or TV show where you'll be asked about your particular field of expertise or your particular product or service.

As an expert in a particular service or product, you may write articles about it for publications. Thus, you may receive free publicity for your business.

Seminars and Speeches. You may give seminars or speeches. In some instances when the occasion warrants it, after the seminar or after a speech, you may mention the benefits of your products and services and offer them to the audience.

Be a Seminar Speaker

Direct Marketing

Direct marketing may involve *classified and display advertising, direct mail, samplings, contests, sales seminars, contests, newsletters, trade shows and exhibits,* and *flea markets.*

Classified and Display Advertising. This involves placing classified and display ads in the right newspapers and magazines. (See Chapter 16, *How to Start & Operate a Mail Order Business,* page 147.)

Direct Mail. Direct mail means the mailing of promotional pieces, which may include a brochure, a letter, and a return envelope offering products or services to prospective customers. You may mail a one-piece brochure, with or without a cover letter, if you have only one product or one service to offer or a catalog if you have several products or services to sell.

Sampling. Sampling may involve giving away samples of products to a certain sector of the population or to a group of authorities who are known in their professions. For instance, if you have an educational book, you may send a free sample to a school principal to have it reviewed for possible comments or for recommendations to teachers and parents. If you have a new brand of lipstick, then perhaps you may give away samples of it to have it tried by your market.

Contest. One way of promoting your business is to launch a contest that may involve your particular product or service.

For instance, you may launch a contest about how the product you sold to customers benefitted them. In that way, such a contest may result in many sales of your product.

Newsletter. Publishing a newsletter about your products or services is a good way to frequently get in touch with your current customers and prospective customers. With a newsletter, you can show how they may use your products or how they can be serviced continuously by your company. In the newsletter, you may also publish other information that may be of help to them in their daily living, whether at home or out of home. You also announce your forthcoming products. A newsletter may be offered free or with a yearly paid subscription.

Trade Shows and Exhibits. It's a good idea to display your products in trade shows and exhibits sponsored by a national organization covering the industry you're in. In these shows, you'll also see products sold by your competitors. You'll know what and how they're doing and may get some manufacturing or marketing ideas from them. Your competitors, in some ways, can also be your friends with whom you can network. You'll know who distributes their products and you'll know what methods of marketing are effective to them.

Flea Markets. Flea markets, which are now booming, are one of the oldest sales methods—one person sells directly to another. Saleable in flea markets are items such as collectibles, antiques, crafts, imports, or new American merchandise.

Hence, if you have products appropriate for the flea markets, then learn how you may find flea markets that want new dealers.

One source is a book entitled *Flea Market and Swap Meet Fun and Profit Manual* by Howard Hicks. The book is available from Fun and Profit Publishing, P.O. Box 53, Fountain Run, Kentucky 42133.

Advertising

Placing classified and display ads in magazines and newspapers is involved in direct marketing. However, there are other advertising media: *yellow pages, radio, television, business directories,* and *outdoor signs.*

Yellow Pages. In 1878, the first telephone directory was published by the New Haven District Telephone Company. It was a single-page directory listing customers of the telephone company. Several years later, a printer ran out of white paper and substituted a yellow paper. Thus, the Yellow Page directory was born.

Directories are targeted at various markets. For example, individual directories may be aimed at teenagers, college students, women or the elderly. For more information about Yellow Pages, write to the American Association of Yellow Page Publishers, 500 Chesterfield Center, Suite 250, Chesterfield, MO 63017, (314) 632-6515.

Radio. You can reach target audiences if you select appropriate stations and time periods. It's less expensive to advertise on radio than on TV.

Television. Since the viewers can see products being used, television is a good medium to advertise any product. However, you must only advertise a product on television if it's highly priced, maybe $35 or more to compensate for the high cost of advertising.

Business Directories. Associations of most industries usually publish business directories. You may advertise your products or services in these directories.

Outdoor Signs. Outdoor advertising may include billboards on highways, signs in airports and rail terminals, and posters on buses and taxicabs, etc.

V. The Product Life Cycle

The *product life cycle* (PLC) concept is of importance to entrepreneurs, especially to a one-person company owner. Like people, products go through different stages of life. Even before you conceive the idea of manufacturing or launching a product into the market, you must be aware of its life stages. The life cycle of a typical new product involves the following stages: *introductory, growth, maturity* and *decline*.

Introductory Stage

When you introduce a product into the marketplace, it is unknown to most of your targeted audience. That is why you must make preparation for its launching. For instance, you must know beforehand what type of distribution channels you will be using and how you are going to reach your market.

If you're an established company and you already have a network of distributors or wholesalers, you must have contacted them beforehand and you might have received some feedback on the saleability of this product to their market or established customers.

If this is your first product to market, then it will be difficult for you because there are no established products to support the new product financially. So introducing the new product will be expensive. You must think of the costs involved in design-

ing the product, in having it produced by a manufacturing company or a group of individual producers, in promoting the product, and in having it distributed by your distribution channels.

Distributors and dealers cannot simply add your new product to their line. Since its marketability is not yet proven, they may need only a limited number of items to be purchased and resold. The dealers may also ask for free counter displays or floor displays for your new product so that it will stand out in their stores. They may also ask for full return privileges if it is not sold.

In the introductory stage, sales may increase little by little, but your profits may be low because of the high cost of penetrating the market.

Growth Stage

Provided you have done your homework—sending out brochures, announcing the product in the New Products section of magazines and newsletters, and running ads in a few appropriate magazines—your targeted market will now be aware of the new product. In fact, sales and profits will increase and the product will be in many locations.

As sales begin to multiply, your start-up costs will be substantially absorbed by your increased sales. As the demand grows, you may need to go back to production. This time, in the case of books, you'll go into a reprint; pre-production preparation, such as shooting the camera-ready copy and other procedures are eliminated. The same is true with other products, the pieces of machinery needed for new productions are already set and ready to make a mass production of your product if it is needed.

At this stage. the advertising of the product is increased. When the product is already well-known, then you can expect that new competition may appear on the market.

Maturity Stage

At this stage, the product is already established. It has been recognized as a good and useful product by a large segment of the market. At this time, however, competitors offering the same type of products will appear on the market. These competitors, to get a slice of the market you have established, may offer competitive prices or, most of the time, lower prices. You should then launch new promotion efforts to protect your market. At the later part of this stage, sales start to taper off and you may expect profits to drop due to increased competition.

Decline Stage

Both sales and profits decrease at this stage. When the product has reached this stage, then you must do special promotions to get rid of your inventory and your distributors' inventories. Your dealers may eventually phase out your product if you can't revive it anymore.

VI. New! Improved !

After your product has reached the decline stage, you may give new life to it by doing new versions, new packaging, new colors, new materials, and new prices. You'll have new products on the market that say: "New! Improved!"

In the case of a book, you may revise and expand it. Eliminate the obsolete information and add new information. Thus, a book may contain these words on the cover: "New Edition!" "Second Edition!" "Revised and Expanded Edition!" "Complete Revised Edition!" etc. One more thing, the cover has a new design!

By improving or introducing a new version of a product with a new package design, it becomes a new one. Thus, if properly promoted and it's really useful, a product may experience again the different stages of life: introductory, growth, maturity, and decline. (Of course, not all products can be revived into a new one. It depends on the product's usefulness, the use at a certain place and time by a particular segment of the market.

VII. Testimonials

Wait for comments about your products to come to you. Usually, some people write letters to the manufacturer or distributors if they liked products they bought.

If they don't come, then seek them. Send samples of your product to appropriate persons or prospective customers and ask for their comments. Try to send some free samples of your products not only to authorities in different fields, but also to celebrities, and/or politicians. Favorable comments can serve as testimonials. Of course, you write them to ask for their permission to use their comments in your promotion. Testimonials—comments praising products (their effectiveness or usefulness) do help to sell products.

VIII. Awards & Recognition

You may mention in your promotional ads the awards and recognitions you have received for your efforts in community services and/or good products. Such awards and recognitions will enhance your image as a successful company in your community and industry.

Local Recognition

Whether you offer products or services, you should be involved in your local or statewide community activities. You may support local schools, clubs, sports teams, and civic organizations, such as Lions and Jaycees, in your city and state. If you're already known in your locality and if you have been of good service to organizations and institutions, you may receive some awards in the forms of certificates of appreciation or achievements or of plaques.

As a result of such awards and recognition, you may have the opportunity to be published in your local newspapers and magazines. Any publicity done by the sponsoring organization will ultimately add to your good image as a first-rate organization. If they don't issue a press release about your awards, then you should do it

yourself! You can't land in the newspaper if you have not done any outstanding accomplishments or received any awards!

Industry Awards

Participation in your particular industry's national contests, especially those sponsored by organizations that you are a member of, is another way of gaining recognition locally and nationally.

For instance, join competitions that recognize product designs and packaging, product uniqueness or usefulness, etc.

For example, as an author-publisher, I'm a recipient of two Benjamin Franklin Book Awards from the Publishers Marketing Association that sponsors a yearly Benjamin Franklin Awards competition. These awards are the most prestigious ones in independent book publishing, participated in by many small- and middle-sized book publishers in the country and some giant publishers in New York, including Random House. Also, I've won four other book publishing awards from Mid-America Book Publishers Association.

In addition, I (and my one-person company, of course), received the "1990 Small Press Publisher of the Year Award" (an award given only to one person or one company a year) from Quality Books, Inc., for having distinguished myself "by maintaining a high standard of excellence in independent publishing." Quality Books, Inc., is the largest distributor of non-fiction books to libraries in the U.S. and Canada.

Winners and finalists of Benjamin Franklin Awards are publicized every year in *Publishers Weekly* and other magazines and newspapers. As a result of such publicity, my books have been recognized as excellent books, resulting in thousands of library and bookstore sales throughout the country.

In short, due to recognition and awards I've achieved, my company and I have gained recognition within and outside the industry.

Therefore, you must exert your efforts in producing good products or rendering excellent services to win awards and recognition.

To win awards, you must, for instance, hire professionals in designing your products and packages. In the case of books, hire only good professional graphics designers in designing the covers, etc.

Also, enter as many national contests as possible.

IX. Bottom Line

■ It doesn't matter whether you enter the general market (mass market) or a niche market. If you have general distributors to the mass market, then you can introduce products for that market. The same is true with the niche market. If you must look for a special distributor for your niche market, then you can enter this market too. In other words, either one of them may be appropriate for you, but it would be better if you have products for both markets. As a one-person company owner, it's best to have your product handled by a master distributor (a national distributor selling products to other small distributors, wholesalers, dealers, and chain stores). In short, use the rifle-shot approach (niche market) and the shotgun approach (mass market) in promoting and marketing your products or services.

■ Get free publicity by sending press releases about your product or service to appropriate publications or by appearing on radio programs or TV talk shows.

■ Don't repeat an ad if it doesn't sell. If a test ad doesn't pay, disregard advertising in that publication.

■ Direct mailing is expensive. In direct mailings, it's best to send letters and brochures to associations, clubs, or groups of people — not to individuals, to get orders. In other words, *sell wholesale, not retail.* (You, of course, may receive unsolicited single orders from people who may have seen or read about your product.)

■ Don't attempt to sell door-to-door yourself! Hire people or sales groups to sell them for you.

■ If a product can't be revived (after its decline stage, eliminate it! You may then introduce a new product or a line of new products whether you manufacture them or obtain them from other suppliers.

Wise Ways to Manage Subcontracting & Partnering

14

■ *Outsourcing* (another term for subcontracting) and *partnering* are nowadays forged by small and large companies. To survive and progress in today's competitive business marketplace as a one-person business owner, you should delegate to outside sources your works: from manufacturing to promoting to marketing of your products. In that way, you can devote more of your time to launching more products or services and to operating your one-person business!

I. Outsourcing

Today's hot new business strategy known as *outsourcing*, which is actually *subcontracting*, is used by small and large companies. The word simply means delegating to outside sources some of the ordinary day-to-day functions of a business, such as data processing, payroll administration, and other matters. These outside sources are simply called *subcontractors*.

The Way to Do It

Many large companies do assign some administrative works to outside sources. I do the opposite: I do the mundane-but-necessary parts of my business, such as filing, networking, bookkeeping, cash management, inventory management, etc.

I, therefore, delegate the big tasks, such as production, promotion, and marketing, to outside subcontractors, including product designers, manufacturers, distributors, dealers, publicists, etc.

I operate my business in the kingdom of my house as if by remote control. My business operates even during my absence whether I'm attending a seminar in Hawaii or vacationing in Asia. You can do the same if you establish a network of subcontractors and other partners in business.

Different Industries, Different Subcontractors

Different industries have different subcontractors.

Subcontracting. Subcontracting is an agreement between two parties, in which the first party promises to pay the second party for the rendering of services or for the manufacture of parts of a product or a whole product. The agreement may be in writing or it may be verbally.

Such rendering of services or manufacturing of products are done for companies by other companies or individuals who may be considered as independent contractors. These contractors are called subcontractors because they are doing the things the service- or product-providers are supposed to do. In other words, the jobs are subcontracted to them by principal companies rendering or providing products to their clients or customers.

Partnering. There's also the new trend of business relationship between large and small companies. They call this business relationship *partnering*, which in fact, is directly related to outsourcing. In simple words, outsourcing and partnering are cousins.

Let George Do It

Your Partners in Big Business

The one-person business owner, more than anyone else, needs subcontractors. Selected carefully, subcontractors can provide you the big business you never dreamed of. Your company is small in size only because it has one employee (you), but your bank account is bulging with cash, and your operations cover the vast territory of the United States and even some parts of the world.

You have no problem with payroll. You have no problem with healthcare costs. All you have to do is operate your one-person commercial ship that plies the stormy seas of business with ingenuity, smartness, and common sense.

You'll be like a coach when you operate as one-person business owner. You select your players to do different tasks in playing in the fields of dreams of business. Whatever will be the results of a joint effort depends on the implementation of your strategies and techniques in operating a business, based on your overall business plan. Only, you select your subcontractors carefully. If you select the wrong subcontractors, your ship may run aground in the rough seas of competition.

Subcontractors

A subcontractor may be a manufacturer, a printer, a distributor, a wholesaler, or a dealer.

Since you should sign a written contract with your subcontractor, be sure to know the background of your subcontracting company: how and when it was established, its number of employees, its current financial condition, its facilities and equipment, etc. (This applies whether the subcontractor is a manufacturer or a distributor.)

A Distributor's Warehouse

It's wise to have a contract that spells out clearly all of the following details:

■ Who pays for the freight for the shipment of goods to be stocked in a distributor's warehouse? How about when any damaged or unsold goods are returned to you (in case products are on consignment)?

■In the case of manufacturers, when will be the definite shipping date of products manufactured? You need this to inform your distributors and wholesalers of the date of release of your goods to the market.

■The contract should have a provision that specifies that either of the contracting parties can terminate the contract if the cancellation request is received at least 90 days in advance, and if any other provisions or conditions of the contract are followed and implemented.

Of course, to look for subcontractors, you need to ask other entrepreneurs and leaders of your industry for information. You may also ask information from your industry's trade association. To look for manufacturers, see the *Thomas Directory of Manufacturers* in your local directory. Also, you may ask references from your subcontracting candidates.

A Dealer

Decision Sharing

Nowadays, since outsourcing has become a new business trend, subcontractors look more like partners and less like suppliers or distributors.

For instance, subcontractors now share in such decisions as the design of new products, the selection of raw materials, and the manufacturing processes.

In such a relationship, conflicts may occur. Here's a sample case:

If you're a publisher, you hire a book cover designer, who you think can create an attractive cover. In hiring a designer, naturally, you must make it clear that the rough layout of design must be approved by your distributor before a final design (or mechanical) is made.

When you (or your designer) submit one or two sample layouts, the art director and other people at your distributing company will make comments about the cover and how it can be improved.

Sometimes your designer may balk. He may tell you, "I think this is too much intervention! Several changes have been made already. I don't agree with their concepts of a good cover design. If we make more changes, I'll charge you for extra work time. You commissioned me to do this job and now I'm dealing with your distributor."

You must remember that the final decision is still yours. Although you're receiving feedback from your distributor, you may also have some ideas of your own on how the cover should look. The best thing that can happen is that you and your distributor may like the first layout with only minor changes. However, a problem may occur when you or your distributor is not in agreement with your designer's ideas.

In such a case, your distributor may make some suggestions involving minor changes, additions, and/or subtractions to improve the design. If you can get some good ideas from your distributor and can provide some of your own, and those of the graphic designer's, then you have enough ideas to improve a design. How to incorporate those ideas involving layout, typeface, graphics, and colors into a single concept requires careful negotiation and compromise to create a cover that can help sell the book. That is, you, your distributor, and your designer will all be satisfied in the end.

Such a situation may occur in any stage of designing any new product or in discussing what raw materials and manufacturing processes should be used.

Just remember, you are still in control of your one-person company!

Temporary Help

I do not hire part-time or temporary employees. But there are some one-person businesses that hire temporary help during business peak seasons or during their owner's vacation.

The three kinds of employees are *permanent, permanent part-time,* and *temporary.*

Permanent Employee. A permanent employee, on a yearly salary or on an hourly basis, is entitled to company benefits, such as paid vacations,

holidays, and sick leave (and medical benefits for companies that can afford them). Of course, as a one-person business, your company must not hire a permanent employee; otherwise, it won't be a one-person company anymore.

Permanent Part-Time Employee. A permanent part-time employee works in a job usually five days a week. However, he or she may not work more than 20 hours a week. The employee is not entitled to paid benefits, such as vacations, holidays, health insurance, etc. Moreover, the permanent part-time employee should not work more than 1,000 hours in any one year. After that, a part timer may be considered as a full-time employee.

Temporary Employee. A temporary employee is assigned to a particular job or project for a specific period. Like the part-time employee, the temporary employee doesn't receive any company benefits. Also, the temporary employee should not work more than 1,000 hours a year; otherwise, he or she may be considered as a permanent employee.

You must remember that if you hire part-time or temporary employees, you are dealing with subcontractors, whether they are high-school students, college drop-outs, or from the unemployed market.

One more thing: some businesses that hire students and others as part-time or temporary employees don't think about withholding taxes from their paychecks. Most of them presume that these part-timers are exempt from withholding taxes.

A part-time employee may be exempt only from tax withholding by complying with the following three requirements:

■ The employee must not have owed any tax during the last year of filing income tax.

■ The employee must not expect to owe any tax during the current year.

■ The employee has more than $550 of income per year (which includes nonwage income). Therefore, he or she may not be claimed as a dependent on someone else's tax return.

It is the employer's responsibility to withhold taxes if needed. If he doesn't and the individual doesn't pay the required income tax and other taxes, the employer can be held liable for those taxes.

Actually, as an alternative the most efficient, hassle-free system by which a one-employee company can obtain extra or part-time employees is to use temporary-help services. If you use temporary employees from these firms, you won't worry about payroll records and tax problems.

Controversies of Subcontracting

Subcontracting or dealing with independent contractors has triggered some controversies. In fact, the Internal Revenue Service (IRS) is strict in enforcing regulations regarding this matter. For the past several years, it has been investigating some small businesses that may be violating laws regarding the hiring of contractors.

In short, the IRS is investigating companies that may be considering some workers as independent contractors, instead of as employees.

The reason is simple: The employer is required to issue W-2 forms and to withhold all federal, state, and FICA taxes if a worker is considered an employee. If the worker is considered as a contractor, the employer gains and the government loses money.

There won't be any problem if you're dealing with companies or self-employed persons filing Schedule C with their tax returns. All you must do is to file Form 1099 with the IRS at the end of the year if the contractor's income is more than $600.00 per year.

Problems may occur only if you hire individual persons who are not filing Schedule C with their income tax returns.

To avoid any challenge to the legal status of contractors, legal experts recommend the following actions.

1. *Self-Audit.* Conduct a self-audit by using the following three-point test to prove that you're hiring an independent contractor:

■ There is sufficient lack of control and direction over the work of the worker.

■ The worker's services are sufficiently different from the company's business. Or the worker does his or her work away from the company's place of business.

■ The worker has his or her own independently established trade, profession, or business.

2. *Contract.* Sign a contract with the worker that specifies, among other things, that the latter fixes his own

hours and he or she is responsible for labor, materials, tools, and equipment for doing the work involved.

3. *Licenses.* Have the contractor pay for any required licenses. Also, let the contractor carry his or her own liability insurance.

Twenty-Point Test for Classifying Workers

The IRS specifically seeks to determine if the employer has the right to control and direct what a worker does. If the employer does *not* have a right, then the worker may be regarded as an independent contractor and not as an employee.

Here is a 20-point test, drawn from principles of common law used by the IRS to determine if a worker is an independent contractor or an employee. (For purposes of discussion, we shall mention the person or company seeking the services of an independent contractor as the "employer" even if the worker is temporarily hired or commissioned.)

A worker is an *independent contractor* if he or she

1. isn't required to comply with the employer's instructions as to *when, where,* and *how* to work;

2. doesn't receive any training or direction from the employer;

3. doesn't integrate his or her services into the business operations of the employer;

4. doesn't provide services that must be rendered personally;

5. can hire, supervise, and pay his or her own workers or assistants;

6. doesn't have a continuing relationship with the employer;

7. sets his or her own hours for work;

8. doesn't provide full-time work and is free to work when and how he or she chooses;

9. does the work in his or her own office or elsewhere and is not on the premises of the person or company for which the service is rendered;

10. does the work in an order or in sequence set by himself or herself;

11. is not required to submit regular reports, either verbally or written;

12. is not paid regularly, such as by the hour, week, or month;

13. doesn't receive payments for business and/or traveling expenses;

14. provides own materials, tools, and equipment in the performance of work;

15. has any significant investment in facilities used to perform the service, such as renting or maintaining the office;

16. can realize a profit or suffer a loss in the performance of the service;

17. works not for a single employer but for several persons and companies;

18. offers services to the general public;

19. cannot be fired unless he or she produces unsatisfactory work, which may be a violation of an agreement; and

20. may not end work without incurring liability.

I am an Independent Contractor!

II. Partnering

In the 1990s, the key to successfully launching new products to the market by small businesses is forming strategic alliances with other large businesses. This results in a small business becoming a big fish in the business world.

Author A. David Silver, in his book *Strategic Partnering,* cites five steps in forming alliances with strategic partners:

1. Development
2. Production
3. Marketing
4. Growth
5. Exit

Your company may seek alliances through this partnering system because you may have a new product that may need huge capital for its research, production, promotion, and marketing. Hence, you may seek companies that may produce and market your product.

In a nutshell, the possible points of alliances between your company and a partner or partners may involve joint research, development, and marketing. Some partners form virtual companies to launch certain products and they disband these companies after the projects have been implemented.

But the point is that you must retain the identity of your company and you must be in control of it. So you must establish your own virtual corporation that can survive even if any partnering is ended. In other words, it's not wise to create another virtual corporation with partners purposely to launch a certain product or products; that will no longer be a one-person company.

For more information on partnering, see *Strategic Partnering* by A. David Silver (McGraw-Hill Inc., New York, 1993, $29.95) in your local library. The book is sold in bookstores and via mail order.

Purposes of Alliances

As already mentioned, a strategic partnering between companies may involve developing, producing, and marketing products.

An example of such an alliance is between a start-up pharmaceutical company and a giant company. The new company may have a good product but it can't fully develop it and market it. So it must seek the help of a large pharmaceutical company. The purpose is to have access to its scientists, stamping machines, customer lists, and sales force to bring the product to a wider market. Such an agreement has been forged between pharmaceutical companies and other businesses for years. More and more alliances are being formed every year. Such alliances are also forged in many businesses, including those in computer and other technological companies.

They call this kind of relationship *partnering.* Actually a partnership, it's not called that name because it's not a *partnership* structure of business. Most of these alliances involved in partnering are temporary in nature, although some may be in effect for many years.

Actually, partnering is an old concept. For example, partnering is practiced by a small builder who organizes a team: a heating and cooling system installing company, an electrical and security system company, a group of workers with different skills, such as brick layers, etc. Besides this, he establishes alliances with financial institutions and good architects so he can build houses or buildings.

In other words, a builder may have only a few employees and only call on contracted companies or workers when houses or buildings are to be constructed. Most of the time, a building company constructs several models of houses at the same time at the same or different sites. They work in different stages. When the project is finished, the group is disbanded. But the group is formed again when another construction project is launched.

Such an alliance is a form of partnering, although in the strict sense, it's also subcontracting: different works are subcontracted to different companies or to different workers with specialized skills.

So you see, subcontracting and partnering are interrelated. As a publisher, when I pay my printer a certain amount of money (for example, $2.10 per copy) to print my books, I'm using the printing company as a subcontractor or as a supplier. But if I receive an order for 50,000 copies of a book and I can't finance it, I may negotiate a deal with my printer and propose that we form a partnering; that is, we co-publish the book and share the profits. If my printer is not agreeable, then I may seek another printing company that may be inter-

ested. That means the printing company may invest in the production cost and receive a certain percentage of the retail price or a certain kind of royalty.

This type of arrangement may also be done for other products. You may use the facilities and equipment of a company for the production of your product and you may use the marketing arm of that same company or any other company in promoting and marketing the product.

Your Partners

While operating your one-person company, your relationship with other companies, such as your subcontractors, may be considered as a type of outsourcing, but not the kind of formal partnering engaged in by companies launching certain products to the market. Your manufacturers, distributors, wholesalers, and other subcontractors are your partners in business.

If you're a service provider, you can also do partnering with other service providers.

Regarding my situation, I do partnering with my subcontractors. I don't have the resources for marketing my books, so I deal with my distributors so I can tap their research departments, their marketing departments, and their sales forces to present my books to other distributors, wholesalers, bookstores, and libraries.

Even at the development stage, my distributor knows what and how I'm doing with my projects. It's because they are also involved in my projects, from inception to production!

It's necessary because they are the ones marketing my products, which happen to be books.

So in dealing with your subcontractors or partners, you may experience that while you're fishing in the lake or shopping in the mall, your products are being marketed because you're using the resources of other companies. Is that the way to do business as a one-person company operator? Yes, it is! I've been doing it for the past 10 years.

In other words, share your profits (but not your losses) with other companies and you'll succeed in business.

You may also do partnering with other independent one-person operators and other small companies. For one, I do partnering with some one-employee companies by participating in cooperative mailings and advertising sponsored by two trade associations. When I participate in cooperative advertising with other publishers in *Publishers Weekly* through Publishers Marketing Association or Cosmep, I receive about a 60 percent discount from the regular rate.

This is partnering in marketing!

III. Bottom Line

As a one-person company, it doesn't mean that you must do all things by yourself. You won't be successful that way: you have only two feet, two hands, one brain, and one body.

As they say, "Let George do it!" Seek the alliances of established and independent small and large businesses as your subcontractors, distributors, and dealers.

Make use of their human and financial resources, facilities, and equipment to bring your products to the marketplace.

In a nutshell, you must do the following:

■ Seek only alliances with companies that you can trust and share your decisions and goals with for mutual benefits. In other words, find subcontracting companies or partners with whom you can be compatible.

■ Don't balk if your subcontractors, especially distributors, get a large portion of your profits based on standard distribution arrangements. Remember, they may stock your products, ship and bill them to their customers, collect the payments for you, and then send you checks every month as if you were a pensioner. (Note: This is the case in the book industry. Maybe it's different in some industries.)

■ If you have invented a unique and useful product and you don't have the capital for research, production, and marketing, you may consider partnering with an established company in your industry.

■ You must seek alliances, not only with established small and large companies, but also with one-employee companies like yours for cooperative mailings, advertising, and other forms of marketing.

■ Subcontracting and partnering are the spark plugs for your growth and huge profits. Make use of them!

Distributors: Your Lifelines to Profits and Growth

15

■ Whether you sell products or services, your distribution system is the key to building a successful one-person company. This is why you should be careful in determining and deciding on which distribution channels you use.

A distribution system may include all the methods, companies, and other intermediaries involved in the process of moving products and services from producers or service providers to the ultimate users.

Involved in these functions are businesses and other intermediaries which are referred to by a number of terms, including distributors, wholesalers, manufacturers' representatives/agents, sales representatives, brokers, jobbers, merchants, auctioneers, and retailers.

I. Distribution Channels

Based on the functions of product distribution intermediaries, a distribution network may be divided into five channels.

Channel 1: *Manufacturer* (or *importer* of products or prime source of products) sells direct to *consumer*.

Channel 2: *Manufacturer* (or *importer*) sells direct to *retailer*. Retailer, in turn, sells to *consumer*.

Channel 3: *Manufacturer* (or *importer*) sells through *representative/ agent* to wholesaler (or *sales representative*), who sells to *retailer*. Retailer, in turn, sells to *consumer*.

Channel 4: *Manufacturer* sells to *wholesaler-distributor*. Wholesaler-distributor, in turn, sells to *retailer*. Retailer then offers goods to consumer.

Channel 5: *Manufacturer* (or *importer*) sells or consigns goods to a *master distributor or national distributor*. The master distributor or national distributor then sells to *wholesaler-distributor* or *jobber*. The *wholesaler-distributor* or *jobber* then sells to *retailer*. Retailer then offers goods to *consumer*.

As you can see, there are at least five channels that you may use to put your products into the hands of consumers.

In Channel 1, as a one-person business company, you may sell direct to consumers if you do it via mail order: advertising your products in appropriate newspapers or magazines (classified and display ads). You may also do it by using 800 (toll-free) telephone numbers. You may use a 900 number (calls charged to your customers' telephone numbers) if you sell consultation or information.

Also, you can use your product as a "premium" or "incentive" item by companies, such as banks, magazine publishers, corporations, and institutions, to be given as a gift, a bonus, or a give-away. It may be given to those people opening new bank accounts or subscribing to certain magazines. (In short, a premium or incentive item is used as a device to obtain or increase sales and/or promote goodwill. Such an item may be a book, a diary, a fountain pen, or a toy. This is known as the premium and incentive market.

Resource:

Premium, Incentive & Travel Buyers
The Salesman's Guide
1140 Broadway, #1203
New York, NY 10117-0130
(212) 684-2985
Focus: 16,000 premium users and buyers

II. Intermediaries

Distribution functions may fall into the following categories of intermediaries to be used by a one-person business: *distributors, wholesalers, middlemen,* and *retailers.*

Distributors

Distributors may operate geographically or nationally. They have different functions.

Master Distributors. In the book industry, there are those companies that are called *master distributors* that operate nationally. Master distributors are not wholesalers or jobbers in this case. The wholesalers have no sales representatives and they buy books from master distributors or direct from most general book publishers to fill orders from retail stores. On the other hand, master distributors actively engage in soliciting orders for books.

In other words, in the book industry, master distributors do the following:

1. *Fulfillment.* Warehousing, packing, and shipping.

2. *Financial.* Credit approving, billing, and collecting payments.

3. *Customer Service.* Phone and mail soliciting, shipping problems, and returns.

4. *Sales.* Publishing catalogs, displaying at conventions, doing cooperative advertising, and soliciting by sales representatives.

Master distributors usually represent medium-sized and small publishers. They sell books to other small distributors, wholesalers, bookstores, and libraries.

They may have in-house sales representatives (who are paid salaries by their companies) or they may be in association with outside sales representative groups who are paid commissions.

Master distributors accept books from publishers on consignment. They usually get big discounts because they also give discounts to other distributors, wholesalers, dealers, and bookstores.

National Distributors. In other industries, there may also be some national distributors. One such industry is magazine publishing. If you can find one in your particular industry, so much the better.

To seek a manufacturer and a wholesaler-distributor you may see *The Thomas Register of American Manufacturers*, which is available in your local library.

Foreign Distributors or Wholesalers. If you want to export your products to other countries, you may contact the U.S. Department of Commerce for leads to distributors and wholesalers abroad. You may also get in touch with foreign embassies and consulates in the United States.

Another way is to contact local or foreign agents who can look for any distributors and wholesalers in other countries. (See Chapter 17, *Running a Home-Based Import-Export Business*, page 161.)

Wholesaler-Distributors

In almost all industries, wholesalers are also called *distributors* (and vice versa). So the terms are interchangeable and are called different names in different industries. In some industries, distributors are also called *jobbers*. In multi-level marketing plans, direct sellers are also called *distributors,* even if they sell directly to consumers instead of to retailers.

Wholesalers are companies whose primary business is to sell products to other businesses, such as retailers or other commercial markets; they do not sell to the final consumer market. The industrial wholesaler may buy from a manufacturer and then sell to another manufacturer that may use the product as a part of another product. Concerning consumer products, the wholesaler buys from the manufacturer. Then the wholesaler resells the products to the retailer who, in turn, sells them to the ultimate consumer.

Wholesalers are always expected to carry a large stock of products from producers to meet retailers' needs. They pay for the products they stock, according to previously agreed payment terms. Usually, wholesalers don't have their own sales forces; however, there are some wholesalers that do have sales forces to promote their business to retailers. Unlike retailers, wholesalers do very little advertising.

Resources:

Food Service Distributors
   Chain Store Guides
Lebhar-Friedman, Inc.
425 Park Ave.
New York, NY 10022-3559
212-371-9400
Focus: 3,500+ food distributors

Thomas Grocery Register
Thomas Publishing
One Penn Plaza
New York, NY 10119-0103
(212) 290-9400
Focus: Grocery chains and wholesalers

Sporting Goods Register
Sporting Goods Dealer
1212 N. Lindbergh Blvd.
St. Louis, MO 63132
(314) 997-7111
Focus: Sporting goods wholesalers

Hardlines Distributors
Chain Store Guides
Lebhar-Friedman, Inc.
425 Park Ave.
New York, NY 10022-3559
(212) 371-9400
Focus: 2,600+ hardware
distributors

Hardware Wholesalers
Chilton Company
1 Chilton Way
Radnor, PA 19089
(800) 345-1214
Focus: Hardware distributors
and chains

Middlemen

In some industries, many small manufacturers use manufacturers' representatives agents and sales representatives. Other individuals or groups serving as middlemen in different industries are brokers, auctioneers, etc.

Manufacturers' Representatives. Manufacturers' representatives/agents are individuals who sell the producers' products, (mostly industrial products) but who do not buy the products themselves for resale to any accounts. They may be working for several companies or manufacturers which have related, but non-competitive, products. They call on wholesalers who then sell to either retailers or industrial users. They are paid after the customer pays for the merchandise.

To seek manufacturers' representatives, you may place a classified or small display ad in *Agency Sales,* a monthly magazine of the Manufacturers' Agents National Association at P.O. Box 3467, Laguna Hills, CA 92654; (714) 859-4040.

Sales Representatives Groups. Usually, these sales agents serve as the link between manufacturers or importers and retailers. Sales representatives may be on their own or be part of a sales group. Like manufacturers' representatives, they are paid commissions. For instance, an educational book publisher may hire a sales agent or a sales group to call on teachers and school supply stores.

To look for salespersons or sales representatives, you may place classified or small display ads in the following magazines:

Income Opportunities
380 Lexington Ave.
New York, NY 10017

Money Making Opportunities
Box Z
Studio City, CA 91614

Spare Time
5810 West Oklahoma Ave.
Milwaukee, WI 53219

Opportunity/Income Plus
73 Spring St.
New York, NY 10012

You may ask for their media kit, sample copies, rate cards, and publication schedules.

Brokers. Brokers are intermediaries whose job is to bring buyers and sellers together. There are brokers who represent manufacturers and call on wholesalers. Brokers, who do not physically handle the products being sold, may work for either the buyer or the seller. They are paid commissions. In the case of real estate, the broker usually represents the seller.

Commission Merchants. Commission merchants are given fees in the sale of manufacturers' goods. This kind of sales arrangement is common in agricultural products.

Auction Companies. Auction companies are involved in bringing buyers and sellers into an agreement. Usually, auctions are held in one central location. Auction companies are given commissions based on the selling price. Auctions are common in such fields as art, antiques, and agriculture.

Retailers

Retailers are individuals or stores whose primary business is to sell products and services to the general consumer market. They buy their products direct from the manufacturer or from distributors or wholesalers. Retailers are sometimes called *dealers.* Retailers may be classified into the following types:

■ *Discount Stores.* Offering a wide assortment of merchandise, discount stores offer brand-name products at low prices. There are, however, some specialty discounters that sell only one product line, such as appliances. They depend on high sales volume to be profitable.

■ *Specialty Stores.* Often clustered together to form shopping malls, specialty stores offer a narrow product line (such as candies). However, they carry many different kinds of these product lines: for instance, different kinds of candies.

■ *Convenience Stores.* Convenience stores, such as 7-Eleven stores, offer "convenience." Usually self-service, they often offer long hours, with some of them being open 24 hours a day. These stores are good places for emergency purchases, although product selection is limited. Usually, their prices are higher than regular stores.

■ *Department Stores.* Department stores sell many product lines. Usually located in centralized locations, their prices may be based on store image.

■ *Supermarkets.* Usually self-service, supermarkets offer a wide selection of groceries, meat, fruits, and vegetables. They offer low prices but depend on high sales volume to be profitable.

■ *Superstores.* Superstores are typically similar to supermarkets in terms of location, hours, and degree of customer service. They may be a combination supermarket, specialty store, and department store. That is, they offer much merchandise sold in retail stores, such as food items, appliances, etc. They may also offer certain services, such as fast food.

■ *Warehouse Clubs and Office Supply Stores.* Warehouse clubs, such as Pace and Price clubs and office supply stores, such as Office Max and Office Depot are examples of other store chains that may carry your products.

■ *Catalog Showrooms.* Usually situated in inconvenient locations, catalog showrooms offer deep discounts on brand-name products. However, they offer less service.

■ *Vending Machines.* Vending machines, which are self-service, are retail outlets for soft drinks and certain food products, such as candy, popcorn, cookies, etc.

■ *Museum Shops.* Typically, museum shops buy art books or art items from imported wood carvings to Oriental artifacts. These can be outlets for your imported products, if they are appropriate for this market. Contact the Museum Store Association to gain some information on what products they usually buy.

■ *Gift Shops.* Mostly located in hospitals, gift shops carry flowers and gift items for visitors to give to hospital patients. They may also carry newspapers, magazines, and books.

■ *Hobby and Craft Supply Shops.* These shops usually buy from distributors. If you wish to sell to them, find out what items they sell and who their distributors are.

■ *Flower and Garden Centers.* If you want to sell items to these outlets, know what products they carry. For instance, these centers can be good places for books about flowers or gardening or gardening tools. These out-

lets, for book publishers, are what we call *nontraditional markets.* Most of these centers, called dealers, also work with distributors, although some of them buy direct from manufacturers.

■ *Arts and Crafts Fairs/Festivals.* Appropriate products may also be sold during arts and crafts shows, fairs, and festivals.

■ Flea Market. The flea market is another good place to sell craft products. There you may also contact some dealers.

■ *Direct Sellers.* These retailers are engaged in face-to-face selling to customers. They may sell door-to-door or in homesales parties.

A Direct Seller

■ *Direct Marketers.* These marketers engage in mail order catalog selling, direct mail, direct response advertising, telemarketing, and television shopping. This type of retailing is gaining popularity because of convenience: Customers may buy goods at home, while watching TV or just plain relaxing.

Resources:

Major Mass Market Merchandisers
The Salesman's Guide
1140 Broadway #1203
New York, NY 10117-0130
(212) 684-2985
Focus: 1,650 mass-market firms

Supermarket & Convenience
    Stores
Chain Store Guides
Lebhar-Friedman Inc.
425 Park Avenue
Yew York, NY 10022-3559
(212) 371-9400
Focus:
Gift, Housewares & Home
Textiles Buyers

The Salesman's Guide
Lebhar-Friedman, Inc.
1140 Broadway #1203
New York, NY 10117-0130
(212) 684-2985
Focus: 6,000 gift & housewares
    stores

Health Marketing Buyers Guide
CPS Communications
7200 W. Camino Rd. #215
Boca Raton, FL 33433
(305) 368-9301
Focus: Health buyers

Home Center & Hardware Chains
Chain Store Guides
Lebhar-Friedman Inc.
425 Park Ave.
New York, NY 10022-3559
(212) 371-9400
Focus: 7,100 home center &
    hardware centers

Publisher's Distributing Company
Terry Sutton
11565 Ridgewood Cir N.
Seminole, FL 34642
(813) 391-6709
Focus: 100,000 sources for flea
market products

Phelon's Discount Stores
Phelon, Sheldon & Marsar
15 Industrial Ave.
Fairview, NJ 07022
(800) 234-8804
Focus: 2,000 discount chains,
    5,000 jobbers

General Merchandise and Variety
Guide
Chain Store Guides
Lebhar-Friedman, Inc.
425 Park Ave.
New York, NY 10022-3559
(2120 371-9400
Focus: 3,550+ variety & specialty
    chains

III. Service Distribution

If you sell a service, that's your "product." In other words, services can also be distributed to individuals or companies. For instance, additional markets for service are now being available during specified times or nonpeak hours. Trade associations assist their member businesses to distribute services through different outlets; for example, hotels offer services to their guests through outside service providers (such as dry cleaning).

As a service provider, you can distribute your services through subcontracting some of your work to individuals or companies. You may also form a partnership with other brothers or sisters in your profession or other related businesses to perform your services to a great number of people or businesses.

IV. Distributor Selection

How you find and select your distributors is one of the most important steps to be taken in distributing your products or services.

John Ettlie, associate of professor of operations management at the University of Michigan's School of Business Administration, was quoted in the *Nation's Business* issue of August 1993 as saying, "In today's competitive world, you have to assume that your manufacturing capability and your product will be obsolete in five years. People who haven't sorted that out will be out of business shortly. Distributors can help in doing product planning for the future."

In the same magazine's issue, Chairman and CEO Bob Trinchero of Sutter Home Winery, Inc., attributed his company's ability to choose good distributors and to build a cooperative relationship with them as one of the major factors in its success as a wine producer.

Case Studies

Smart companies use distributors for marketing their products. Here are two examples:

Crispy Corn. Here's a true story (which came out as a feature article in a local paper) of a company that now relies on distributors to penetrate a larger share of the market for its products.

Otto's Crispy Corn, Inc., a five-shop retail chain in Detroit, Michigan, has been expanding to engage in wholesaling. Dale and his brother, Brad Otto, who runs the wholesale spin-off LTD, Inc., have learned that the right distributors are the keys to opening a big market for any company's products. Although Otto's has been in business for the past 43 years, it still found it hard to get its products into the marketplace, particularly in grocery stores and vending machines. Its products include popcorn, caramel corn, and popcorn with barbecue, cheese, and white cheddar flavors.

"You really have to rely on key distributors that are willing to put you on the shelves, that are already serving the marketplace," Dale Otto said.

LTD, Inc., recognizing the importance of wholesaling in the distribution of their products in the marketplace, has reached an agreement with several independent distributors that can help the company get into its target markets: party stores, grocery stores, and vending machines.

"The product sells once it's there," Dale Otto said.

The two brothers learned that middlemen are needed to really succeed in business. "Manufacturing is one business; distribution is another," said Brad Otto. "We found out in a hurry we can't do both."

With new distributors, LTD, Inc. now hopes to reach the shelves of grocery chains such as Kroger or Farmer Jack/A&P.

Product Uniqueness. Here's another enterprising entrepreneur who succeeded in placing his products on retail stores' shelves.

Dough Foreman, owner of the Guiltless Gourmet snack-food firm in Austin, Texas, found out that retail shelf space for a new product is hard to find. So he started with small stores in his location and worked up to larger stores while he created consumer demand for his goods. Guiltless tortilla chip contains no oil, so he made it as his selling point. He said that his product uniqueness has helped in getting shelf space.

Master or National Distributor

As discussed in an earlier part of this chapter, you may look for a master distributor or a national distributor if you can find one in your industry. If there are none, then it's best to established a network of wholesalers that will act as your distributors.

Finding a national distributor or a few wholesaler-distributors should be carefully done. It may be a short or long process, depending on the availability of distributors in your field.

While there are those companies that are known as general distributors in certain industries, there are also independent distributors that special-

ize in reaching particular markets. For instance, in the book industry, while there are general distributors to the trade, there are also distributors to certain niche markets. As an example, a number of companies distribute only cookbooks to their targeted markets.

Finding Distributors

To find distributors, you may simply make inquiries. Go to retailers that sell products similar to yours and ask for the sources of their products. Get their names and addresses.

Ask who the good distributors are: if they ship goods on time, how long they pay, if they offer good service, etc. If you're a member of organizations serving your industry, seek names of distributing companies that may distribute your products.

Thomas Register of Manufacturers and Other Directories. You may also find possible distributors and wholesalers in the St. Thomas Register of Manufacturers.

Also, check your local library to see, if there are any directories of manufacturers, distributors, and wholesalers in your state. Some manufacturers that distribute their products may also distribute noncompetitive products from other producers.

Publishing Your Product. Publish your product in *the* New Products section of magazines, newsletters, and other publications. You may attract some distributors. Or you may advertise the fact that you're in search of distributors.

Testing the Market. When your product is already in small stores on your own efforts, you may mention this to distributors, saying it is now being carried by most stores in your area. If there's a demand in your local area, then there may also be a demand regionally or nationally.

Selecting Your Distributor

The best way to select a distributor is to ask around. Ask other manufacturers, wholesalers, and retailers of products similar to yours as to with whom they enjoy working.

Here are some questions you may ask:

■ How many manufacturers do they represent?

■ How many sales representatives do they have? Are they in-house representatives (paid by salary) or outside sales representatives (paid by commission)?

■ Do they ask a percentage of net sales (total selling price minus dealer discount) or gross sales (selling price)?

■ How long have they been in business? What are their total annual sales volumes?

■ What markets do they reach? What are their payment terms? Do they pay on time?

Most important of all, inquire into their financial condition. This is very important because if your distributor closes shop due to poor business or to filing bankruptcy, you'll be holding an empty bag.

Distribution Contract

A master distributor, a national distributor, or a wholesaler-distributor may demand a signed agreement. Of course, that will be best for both of you. With a contract, a distributor or a wholesaler-distributor will be committed to you. Some of them may ask for an exclusive agreement.

Of course, it's to a distributing company's advantage to have an exclusive agreement because your products will be included in its marketing efforts. For instance, your products may be included in its catalogs to be presented to their wholesalers.

Sole Source of Products. There are also wholesalers or even retailers for whom you may be the sole source of a product within a specific geographical territory. In many instances, certain territories are assigned to certain distributors who also have been given assigned specific sales goals. That is, in your contract, you may demand an estimated sales goals. If they do not meet such goals, it may be the cause of freeing you from an inefficient distributor.

Certain Exemptions. If you have a distributor to the general market, ensure that although your contract is exclusive, certain markets not served by this distributor should be exempted from your contract.

As an example, the first time my current master distributor sent me a an exclusive agreement, I rejected it because I had already certain dealers in certain markets. We negotiated and certain markets were excluded from the contract. For instance, I negotiated for the exclusion of mail order sales and non-traditional markets for books such as warehouse clubs, grocery stores, and teacher and school supply stores. Of course, my distributor obliged because it actually is not covering them. In other words, I may still look for other distributors to markets not served by my master distributor.

Goods on Consignment

If retail stores and other outlets are reluctant to buy your products because they are not sure of the market, consign the products to them. That is, they will pay only for goods sold, and you'll pick up the balance of the merchandise on a specified date if they are not moving well. If they are, then you can let them continue selling the items.

I tried this method when teacher and school supply stores were first adamant to sell one of our books entitled *How to Teach Your Child: Things to Know from Kindergarten through Grade 6.* I offered them to resell the book on consignment and they'd pay only for total books sold in three or six months, for example. I offered free freight, including return freight for books not sold if they decided to return them. This system worked. *How to Teach Your Child* is now being sold on consignment in many teacher and school supply stores throughout the country. The good news is I found no difficulty in the collection of payments, even from stores in Alaska, Maine, or California. Probably the reason is, if they don't pay, they won't be able to sell the book again!

Maximum Order. It has been proven that consignment generates sales, if your products are really good, unique, or useful. Of course, there should be a maximum order to prevent any large loss if a dealer doesn't pay you. The important thing is to have the goods displayed on shelves and let them sell themselves. So if you think your product is good enough to sell itself, then offer it to dealers on consignment, even to dealers as far as Hawaii or Guam.

Dealership. If you are, for instance, a mail order dealer of other products, you can get goods on consignment and sell them if you have markets for them.

IV. Bottom Line

Distributors (master or national distributors or wholesaler-distributors) and other middlemen and dealers are your necessary partners in putting your products in the marketplace.

Channel 5 of distribution channels (from manufacturer to master distributor to wholesaler-distributor to retailer to consumer) may be the right distribution channel for a one-person business. This is necessary so that you can concentrate your efforts and resources to producing goods, importing products, or publishing books and running your one-person company.

However, you may do some mail order marketing: direct mail, placement of classified and display ads in some publications, etc. (channel 1: direct selling to consumers).

How to Start & Operate a Mail Order Business

16

■ Mail order is one of the best businesses suited for a one-person business. In fact, it's becoming more popular than ever before.

Mail order can be only a part of your operation or it can be your whole operation. Many entrepreneurs engage in it because of the following reasons:

■ It requires little start-up capital.

■ It can be operated part time or full time.

■ It can be operated anywhere, at home or in an outside office.

■ It can sell hundreds of products at the same time to a targeted market or to the general public.

■It can be operated by young or old, men or women.

■It can be very profitable.

Mail order is a business that is involved in the selling of products or services conducted through advertising in the print and broadcast media and direct mail. By engaging in mail order, you have a vast market: the whole United States and even some countries of the world.

Many products can be sold by mail—from kitchen tools to books to swimming pools. In fact, even people can be sold by mail. How? Well, certain businesses act as brokers for people who want to find pen pals for love or marriage. Typically, these businesses offer so-called "mail friends" or prospective "mail order brides." They normally invite women from throughout the world, place their write-ups with enticing pictures in their catalogs and place classified ads in magazines. Then they sell their names and addresses to men who are looking for friends from different parts of the world for possible friendship or future marriage.

You may not be interested in selling people. You want to sell products or services. So let's determine where to get products and how to sell them.

I. Products via Mail Order

You may want to sell products by mail. But where are you going to get them? Here are three ways you can do it: (1) manufacture them, (2) import them, or (3) get them from other manufacturers/wholesalers.

Manufacturing Your Products

The best products are your own. So if you can do it, produce your own books, cassette tapes, newsletters, gadgets, dolls, or whatever. If you do this, you'll engage in light manufacturing.If you can't manufacture them yourself, have them manufactured by other individuals and companies.

Importing Your Products

The second best way to get products is to import them. By importing products, you'll find unique products that are ideal for mail order. Try to find products that you may not find in stores and other markets—products that are light so that they can be mailed easily.

Of course, you have to learn importing. (See Chapter 17, *Running a Home-Based Import/Export Business*, page 161.) You must know the regulations and procedures in importing products into the country. One way is to take a course in importing and exporting given by a community college in your area.

The Mellinger Company can be your key to importing. Based in California, this company, which has been in business for decades, offers a course in import/export. By taking this course, you can become a member of the International Traders organization.

Getting Products from Manufacturers

Find hot products from manufacturers. Where can you find them? The best places are catalogs and mail offers, or products already sold through space ads in magazines, and products published in *New Products* sections of publications. Also see the *Thomas Register of Manufacturers* in your library.

About 3,700 different catalogs are mailed. There are thousands and thousands of products sold through the mail. Find the bestsellers, know their manufacturers, and request that you be a direct marketer of the good ones. These pertain to products whose ads are published again and again in publications.

Getting Products from Wholesalers

If you don't want to manufacture or import products, you may buy them from two companies that are engaged in providing mail order products to entrepreneurs. The two companies are Mail Order Associates and Specialty Merchandise Corporation.

Mail Order Associates. Mail order Associates offers hundreds and hundreds of products to entrepreneurs for sale by mail order. It also offers a drop-shipping program. That is, they can "drop ship" your products directly to your customers with your name and company on the shipping labels, as if the merchandise came from your own company. Through this method, you don't have to tie up your capital in inventory.

The company also packages its products in a gift catalog. Your name can be printed on the front cover of the catalog as if it's your own catalog. When you mail catalogs of this kind, you receive the orders.

For information, write to Mail Order Associates, 120 Chestnut Ridge Rd., Montvale, NJ 07645.

*Specialty Merchandise Corpora-*tion. In business for the past 45 years, SMC offers products that can be sold via mail order, home party-plan sales, and door-to-door selling.

According to some reports, a former car salesman joined SMC's operations and started his own mail order business. He is now making $50,000 a year in mail order.

For more information on SMC, write to Specialty Merchandise Corporation, 9401 De Soto Avenue, Chatsworth, CA 91311.

(You must get information first and then evaluate if any of the programs offered by Mellinger Company, Mail Order Associates, and Specialty Merchandise Corporation is the right one for you. It's a good way to test the small business water, by starting out on a few products on a part-time basis. It's not just mailing out catalogs, and, bingo, you'll be swamped with orders! There are many factors to be considered.

II. Mail Order Methods

At least there are six basic mail order methods that you can use to promote and sell your products. They are selling via *free publicity, classified ads, display ads, card decks, direct-selling salespersons, mail order dealers, catalog publishers,* and *direct mail.*

Whatever promotional method you use, you must always remember the so-called A.I.D.A. objectives, which are as follows:

■ *Attention*—Capture the customers' attention.

■ *Interest*—Awaken their interest.

■ *Desire*—Stimulate their desire to buy.

■ *Action*—Move them to action.

So whatever direct marketing method you use—display ad, flyer, or salesletter—you must focus your attention on these objectives, overlooked by many entrepreneurs.

1. Selling via Free Publicity.

Many magazines have the so-called New Products section. You can send a short write-up that includes your product's name, its specifications, its price and photo. Send it to the New Product section of magazines or newsletters that may be interested in featuring your mail order item.

If your product is unique and of use to many people, you may get a lot of orders.

Another way of getting free publicity is to write press releases about your product and send them to the appropriate editors of newspapers and magazines. Some call it an "editorial." In other words, it's news about your product. Don't make it look like an advertising piece.

The correct method of writing a good press release is turning it into a good feature story.

Here's one of my feature stories that I sent out and published in some newspapers as a feature story during a holiday season.

Teaching Your Child Is a Lifetime Gift

Are you looking for a perfect gift for your child during this holiday season that he or she will cherish forever? The best gift that you can give is to start teaching your child at home to enable him or her to master the "basics" and succeed in school.

Veltisezar B. Bautista, author of the new book *How to Teach Your Child: Things to Know from Kindergarten through Grade 6*, gives the following tips to successfully help your child master the basics of every major subject:

• Know the subject areas taught in whatever grade your child is in. Talk with his or her teacher about them or learn them from teaching aids or manuals.

• Review the basics of these subject areas and share your knowledge with your child.

• Allocate a definite time each day during which you teach your child. Besides imparting knowledge, one-on-one teaching also builds a good parent-child relationship.

Bautista, author of another bestselling book entitled *Improve Your Grades: A Practical Guide to Academic Excellence*, also advises that you teach your child the techniques for proper studying and test taking.

Bautista, a former journalist, offers the following suggestions from *Improve Your Grades*.

• Use images and word keys in remembering dates, formulas, and other important numbers.

• Use an eight-step study system: previewing, speculating, scanning, coding, memorizing, decoding, reviewing, and taping.

• When reading, do "idea-culling," the process by which one picks up key ideas from every sentence or paragraph.

How to Teach Your Child retails at $12.95 plus $3 for postage. *Improve Your Grades* retails for $9.95 per copy plus $3 for postage. To order these books, call toll free 1-800-356-9315 (credit card orders only).

As you can see, in featuring the books, several "tips" in them were given in the feature story to make it appear that it's not a press release but a legitimate story written by the paper's staff member. In other words, there should be some information for the benefit of the newspaper's readers that they can make use of, even if they don't buy the books.

To send out feature stories of this kind, you may contact companies that specialize in publishing "editorials" that they send to about 10,000 major and local newspapers. These companies publish a catalog of camera-ready newspaper features that can be clipped and published by daily and weekly newspapers. There is a fee for this kind of service.

Two companies that offer cooperative marketing services are:

Metro Creative Graphics, Inc.
33 West 34th St.
New York, NY 10001
(212) 947-5100.

News USA
1127 National Press Building
Washington, DC 20045
(202) 682-2400

Media Syndicate Newsmakers
P O Box 2282
Boulder, CO 80306
(800) 533-2324

Selling via Classified Ads

If you look at the classified ads in magazines, you'll notice that the majority of them don't give a price for the products. Classified ads typically contain words such as "for more info, write," or "free details," or "free brochure." An inquiry means a request for further information about a product or service offered in a classified ad, from a telemarketing program, or from a TV commercial offering an 800 number. Such inquiries may be in the form of letters or reply cards as a result of classified ads or giving their names and addresses in the case of telemarketing or the use of a 900 number.

Certainly, we use classified ads in selling products or services or in becoming brokers of people (for friendship or marriage).

In magazines, the classified ads may say:

"Emergency alarm that talks! Will drive your attacker crazy! Free details."

"Men! Be acquainted with women from Asia, Europe, and Latin America who want a U.S. passport! Hurry before they change their minds! Free brochure!"

A low-cost classified ad, which is paid per word, is used to invite inquiries only and not to get orders. Then when you receive responses asking for more information about your product, you send the prospect a flyer, a salesletter, or a brochure with an order form and a reply envelope to make it easier for him or her to send the order.

The benefits, features, prices, etc., are mentioned in these mailing pieces to entice the prospective customers to buy the products.

To make classified ads work for you, choose only publications that carry heavy classified sections where you'll find a lot of ads for various products and services. If you're selling services, then it's best if you place an ad in the Sunday classified ads section of local newspapers and magazines. If your services are operated nationally, then you can use national publications.

Selling through Display Ads

Selling through these display ads means the product is sold directly from the ad. That is, the ad contains a picture of the product, its benefits, its features, its price (shipping charges), and how to order it.

The ad may include some of these words:

"Order it now, today, at this very moment, or else you may forget about it!"

"It's your chance of a lifetime to own this unique, marvelous product!"

"Price is only $9.95, battery not included."

So through this method, the reader will or will not buy your product based on what he or she sees and reads.

This kind of ad is more expensive. It's best to first try the classified ad and then when it generates a lot of inquiries, you may try a display ad.

Media Selection. Display advertising is expensive, so be careful in selecting the media where you want them advertised. Certain magazines appeal to certain groups of people. Learn about the income range, occupations, age range, and place of residence of people reading the publications.

For example, to advertise tools for men, you may advertise in *Mechanics Illustrated* and other men's magazines.

Magazines. Magazines are classified geographically as local, regional or national and demographically by types of readership. Ads have longer life in magazines than in newspapers and may generate readership and response for some time. Write the appropriate magazines for their advertising rates for classified and display advertising.

Newspapers. Ads in newspapers can be read the same day they are published. However, they have a shorter life because after a day or two, most newspapers are thrown away. Typically, it's better to use newspapers that give the highest circulation at the lowest cost. You can advertise in newspapers to get immediate results or responses. Normally, placing classified ads in newspapers is effective if you're offering local products or services.

Before placing a big display ad, 5 x 7 inches for instance, you may try first classified ads.

Keying. All ads, whether classified or displays, should be keyed to know the number of inquiries or orders you get from a particular ad or publication. For instance, you may add a letter to the number of your address, such as P.O. Box 9502-P, Somewhere, Michigan. (The "P" that follows the P.O. box number is the key; it may be the first letter of the magazine.) Or you can add a department number to your address, such as 310 Lovers Lane, Dept. 393-U, Anywhere, Alaska. The department number "393-U" may represent the month and year and the name of the magazine (393-U: March 1993, *UFO Magazine*) where the ad was placed. So everything must be keyed to differentiate the ads you place in publications. Reason: you don't have to repeat ads that are not profitable.

Cooperative Advertising. Cooperative advertising is between a manufacturer and a distributor. You may participate in your distributor's co-operative advertising program. As an example, I usually participate in my national distributor's cooperative advertising program. That is, when it advertises several items it distributes, it includes mine. Of course, it does that with my consent. The distributor shares the advertising cost with publishers. I pay a certain percentage of the cost.

Ad Writing Strategies. You must use certain strategies to write display ads that sell. Some of them are as follows:

Strategy 1. Write an attention-getting headline to flag your prospect. Write a headline that whispers, "Hey! you've got to read me! This is good news for you!"

The headlines may be something like these:

"Get a Job in One Day!"

"At last....Here's a Knife That Does It All!"

"Finally, You Can Earn $100,000 a Year!"

"Now! Earn $500 a Day Using This Tool!"

As much as possible, compose a benefit-oriented headline. That is, you're mentioning what benefit your buyer will get from the product you're offering.

Strategy 2. Use the KISS principle—"Keep it short and simple." Also, you should support the headline with secondary benefits and selling points (including why they should buy the product) and then add some features of the product, such as what it's made of and its size, shape, color, taste (if it's food), etc.

Strategy 3. Use testimonials. Use comments from satisfied customers. One testimonial is enough for a small display ad.

Strategy 4. Ask for action. In closing, you have to ask for the order. "Send your order now! Stock is limited!" "Limited time to order!"

Strategy 5. Send a free gift or a bonus. (In a salesletter, it's usually mentioned in the postscript.) For example: "If you send your order within 10 days, we'll send you a free book ($8.00 value!) entitled *Where Are You, My love?* So rush your order now!" Giving a deadline to send the order is a good way of getting an immediate action.

Strategy 6. Offer a money-back guarantee. You may include it in the last part of the ad, the salesletter, or the flyer. You may say it in this way. "There's nothing to lose but there's something to gain! Try our product now! If you don't like it for any reason, just send it back to us within 15 days, and we'll send a refund of your payment. No questions asked.

Selling by Card Decks

Card decks are composed of several cards with product information contained in a plastic package. It is usually mailed bulk rate. The available advertising space of each card is only 3 x 5 inches. One-third of this must be used for prospect response information, such as name, address, phone number, etc. So the message must be brief and to the point.

Typically, a card contains a photo of the product or the service and some information about it. Usually, the card seeks only inquiry and says, "Call or write for more information." Some cards, though, ask orders directly from the ad.

Card deck mailing is a cooperative advertising program of manufacturers, dealers, or service providers.

Each advertiser pays for its card (printed usually printed on both sides), costing from $600 to $1,700, depending on the mailing list size and the category. Each advertiser provides its own camera-ready copy.It is said that an average response to a card deck mailing is from 1/4 percent to 1 percent.

Generally, deck cards are mailed to businesses, schools, teachers, multilevel marketers, and business opportunity seekers. That is, they are mailed to a specific, targeted market.

To know several card deck publishers that may be serving your industry, you may look at them in card deck directories. Two such directories are:

Card Deck Rates and Data
Standard Rate & Data Service
3004 Glenview Rd.
Wilmette, IL 60091-3065
(800) 323-4588

Directory of Postcard Deck Media
Caddylak Systems
201 Montrose Rd.
P.O. Box 1817
Westbury, NY 11590-1768
(516) 333-8221

Selling through Direct-Sales Persons

You may use sales representatives in selling your products. You contact salespersons through the mail. You can rent a mailing list of sales representatives who sell your kind of product or you can advertise either through classifieds or through display ads in sales magazines, such as *Opportunities Magazine.*

Selling by Mail Order Dealers

There are also other mail order dealers who may carry your products if they are compatible with other products they sell.

Selling via Catalog Publishers

Catalog publishers mail out millions of catalogs each year to their customers and other prospects. Contained in their catalogs are hundreds of unique products, gift items, books, and even equipment.

If you are the manufacturer or the sole source of a unique product, catalog publishers are its ideal sellers.

To test the saleability of a product, you may offer sales agents or mail order dealers a sample product at a wholesale price. But you have to send a free sample product to catalog publishers, with a black-and-white photo and/or a transparency. But select only catalog houses that you think may carry your product based on what products are included in their catalogs.Or you may inquire first before you send samples.

With sample products, they may offer it to prospective customers—individuals or businesses. Naturally, if it sells, then they'll place an order with you.

Of course, in the beginning, they may get the products from you on 30 or 60 days net. Or you may offer the products on consignment if they are big sellers.

Selling by Direct Mail

Selling by direct mail means the sending out of a mailing package to sell products or services to current customers or prospects.

A direct mail package is mailed to your current customers or to inquirers (those who respond to classified ads or TV commercials) or to a mailing list. The mailing list may contain names of persons who are known mail order buyers of particular products, such as cookbooks, kitchen utensils, etc. (Direct mail is a term that also applies to grocery store food circulars that you often find in your mailbox. It also applies to all retail promotions that are mailed out to prospective customers.)

Selling goods or services through direct mail is quite expensive because of the high cost of printing and postage. So if you're mailing over 200 pieces, you may consider applying for a bulk mail permit with the post office.

If you're selling to a niche market, you may rent a mailing list.

Basic components of direct mail packages may include any or some of the following: a cover letter, a flyer or a circular, a salesletter, a brochure, a self-contained piece that can be turned into an envelope for return of an order or an inquiry, a catalog, an order form, and/or a business reply envelope.

Cover Letter. Usually, a cover letter is the first piece of mailing package with a circular, a brochure, or a catalog. It greets the prospective customer and introduces the product contained in the promotional piece.

Flyer or Circular. A flyer is also called a circular. A flyer or a circular is a one-piece promotional material that contains a photo of the product and its benefits, features, and specifications. It may or may not be accompanied by a cover letter. The size of the flyer may be 8 1/2 x 11 inches or 11 x 17 inches, which, when folded in half, measures 8 1/2 x 11 inches.

Salesletter. A sales letter may contain only in an 8 1/2 x 11-inch paper printed both sides) or 11 x 17 paper. It may be mailed with a reply envelop by itself; that is, there is no flyer or catalog. A sales letter is like a display ad or a flyer. It has also a headline and it contains all the strategies mentioned under the heading *Selling through Display Ads*. The only difference is that it has a greeting and a closing, such as *Sincerely yours*. The salesletter may be printed or typewritten. In short, the salesletter is more personal than a flier. If you can't compose an effective salesletter, you may have someone else do it. You may wish to obtain the help of an expert.

Brochure. A brochure is a pamphlet, especially one promoting something. It may or may not be accompanied by a cover letter.

Self-Contained Piece. A self-contained piece, whose size may be 8 1/2 x 11 inches or 8 1/2 x 14 inches is a promotional piece that, when folded into three, serves as the envelope itself. In short, it's a promotional piece, serving as a salesletter or a flyer, mailed by itself. It may contain a product or a service photo and its descriptive copy, an order form that may be detached and mailed, or an inquiry section if the piece is lead generating.

Catalog. A catalog is a promotional piece that may consist of several pages. It contains a photo of each product or service and its descriptive copy. The catalog's second page may also contain a letter from the manager or the sales director of a company next to the cover or on page 3.

Order Form. Most often, the order form is incorporated into a mailing piece, whether it's a salesletter or a flyer. However, some individuals and companies prefer to have a separate order form.

Envelop. Most often, "teasers" are placed on the front of a mailing envelope. Such a teaser may be "Discover the secrets of a unique business that makes $500,000 a year. Details inside!"

One of Your Best Friends

III. Mailing List

A flyer or a direct salesletter is mailed to a list of names. Lists of names are available by customer category from mailing list brokers. They may be buyers of certain products or books or they may be prospects who have responded to mail offers (but who are not proven buyers). When you rent a mailing list, you may pay from

$50 to $75 per thousand names, depending on name categories.

Kinds of Mailing Lists

There are at least three kinds of mailing lists: *buyers' list, inquirers' list,* and *compiled list.*

Buyers' List. A buyers' list is a list of proven buyers of products by mail. They have responded to mail order ads and direct mailings.

Inquirers' List. An inquirers' list is a list of people or companies who have responded to ads or mailings, but who have not yet bought products by mail.

Compiled List. A compiled list is a list compiled from telephone books, directories, or subscribers to certain publications.

When you rent a list, it's for a one-time use only. You send your order to the broker and the broker sends it to the list owner. Most mailing lists are computer-generated. So what you receive are mailing labels.

Be careful in renting a mailing list—if you get the wrong one you'll only throw away your money! Be sure to know if the names are proven buyers, inquirers, taken from a phone book, etc.

After you have rented a list, you monitor the result of your mailing as to whether it's profitable or not. For instance, if you receive 30 orders on your mailing to 1,000 names that's a return of 30/1,000, or 3 percent. If you are to mail ten times as many salesletters or flyers, or 10,000, you can expect to receive 10 times as many orders, or 300. You can now decide if a 3-percent return will give a profit after calculating your sales and cost of materials and postage. According to experts, a 3 percent return is considered to be excellent.

It is also interesting to note that not all products are ideal for direct mail. Your product should have a list price of at least $25.00. Of course, it's best if you can promote several products at the same time, as in a flyer or in a catalog.

Most list brokers are located in Chicago, New York, and Los Angeles. You may get their names and addresses from publications such as Direct Marketing, 224 Seventh Street, Garden City, NY 11530. Also see the yellow pages of large city telephone directories.

Here are two directories of mailing lists:

Direct Mail List Rates & Data
    Standard Rate & Data Service
3004 Glenview Road
Wilmette, IL 60091-3065
(800) 323-4588
Focus: Direct mail list

Directory of Mailing List Houses
B. Klein Publications
P O Box 8503
Coral Springs, FL 33065-8503
Focus: mailing houses

Cooperative Mailing and Package Inserts

Cooperative mailing is another way of saving postage. It can be done in two ways: 1) insertion of flyers in a mailing package, usually mailed bulk rate, and 2) insertion of flyers in packages sent out to current customers.

Cooperative Mailing. You include your piece of mailing in a cooperative mailing (or you include your flyer in another mail order dealer's mailing). The process works this way: A person or a company does a mass mailing to a certain targeted market. Several pieces of brochures are included and each participant or company pays a certain amount as part of the postage. Of course, the participants' products should be noncompetitive, although they may be similar, such as products for cooks or cooking.

As an example, I often participate in cooperating mailing programs sponsored by the Publishers Marketing Association that sends out mailings to libraries, bookstores, and book reviewers.

Package Inserts. Several flyers are inserted in packages sent out to customers. To obtain information on companies engaged in package inserts and co-op mailing, see:

Package Insert & Coo-op Directory
50 Lake Drive
P. O. Box 930
Highstown, NJ 08520-0930
(609) 443-1298

Package Insert Directory
Walter Karl, Inc.
135 Bedford Road
Armonk, NY 10504-1831
(914) 273-3353

IV. Services via Mail or Telephone

We are in an exploding information age. More and more entrepreneurs are now using 900 telephone lines to make big money: legal hotlines, financial advice lines, and other advisory sources. The 900 lines are sprouting in many parts of the country.

The 900 number is usually best for selling advice or information. The typical 900 number charges are from $2.00 to $3.95 for the first minute, and at a lesser cost for each additional minute.

About two thirds of the amount billed to callers goes to you; the balance goes to the telephone carrier. Usually, the 900 number works like computerized voice mail, somewhat like this:

"To talk to a live person giving advice on your particular problem, press 1."

"To get information on how to get free travel to the Bahamas, press 2."

"To live in a million-dollar house tax-free, press 3."

Etc.

However, you must set your voice mail in such a way that there is a pre-recorded message informing the caller about the cost per minute of the call. Otherwise, there might be a problem when the caller receives the telephone bill.

In running your service-oriented business, you may also use mail order methods used by entrepreneurs who sell products: via free publicity, classified ads, display ads, and direct mail.

Also through the telephone, you can set a specific time for a client to call you regarding a certain course or whatever. In this way, the call cost will not be too much for your client. Of course, the fee for your service must be prepaid to avoid any problem in collection.

Some services can be operated nationally. If you're a psychic, for instance, you have to advertise your service in a classified ad with your regular telephone number or your 900 number. Hence, you can operate nationally.

If you are operating locally, you can advertise in the Sunday classified ads of your local newspaper or your local monthly magazine.

V. Bottom Line

In marketing your product, you can use any, some, or all the mail order methods. Classified advertising is a good tool and when it proves that advertising through magazines is the best way to do it, you can do so. If your classified advertising is effective, then you can start with a small dis-play ad, graduating to large ads. To save money in display advertising, you may wish to participate in cooperative advertising.

Direct mailing by yourself is expensive, so unless you have a high-price product and you find a good mailing list, it might not be the right route to follow. But you may try cooperative mailing, one which may be sponsored by an association in which you are a member or with certain individuals or companies doing mass mailings.

However, it's best to sell products to clubs or associations than to individuals. That is, instead of mailing letters and brochures to buyers of certain products or services you may write associations, such as the National PTA (National Parent-Teacher Association) if you're selling books and other products for parents or teachers.

Of course, the best way to market your product via mail order is to let other mail order dealers, sales representatives, and catalog publishers handle it. In that way, you can concentrate your efforts in producing or importing other good products.

Running a Home-Based Import/Export Business

17

■ When you import, you must know the products abroad and their possible market here. When you export, you may export your own products or you may find products produced by other manufacturers for export to the foreign market. That's what the import/export business is.

So you see, import/export business is a two-way street.

However, you may engage in import only or in export only. You play either of two roles: a *merchant* or an *agent*. Import and export will be discussed separately in this chapter.

Import-Export is Big Business

I. Import

We import some foreign goods because we don't have everything that we need in our daily lives. Whether they are luxuries, novelties, arts, or crafts, import goods add to the competition and make them priced at reasonable levels affordable to many people. The beauty of it is that the cost of labor and materials in most countries abroad is usually low. For this reason, manufacturers abroad can afford to offer their products at lower costs. Naturally, this low buying cost gives you the opportunity to enjoy big profit margins. That is why, even if you quadruple the buying cost of the product, the selling price here will still be very low.

A. Import Merchant

As an import merchant, you buy goods from abroad for sale in the United States.

Trade Lead

The very first step in importing is to know what products you are interested in, or what products abroad are appropriate for export to the United States. We call this first process a *trade lead search.* That is, you have to do some research work to find a trade lead that usually takes the form of an offer made by a foreign manufacturer or supplier.

Trade leads can be found in trade journals, business magazines, and sometimes in business sections of large newspapers, such as *The Wall Street Journal.* Trade leads can also be provided by the U.S. Department of Commerce, foreign trade commissions, foreign chambers of commerce in the U.S., and chambers of commerce in foreign countries.

U.S. Department of Commerce. The U.S. Department of Commerce offers several publications that give advice on import and export.

Foreign Trade Commissions. After you have learned importation, you may also contact the trade commissioner of any country from which you want to import. Trade commissions are situated in many cities of the world. They are generally connected with foreign embassies. For a list of consular offices, consult a copy of the *Export-Importer's Encyclopedia,* which is available in most libraries.

Foreign Chambers of Commerce. Find names and addresses of Chambers of Commerce of principal trading nations that maintain offices in the United States. You may try the library.

Chambers of Commerce in Foreign Countries. You may contact the chamber of commerce in the capital city of a country from which you may wish to import.

Other Sources of Trade Leads. You may get good trade lead sources listed in U.S. government publications and non-government publications.

The Mellinger Company. To me, the easiest way to import as a beginner is to take a course with a company that can give you some leads. There are several companies offering books or manuals on import-export that serve as courses. One of them is The Mellinger Company in California.

Way back in the 1980s, I bought the Mellinger World Trade Mail Order Plan. Today the plan consists of a five-manual course in import-export that includes the monthly *Trade Opportunities* magazine, and a *Trade Agreement Catalogs Book.* The program currently costs $200. Buyers of this course become members of Mellinger's International Traders organization.

Of course, being a member of this organization doesn't guarantee one's success in the import business. Usually, it all depends on one's ingenuity, resourcefulness, and knack in business.!

If you are interested in this program, you may send your request for information to:

The Mellinger Company
6100 Variel Avenue
Woodland Hills, CA 91367-3779

However, you must evaluate carefully if this is the right course for you. At any rate, if you decide to enroll in the course, you will be given a few days within which to return the materials if you're not satisfied with them.

My first import as an International Traders member was a unique product which was called a car's back-up horn. Actually, the horn, attached to the car's back-up light wiring, emits a chirping sound (like a bird) every time that you back up your vehicle.

I sold the import through mail order, sales agents, and stores.

I was quite successful in my import business for sometime, but I switched to writing and publishing my own books because this is my real love.

The New Products

As a one-person business, it would be best for you to import small and low-cost products, such as watches, solar radios, calculators, small shop and kitchen tools, and gift items.

You don't need an import license to buy these products from abroad. Being an importer, you just need the standard license to operate a business in any locality. In many instances, you're not even required to get a business license. As long as you register your business name and pay the corresponding fee, you'll be in an import business. (However, you have to get export licenses for exports, which is discussed in the latter part of this chapter.)

You may have a good chance of successfully selling a product if it's a new one. Usually, some of these products are mere improvements or new versions of old products. So when you advertise it, the most important words in your ad are "It's unique!" or "This unique product can make you cry and laugh at the same time!"

Naturally, you have to select very carefully your prospective supplier. Know about its financial condition, its manufacturing ability and its promptness to respond to your requests for product modifications and/or samples.

Also, you must learn how to bargain with your supplier. In other countries, prices are not usually fixed. But remember that price alone is not the only important thing in a good deal. Other factors enter into a good deal: quality of product, reliability of supplier, and good packaging.

If you're already adept at importing, then you can graduate to bigger and higher priced foreign products.

The Request for a Sample

When you have found your product through whatever means, you may request a sample. Usually, samples are paid for and sent via airmail if they are light, low-priced products. Or, if you wish, you may buy a few pieces so that you can use them as samples in testing the market.

You may pay for your sample in bank money order, international bank draft, postal money order, or foreign currency check.

The bank money order and international bank draft may be obtained from your local bank, for a fee.

A foreign currency check may be obtained from Thomas Cook Foreign Currency Services, while a postal money order may be obtained from the Post Office.

Market Testing

When your sample arrives, you can show it to friends, relatives, or anyone you meet on the street, in restaurants, or in recreational areas. If you bought several pieces, one dozen for instance, try to sell them.

Also contact distributors, wholesalers, and dealers, and tell them that you are an importer. See if they are interested in your sample, and would want to sell it. You may also try a small display ad in an appropriate magazine to try mail order.

In other words, you may try selling the product either through distributors, wholesalers, etc., or through sales representatives or mail order, or a combination of all of them.

The First Order

If you have determined that you have a market for your import product, you can place your first order with your foreign supplier; that may be a manufacturer or a distributor.

Ask your supplier, if it is familiar with U.S. Customs regulations and about guidelines for suppliers who mail products from foreign countries. You may have your first order sent by air parcel post if the shipment is not too heavy. But the size should be acceptable by the post office.

Some guidelines for products mailed from abroad are as follows:

1. There should be a marking showing the country of origin.

2. Usually, packing charges are included in the price of the goods; however, postage and shipping charges are not. If the invoice value of the goods, including packing, is not more than $5.00, no duty is assessed.

3. A customs statement should be attached to the outside of the package with the following information:

a. The phrase "May be opened for customs inspection"

b. Merchandise description

c. Merchandise weight

d. Invoice value shown in the currency of the country from which it came. An invoice is enclosed if the value of the shipment is over $1.00. A duty may be collected on small shipments valued at more than $5.00. But actually, duty on low-value imports is seldom collected.

In placing an order, have a purchase order filled out, which may, more or less, contain the following information:

Name and address of supplier; purchase order number; date; your name and address; date of shipment (for example, "as soon as possible"); method of shipment (via air surface parcel post); terms of payment (international bank draft); quantity; description; price per unit,; and total amount.

You may have the invoice in triplicate or quadruplicate, retaining one copy and sending the rest to your supplier.

If your first order is too heavy to be shipped via air parcel post, you may have it shipped air freight. Ask your local post office of the requirements when you use air freight, which cost is higher than air parcel post.

Then check with your customs broker and freight forwarder about costs of shipping goods from abroad.

The Large Order

If your order is large enough and too costly for air freight, have it shipped by ocean freight. Again, you may send three copies of the invoice to your supplier and retain one copy.

The purchase order must contain information (same as required on a small order) but with some modifications. For instance, you may specify how it is to be shipped (ocean freight collect) and how it is to be paid (an irrevocable letter of credit). There also should be a notification on your purchase order; for instance, mentioning the name and address of your broker at the port of entry.

Via Ocean Freight

The Customs Broker. The customs brokerage company is the one that will clear your import through the customs, processing your import for entry into the United States. Usually, customs brokers are located at ports of entry; for instance, in New York or in Los Angeles. Some customs brokers also act as freight forwarders. (In export, freight forwarders handle the shipping paperwork.) But you may select a customs broker from those located in your area. See the yellow pages for a list of customs brokers. It's best to tell your supplier to ship your order in care of your customs broker. Your customs broker will take care of all the paperwork and pay the duties, but you will be billed later for the customs duty and other fees.

Your customs broker will explain to you about the requirements and documents for your import's entry.

The processes involved in the handling of the paperwork for the arrival of your import are *entry, inspection, valuation and appraisement, classification,* and *liquidation.*

So with a customs broker, you don't clear your goods with customs: all is undertaken by your customs broker.

Irrevocable/Revocable Letter of Credit. An *irrevocable letter of credit,* when opened with a bank, cannot be cancelled. The only way it can be cancelled is if your foreign supplier does not ship the product on time or if the letter of credit expires or if some other condition provided for in the letter of credit is not fulfilled. On the other hand, a *revocable letter of credit* is one that can be cancelled by either the seller or the buyer. The letter of credit is used to pay for large orders.

Naturally, when you import, your supplier will ask for an irrevocable letter of credit, knowing that a payment "has been reserved." Then your supplier can start to manufacture the product and ship it as soon as possible.

Your local bank can explain the procedure to you. Usually, to obtain a letter of credit, you must have an equivalent amount in your account. If not, you have to make the additional deposit. Of course, if you're already an established importer, you can have your import financed by your bank.

As an example, I hired a customs brokerage in Detroit, Michigan, when I placed my first order for a few dozen vehicle back-up horns with a Taiwan importer as mentioned earlier.

Then, I went to my bank and inquired about a letter of credit. Actually, it is not a letter of credit in the strict sense of the words on my part. I just bought this "letter of credit" (cost of the goods) from my bank. It was addressed to a bank in my supplier's locality. In short, I paid for the "letter of credit." It's as simple as that!

Marketing Your Import

After a reasonable time, your product arrives. Then you start your promotion for it, granting that your promotional materials are ready. Decide whether you will sell it via direct marketing (placement of ads in magazines) or direct mail or through sales representatives or distributors or wholesalers. You may use any or all of the above.

Thus, you have become an importer. If you're successful with your first product, then you may import others to sell a line of goods for your business.

B. Import Agent

If you wish to be an import agent, it simply means you'll become a selling agent for foreign products. That is, you may contact some companies in the U.S. that import. Your primary role is to be the intermediary between a supplier from abroad (foreign exporter) and a local importer. So as an import agent, you don't have to deal with paying for the goods; you'll be paid commissions by your local importer. Of course, you'll have to have a written agreement with your local importer regarding your commission if you find a foreign supplier.

The Product Search

Before you look for importers, you may do your product search abroad.

For example, if you are familiar with a country's products, that can be a big plus for you.

You can be that importer if you're, for instance, a native of a certain country who immigrated to the United States. You may know your old country's unique products and how they are manufactured. Such products may be woodcarvings, floor mats, crafts, and the like.

If you're are not familiar with any foreign country's products, then you may search import products, as if you're an importer. Then you search for trade leads, as mentioned in the early part of this chapter.

As you make arrangements with a foreign supplier about its products, you may search for any importer that may be interested in the product that you found.

You may seek importers in directories. You may go to your local library and inquire if it has such directories. In some libraries, you may find the *Import Bulletin,* a weekly publication, and the *Directory of U.S. Importers,* both published by the *Journal of Commerce.*

As a specialized directory, the *Thomas Grocery Register* provides names of manufacturers, wholesalers, importers, and brokers of nearly every food product sold in supermarkets.

If you find an import company of a product you found, negotiate with it. Then you may asked for a product sample from your contact abroad (foreign exporters) if it's not heavy, or for brochures and other literature (if it can't be shown physically).

As an import agent, you get the orders from your local importer and forward it to your supplier abroad. Your supplier then ship the goods and the local importer pays you the commission.

Thus, a deal is closed. You may become involved in importing although you don't invest any money.

II. Export

You will receive more help from the government if you export products. The reason is, exports can help reduce the nation's trade deficit. (As of now, we import more goods than we export.)

A. Export Merchant

Export is the opposite of import. If you become an exporter, you are an export merchant. When you become an exporter, you have to sell your products or any other products to foreign countries.

There are three ways by which you can export products.

Selling to Exporters

You may sell products to merchants in the U.S. Some of your products may land in the hands of exporters, without even your knowing it.

Also, you may look for export companies that advertise themselves as such. In either way, you are exporting indirectly and you don't have to worry about negotiations and all the hassles involved in export.

Hiring a Consultant or an Exporting Firm

You may hire a consultant or an exporting firm to find foreign markets for your product. Certain specialized firms, such as export management companies (called EMCs) and Export Trading Companies (known as ETCs), can function as your "Export Department." An EMC or an ETC, for a fee of course, will help you find buyers abroad and handle all the negotiations and the paperwork. In this way, you're involved in indirect export through a third-party under contract.

Selling Directly

You can directly sell your product to a foreign importer. In this way, you'll earn big profits. However, you'll handle all the things needed for exporting: manufacturing your own products, searching products supplied by other manufacturers or suppliers, and negotiating.

If you have to deal in direct export, you need help from the following agencies:

The U.S. Department of Commerce. You have to visit the branch of this department called the U.S. and Foreign Commercial Service (US&FCS). This department also sponsors district export councils through local offices of the US&FCS. The council participates in seminars, workshops, and clinics on exporting. The US&FCS has over 100 officers working in more than 60 countries to gather market trends. There are more than 500 foreign nationals who assist in establishing programs to help U.S. companies sell products abroad.

Also, through the local district of the US&FCS, you may subscribe to *Export Administration Regulations* to learn about all the legal details in export, such as the acquiring of an export license to be an exporter.

The US&FCS can also help in finding an agent or a distributor abroad (for a fee, of course). The Agent/Distributor Services (A/DS) section of US&FCS provides a custom search for foreign import agents and distributors who are interested in importing products. An officer of this agency assigned abroad will search and prepare a report giving names and addresses of agents and firms you may contact; their phone, cable, telex, and fax machine numbers; and some comments about them. Application

forms for this service are available at the US&FCS District Office.

Small Business Administration. This government office gives information and counselling not only to small businesses, but also to exporters. It has Small Business Institute/Small Business Development Centers in over 450 colleges and universities.

State Governments. Many state governments also provide help to exporters. In particular, they provide export education and marketing advice. Look in your phone book, under State Government, for your State Development Agency.

Department of Agriculture. The Department of Agriculture is involved in promoting the sale of farm products abroad. It can provide you with advice and information.

Commercial Banks. Go to the foreign division of your local bank for world trade banking advice.

Other Agencies. You may also seek help from the chamber of commerce, trade associations, state and municipal agencies, Eximbank, and other commercial banks dealing in world trade.

Advertising in Foreign Countries. If you're seeking importers from abroad, you may also place low-cost advertisements in a monthly publication, *Commercial News, USA* of the US&FCS. It's a publication that promotes American products and services in overseas markets. You may feature your product in its *New Production Information Service* (NPIS) and hope that some individuals or companies contact you. This publication is distributed to 240 U.S. consulates and embassies throughout the world. There are also products that are broadcast over the Voice of America (VOA).

Export Licenses

As an export merchant, you need export licenses because the U.S. Government controls the exporting of all goods and technology. The reasons are national security, foreign policy, or short supply of domestic products.

As a merchant, you don't need to have an overall export license to cover all your exports. You need a license on every export.

The two types of export licenses are *general license* and *validated license.*

General License. A general license is granted to all exporters of certain categories of products. That is, it covers a list of products that can be exported without any questions and/ or screening. There is no need for individual exporters to apply for general licenses. The license is automatically issued for certain kinds of products.

If you look at the regulations and know that a validated license is not needed, you can then ship goods under a general license. Your broker/ freight forwarder will then comply with certain requirements, such as a "destination control statement" appearing on your shipping documents. Also, a "shipper's exporter declaration" (SED) must be completed for shipments valued at more than $500.00.

Validated License. A validated license is a specific grant of authority to particular persons or companies to export a specified product. This is done on case-by-case basis either for a single transaction or for a specific period of time. For example, if you're to export some kind of technology, you have to apply for a validated license.

You may apply for a validated export license with the district office of U.S. Department of Commerce.

All shipments must be recorded on the back of the validated form. When all shipments are made, or when the license has expired, it must be returned to the Department of Commerce.

Trade Leads

Like in importation, you need trade leads to export your product.

Trade Opportunities Magazine. If you're a member of the International Traders organization of the Mellinger Company, you can get leads from its *Trade Opportunities* magazine. It has a section that covers trade leads. It lists names and addresses of companies that have desires to buy certain products—from consumer products to tools to equipment.

Business America. The U.S. Department of Commerce has its *Business America,* a biweekly magazine that provides a good source of trade leads and articles of general interest to exporters. You can obtain copies, however, only on subscription. You may write or call the district office of the US&FCS (U.S. Department of Commerce).

Journal of Commerce. The *Journal of Commerce* also provides trade leads. You may write to its address.

Journal of Commerce
U.S. Department of Commerce
10 Wall Street
New York, NY 10005.

Product to Export

To be an exporter, you have to carefully evaluate what product to export. Not only that, you must determine which country will likely need your export.

The Product Search

As mentioned before, it is to your advantage if you're a native of a certain foreign country. As such, you know what products your old country lacks and as an American, you know what exportable products the U.S. has.

If you're not a native of any country abroad, then study the market in a particular nation and what it needs. If possible, learn a few words or phrases in the language of that country.

Negotiations

Before negotiations, you should take the following actions.

Conduct Research. Talk with trade experts and people of consulates representing the country with whom you would like to do business. Or call the Small Business Foundation of America (800-243-7232); it has information files on individual countries. Many of its services are free, while there are nominal fees for some publications and access to databases.

Get References. Check with your banks, trade sources, and the U.S. Department of Commerce to see if you can find any leads about your buyer.

If you find an importer abroad that wants to buy your product, you have to send a sample if it's easily mailable. You send a brochure and other literature only when your product is heavy and costly.

When you negotiate with an importer, be sure to present your company as a reliable exporter. You have to use a nice letterhead with a logo. The letterhead must contain the name and address of your company, telephone number, fax number, telex number (if any), and your name with a designation (for instance, Michael Vinson, President or General Manager or Michael Vinson, Manager, Export Department) printed on a high-quality paper. It is sealed in a high-quality envelope. In other words, protect the image of your company. (You should also do this when you negotiate for an import.)

In other words, don't make the mistake of exposing yourself as a one-person business.

When you offer to sell to an importer abroad, you must be specific about it: quantity, price, description of product, method of payment, and shipping terms. (Of course, you can also do a credit check of your prospective customer. Go the district office of the Department of Commerce to see how you can do it.)

In the case of shipping terms, specify whether it's F.O.B. or C.I.F.

1. F.O.B. (free on board) New York. This simply means that your quotation price covers the product cost and all expenses (insurance, inland freight, etc.) in order to load the goods on an international carrier in New York. Then it's your buyer's responsibility for all freight to be incurred from New York to the importing country.

2. C.I.F. (cost, insurance, freight), Manila. Thus, the quotation price covers cost of goods plus all in-transit expenses to the port of Manila.

Naturally, it is to your advantage if your price quotation specifies F.O.B.

Like in import, you have to deal with your freight forwarding company to have your product exported. It will handle all the paperwork.

If you can't have your broker as your freight forwarder, then you have to look for an inland freight forwarder. Forwarding agents are listed in the yellow pages of city phone directories.

Shipping Documents. The three basic fundamental forms for export shipping are the *bill of lading,* the *invoice,* and the *insurance policy.*

The bill of lading shows the shipping contract; for instance, the terms and details of the agreement between the exporter (you) and the carrier for transporting your goods. Either the carrier or your freight forwarder fills out the blank forms in multiple copies. In the case of goods shipped by air, the bill of lading is replaced by the air waybill. The majority of countries served by air will accept the waybill in place of the standard consular and commercial invoices and bills of lading.

Several copies of the invoice may be needed. Some countries, especially in Latin America, require a special form of invoice, in addition to the regular commercial invoice, which is called *consular invoice.* This form should be prepared in the language of the destination country. Such forms may be obtained from the consulates of countries requiring it.

The insurance policy is the third primary export shipping document. The insurance guarantees against the hazards of sea transportation.

For any other additional documents, you may ask your freight forwarder.

Irrevocable Letter of Credit. As mentioned before in the import section of this chapter, your seller abroad will naturally ask for an irrevocable letter of credit so that it can't be cancelled. Now that you are an exporter, you'll do the same: you'll ask your buyer to open an irrevocable letter of credit.

Back-to-Back Letter of Credit. If you are not the manufacturer of the product you are exporting, you need to open a *back-to-back letter of credit.* Let's suppose you found a trade lead offering to buy a certain product. At the same time, you found a local manufacturing company that can fill the order. All you have to do, after negotiation, is to ask for an irrevocable letter of credit (payable in U.S. funds) in your favor from your foreign buyer. Since the original letter of credit is under your name and it can't be paid until after the product has been placed on board bound for abroad, you have to open the back-to-back letter of credit. It's good if you have the capital to finance the export. However, if you don't have the necessary funds, you can have the deal financed by your bank by applying for an export loan.

The Eximbank will process your application because it's the one that will guarantee the loan to your regular bank. If the loan is approved, then your manufacturer/supplier will receive the letter of credit from your bank and it can load the goods on board ship.

Since the goods are already on board ship, you'll receive the payment on the letter of credit that you hold, which was sent by your foreign buyer.

As you can see, two letters of credit are involved: the LC sent to you by your foreign buyer, and the LC issued by your bank for your local supplier.

Hence, you can export goods that you don't manufacture as long as you have a buyer abroad and a local supplier.

Case History

Here's the true story of a man who became a successful exporter because of his fluency in Finnish, his love of travel, his technological expertise, and his having been an engineer. Let's just name him Mark Stevenson.

In June 1988, Stevenson started a company to export U.S. technology to Finland and the former Soviet Union. Let's call his company, American Trade International. Seeing Finland as a gateway to what was then the Soviet Union, he thought of exporting computers and peripherals and offering support, service, and training in Helsinki. Using a spare bedroom as his company headquarters in his home in California, he bought a computer and used a nearby mailbox center's fax machine for telecommunications.

Then armed with 500 printed business cards, he flew to Helsinki to attend an office automation show. Within six months, he generated sales of $4,500. (At that time, he was still studying for his MBA at California State University.) In 1991, Stevenson claimed that he had over $1 million in sales.

That was the beginning of his export business. Since import/export is a two-way street, his company also began importing a Finnish idea-generating and problem-solving software package.

B. Export Agent

If you don't desire to be an export merchant, then maybe you can be an export agent.

As an export agent, you don't invest any money and you receive the agreed commission on any business deals.

You may choose a country where you find importers and distributors of products looking for American products. Then you have to find local exporters selling such products.

Like an import agent, you'll be the middleman between a seller and a buyer. As such, you'll get a commission from the person or company that will do the actual exporting. Be sure that you have an agreement on what commission you are to receive and what particular deal your contract covers. For instance, you may provide in the contract that you'll also receive commissions not only on the first order, but also on possible succeeding orders.

C. Commission Agent

When you become a commission agent, you're the buying agent of a foreign company. You look for products that it likes and you become the intermediary. When a deal is closed, you'll receive a commission from the foreign merchant or distributor. So you don't have to invest any money in the product and you don't have any title to it.

Of course, you should have a contract that specifies the services to be performed and the commission to be given to you when a deal is made. Of course, being a commission agent is

harder than being an export agent because you'll be dealing with a company that is abroad. But everything will be fine, if everything is specified in the contract.

III. The Bottom Line

With the help of many agencies involved in import/export, you don't need to find it hard to start this business. As a one-person company, you'll deal with the bank and the customs broker, who can also act as your freight forwarder and do the paperwork.

Like any other business, however, an import/export business is risky. To test the water, you have to start small and grow as you go along.

If you're determined to make money in the import/export business, and if you do your homework, there's no way you can't succeed. Knowledge is power, and once you have it, there should be no turning back for you!

An Import Item

How to Run a One-Person Book Publishing Company   18

■ Whatever your present occupation or whatever your educational background, work experience, and life experience, you may become a sucessful publisher of nonfiction books in three ways: by writing them yourself, by collaborating with an established writer, and by publishing the works of others.

Self-Publisher. This means you write your own book and publish it yourself, not only with your writing ability, but with your own money to finance the project.

Co-Author. This means you must seek a co-author to help you write your own books based on your life, or your work experience, or your technical expertise. You may pay the writer an agreed one-time fee or give him or her a royalty based on the net or gross sale per book.

Publisher of Other Authors. This means you must seek authors or prospective authors.

For the past several years, more and more people have become publishers of *self-help* or *how-to* books due to the widespread use of desktop publishing. I was one of them.

But it took me several years before I considered myself as a successful author and publisher of my own books. That was after I won several book-publishing awards, including the "1990 Small Press Publisher of the Year" award from Quality Books, Inc., the largest distributor of nonfiction books to American and Canadian libraries.

Of course, awards should be accompanied by money to be a real successful author-publisher. That same year, I obtained my first $100,000-a-year net sales (gross sales minus discounts) with only two books in print. Up to 1993, I had so far written and published five nonfiction books, three of them award winners, while operating a one-person publishing company.

You, too, can become a successful operator of a one-person publishing company if you have the knowledge, patience, persistence, and determination to succeed.

Whether you publish your own books, collaborate with others, or publish the books of others, the processes in publishing, such as in the production and marketing of your books or in running your company, are all the same.

I. Who Is Your Buyer?

The first thing to know is what your market is. In other words, before you write and publish a book, you must know who will buy your book or why people will buy it.

The two markets are the *general market* or *the mass market* and the *niche market* or the *single-target market*.

General Market

General market means you sell to a larger portion of the population, which really is expensive to reach. Without the help of distributors, wholesalers, and retailers, you'll have a hard time serving this market.

Niche Market

Niche market, as stated in Chapter 13, *(Savvy Marketing* page 113), can be narrowed down to various groups or segments. If you sell a particular cookbook to buyers of these books, you have a niche market or a targeted market. Selling a book for pediatricians also means you have a niche market.

The Market I Like

Publishing experts say small publishers should confine themselves to going after the targeted market. Of course, most self-publishers succeed in this method.

However, I do the opposite. I go for the big one—the mass market that has millions and millions of prospective buyers. My books, *The Book of*

U.S. Postal Exams and *Improve Your Grades* and other books are displayed side-by-side in bookshelves (particularly in B. Dalton, Waldenbooks, and Crown Books) with books produced by the Goliaths of publishing.

Of course, I also sell books to several non-traditional markets.

II. Writing Your Book

The writing process involves several factors: knowing what to write about, knowing how to write it (or writing style), and having it edited. This section discusses those elements and other factors that you should consider.

What to Write About

The best books you may write should be about things you know or with which you are familiar.Not only that. You must support them with materials that you should have researched

Experiences. My books are all based on my experience and exhaustive research. I scored 95-100% on several U.S. Postal examinations, so I wrote a book on this subject, entitled *The Book of U.S. Postal Exams: How to Score 95-100% and Get a Job.* I became an honor student during my college days (after having been an average student in elementary and high school) by devising and using a study and test-taking system. Hence, I wrote and published *Improve Your Grades: A Practical Guide to Academic Excellence.* Then followed all other books, all based on experience.

Interviews and Thorough Research. Of course, you may write books that are not based on experience. Merely be an active observant. Know what people complain about. Try to help them solve their problems. If they need information on a certain subject, do a research work and write a book about it. If you're not an expert on the subject, interview the experts and let them talk in your book. In addition, add materials you get from your research.

Other Book Ideas. You may discover some book ideas in your local library. For instance, I went to our local library and found a flyer concerning a course entitled *Career Building: Preparing for Change* offered by Oakland University. This course is only offered locally. So if I were to publish such a book, I would attend such a course, do some research work, and write a book on the same subject. I may also interview some authorities on the subject and fill the books with authoritative theories and ideas, with quotes from the experts.

One more thing, instead of writing a book on the same subject, I might offer, to the "presenter" of the course, to publish it into a book with the same title. That involves royalty! (But I'm not interested because I've so many books in my head that I can't publish all of them in my lifetime.)

If you want to write a book, then you may go to your local library to find flyers about courses offered by your local college or university. If you merely want to be a publisher, contact the authorities on any subject you think may be appropriate for a book.

Know What to Write About

Books That Last! Write books that will sell forever. All my books are good backlist titles with a wider audience. They sell every season, spring or summer, fall or winter. They have been selling for the past several years, and I keep them new by revising and expanding once every two or three years. Write and publish useful books and they will last for a long time!

Writing Style

If you're to write and publish nonfiction books, particularly how-to or self-help books, write in a simple, concise, lively style. Talk to your readers as if they were in front of you. Remember that in writing nonfiction books, you don't have to use high-sounding words; you're not writing a novel. Your object is not to impress, but to give information, to offer advice, to motivate, or to entertain people in order to help them accomplish their dreams or solve their personal problems in life.

Your Writing Style

In my books, I always try to spice some paragraphs with some kind of humor. I also include some funny, attractive graphics to make the pages come alive. I've mentioned in my books, *Improve Your Grades* and *How to Teach Your Child*, the names of Madonna, Vanna White, Imelda Marcos (and her shoes), Saddam Hussein, and other personalities, although they have nothing to do with improving one's grades or teaching a child. Many of my readers like my books, not only for their contents, illustrations, and graphics, but also for my easy-reading writing style.

List of Chapters

Many writers suggest that you make an outline before you write a book.

Instead of an outline, I'll have a complete listing of chapters of my book. Then I submit this list of chapters, with tentative headings, to my editor for comments. Organization is very important in writing a book; that's why I always want to be sure that the chapters are in order.

Editorial Help

You should have an editor to check your manuscript. A copyeditor can give you feedback and check on several factors, some of which are follows:

Clarity and Readability. Is it clear what you're trying to say or convey? Is it easy to read?

Spelling, Word Use, Style, and Punctuation. The editor can check on spelling, word use, style, and punctuation —eliminating grammatical errors and redundancies.

Choose a Good Editor

Organization. A good editor also can see to it that the book is well organized into paragraphs, chapters, and units. In other words, the transitions should be smooth and not winding from sentence to sentence, paragraph to paragraph, chapter to chapter, and unit to unit. Moreover, a good editor must pay particular attention to titles, headings, subheadings, and italics and boldface in the text.

Before you write your book, you must submit your title and subtitle to your editor for comments or suggestions. For instance, ask the editor if they convey the general content of the book.

You may also ask your editor how it differs from other books of the same subject. Also, the editor may be able to suggest how you can make it different from the competition.

Choosing an Editor

Search for a professional freelance editor who does editing as a sideline or as a full-time work. Many freelance editors place classified ads in the *Writer's Digest*, which is available in most large bookstores, such as B. Dalton and Waldenbooks stores.

You should select your editor from a list of at least three persons. That is, find three names in the classified section of the above magazine. Then have each of them edit one or two chapters of your manuscript and see how different they are in editing your work.

For instance, if one editor deletes a few sentences or paragraphs that you think is very important, that means he or she is not the one for you. If an editor says you must go back to school to learn about grammar and punctuation, maybe he's not the right one for you, either. In short, find out their writing styles and ways of editing and then choose one with whom you may be comfortable. Also ask for a biodata of each of them.

After you've decided to choose one, then have a contract with the editor, specifying fees, time schedule, and other matters. One such matter involves the fee, which is to be considered as a one-time payment for services and that he or she has no rights for any royalty on sales. Most editors provide their own contract.

Writing the Manuscript

To write a book is overwhelming, especially if you think that you'll write a 30-chapter book.

Write a Booklet. If you think it will be hard for you to write a book first, write a booklet. Sometime in the early part of the 1980s, I wrote a 32-page booklet entitled *How I Got 95-100% on Postal Exams and How You Can, Too!* I sold it for $5.00 each through classified ads and by sending out flyers. The booklet turned into a 90-page, spiral-bound book, which I sold successfully through local bookstores, especially when postal exams were held in my area. That inspired me to turn the booklet into book form.

Eventually, a new paperbound book entitled *The Book of U.S. Postal Exams: How to Score 95-100% and Get a Job!* landed in bookstores throughout the country, and finally it became a silent bestseller.

You'll Write Articles. If you write a manuscript, don't think that you're writing a book. Consider that you're writing related articles, with each consisting of several pages, known as a chapter. Then these articles will be combined into a book. But of course, the transition from chapter to chapter should be smooth, as mentioned earlier.

"I've No Time! I've No Time!" This is the excuse of many people who aspire to be a writer, but can't begin writing. They don't know the secret! The best thing to do to finish your manuscript is to write at least two or three hours a day. Whether it's at 12 midnight, at 6 o'clock in the morning, or at 7 o'clock in the evening, you may finish two or three pages a day.

If you write 2 pages a day, you can write 14 pages a week: 14 pages x 24 weeks (6 months) = 336 pages. So in six months, you have a manuscript! If you wish, write 4 pages a day and

you've a 336-page manuscript in only three months.

My Own Writing System. I don't wait for the completion of writing a manuscript before I submit it to my editor for editing. Usually, I have an agreement with my editor that I'll have to submit my manuscript in installments.

A few years back, after having a chapter or two edited, I would start typesetting them by sending my computer files via modem to my typesetter in Virginia. The next day after I sent it, I received the typesetting on Kodak paper, ready for pasteup on board for layout purposes. Now, I have my own desktop publishing program, and everything is automatically typeset when a file is printed by my laser printer.

In having manuscript in installments, I feel that I am committed to finishing the book. And one more thing. At the time of my writing, I'll have the cover design finalized. That's my way of having an inspiration to have the book published!

III. Book Production

Self-publishers usually don't have their books typeset by a commercial typesetter, which is costly. The standard practice of self-publishers is to have their book in camera-ready copy.

Camera-ready Copy

Camera-ready copy is manuscript that has been typeset and laid out on board or typeset by your laser printer, with line drawings or other illustrations and graphics. Then the copy is shot by your book printer. This is the cheapest way of publishing books because all the book printer must do is to shoot the pages; make the negatives, flats, and plates; and run the presses. Bingo! You have a book!

Also, there is now a new technology in book printing. Ron Mazzola of McNaughton & Gunn, a short-run book printer in Michigan, in a talk before the Michigan Book Publishing Association, said that it's better to submit the book on disks as opposed to camera-ready art. (However, be sure that the printer's specs meet your own.)

He also offered the following cost-saving ideas for publishers (as published in *The Communicator*, a newsletter of the Michigan Book Publishing Association):

1. Avoid putting rule lines around halftones because it is difficult and time-consuming to match them up.

2. Use standard signature sizes in determining the length of books. (A signature is a bundle of pages printed and bound as a unit. All books are bound to the spine in such units.)

3. Use standard trim sizes (mentioned in this chapter).

4. Plan the selection of colors by using only standard or PMS mixed colors.

Size of the Book

Determine the ideal size for your book, depending on the subject matter. The standard sizes are 4" x 7", 5" x 8", 7" x 10", and 8 1/2" x 11".

As an example, I decided to have this book in a 8 1/2" x 11" size, so that I could fit in enough text. I used a two-column text format.

You Don't Need This Machine

Typefaces

You must have a good interior design for your book. Use letters, numbers, and symbols that will make the text easy to read.

The typeface is either *serif* or *sans serif*. *Serif* has "feet" at the edge of each letter, while *sans serif* does not. Examples of serif types are those used by newspapers.

Examples of serif types (set in 11-point size) are as follows:

(**Century**)
The quick brown fox jumps over the lazy dog.

(**Times**)
The quick brown fox jumps over the lazy dog.

(**Garamond**)
The quick brown fox jumps over the lazy dog.

(Times New Roman)
The quick brown fox jumps over the lazy dog.

Examples of sans serif types (set in 11-point size) are as follows:

(Futuri)
The quick brown fox jumps over the lazy dog.

(GillSans)
The quick brown fox jumps over the lazy dog.

(Helvetica)
The quick brown fox jumps over the lazy dog.

(Univers)
The quick brown fox jumps over the lazy dog.

Books, like newspapers and newsletters, usually are set in serif, not sans serif type, for faster reading. For easy reading, 10 to 12-point type is used for the body text. For a 10-point type, the subhead is usually in 12 points. (For my books, I use 10.5 point, 11 point, and 12 point for body text.)

Alignment of Types

The two types of type alignments are *flush left* (ragged right) and *justified*.

Flush Left. In a flush-left-type alignment, only the first letters in each line of type (except the indented first line of a paragraph) are aligned. An example of a flush-left alignment, which is ragged right, is shown below:

Tadpoles are young frogs and toads which lose their tails when they reach adulthood. The majority of frogs or toads can use suction cups on their toes in climbing trees and hanging upside down. "Look, Ma, I'm upside down!" one might be saying while doing it.

As you can see, the informal ragged right gives visual variety on the right margin. It gives only few or no hyphenated words.

Justified. In a justified alignment, the first letters (at the left margin) and the last letters (at the right margin) are aligned. Hyphenated words are incorporated into the text.

Here's an example of justified text.

Like humans who have their Patriot and Scud missiles and poison gas, animals have their own weapons, too. They use them to fight their enemies and predators. For example, the cat has claws and teeth to grab and kill its prey, as if saying "I got you!" The hognose snake just lies down motionless, as if saying, "I'm dead, leave me alone!" The skunk bombards his enemy with a foul-smelling liquid, as if shouting, "Come closer and you're dead!"

The Cover Design

Before you bring the camera-ready copy to the printing press, you must have a good cover design for your book, which I always do. It should be done, if you can afford it, by a professional graphic designer whose job is designing book covers. As the saying goes, "Covers sell books!"

I had the covers of two of my books redesigned a few years ago. I told my new two graphic designers for two books to make covers that say, "Hey, come and get me!" And they did! My sales during the first month of publication of those two revised editions doubled (as compared to a month's sale with their original covers). The two books sold 13,000 copies with a total amount of $60,000 in a month's time (August 1990) which was a record sale. (Of course, the sales levelled the next month.) Not only that. *Improve Your Grades* won three awards (including one for Best Cover Design) in a contest sponsored by Mid-America Publishers Association. *The Book of U.S. Postal Exams* got an Honorable Mention, Total Sales award in the same contest. And *The Book of U.S. Postal Exams* won the 1991 PMA Benjamin Franklin Award for Most Improved. Covers do sell books!

Ingredients of a Good Cover Design. Among the ingredients of a good cover design (front and back) are the following:

■ The cover must attract attention.

■ The title and the subtitle should stand out and convey what the book contains.

■ The graphics, if there are any, should help the title and the subtitle communicate with the reader what the book is all about.

■ The title, the author, the bar code, the spine, and the price should appear in their appropriate sizes and proper positions.

■ As much as possible, the front cover must not be cluttered. If possible, just have the cover with only the title, the subtitle, the author's name, and a simple graphic, depending on the book's subject matter.

■ The size of the title should be large enough on the spine because,

usually, it's the only one seen when a book is displayed on a shelf in bookstores.

■ The category of the book (whether it's a business book or a travel guide) must be stated at the top left corner of the back cover. The bar code, meanwhile, should be on the bottom left or right of the back cover. Usually, the price is placed on the top right corner of the book.

■ Advance comments about the book, if there are any, should be placed at the back.

Hiring a Cover Designer. It's difficult to select a graphic designer. It's because there are designers who will not let you incorporate your ideas into their own design concepts.

So it's better to hire one whom you think is compatible with your own ideas of creating an attractive cover. I once hired a woman designer. I requested her to make my name a little bit larger on the front cover. She did the opposite; she made my name so small that I almost couldn't read it—probably thinking that I wasn't a known author. For my next book, I commissioned another designer! In short, almost all designers hate to change their ideas about the book cover.

When you contact several cover designers for possible selection of a good one for your particular book, ask for their resumes and sample covers they have done. See if you like their own style of cover designs.

Designers ask for a certain fee, $650 for example (for designing only), and extras for supplies and materials.

So actually, you won't know how much the total cost will be at the beginning. At least, a few graphic designers make an estimate for the total package. Cover designs for my books usually cost over $2,000 (designing fee plus materials).

For your information, here are few cover designers who serve the independent publishing industry:

Robert Howard Graphic Design
111 E. Drake Rd., Suite 7114
Fort Collins, CO 80525
(313) 225-0083

Robert Pawlak Design
2411 Webster #2
San Francisco, CA 94115
(415) 776-2280
Mike Stromberg, Great American
    Art Company
P.O. Box
Shelter Island Center
New York, NY 11964
(516) 749-4390

Feedback from Your Distributor. If you have a master distributor, you must ask your graphic designer if he or she is willing to have the initial rough to be approved by your distributor.

Once, when I didn't submit a cover design to my distributor for feedback, the art director of the company told me that I should have submitted the design for their feedback. "We sell books and we know what cover designs sell," she said.

From then on, I have always submitted to my distributor the cover design of a new book before the cover design is finalized. Anyway, the feedback is free! (You don't have only the art director, but also the president and other members of the staff of your distributing company offering free services to you.) Like you, they want to sell more copies of your books so that they make money, too.

Interior Design

The typography to be used in the inside pages should be readable. In order to select a typeface appropriate for your subject matter and audience, it's best to go to your local bookstore and look at book formats. Then you can decide whether to put your text in one or two columns.

Making the Pages Come Alive! Select graphics and illustrations appropriate for the subject matter. It is to be emphasized that sometimes you should use line drawings to break the monotony of seeing too much text.

The interior design involves the use of chapter headings, subheadings, sub-subheadings, *italicized* and **bold** words, and illustrations and graphics.

Having a commercial artist to create your illustrations is expensive. I seldom commission an artist to make a line drawing for me. However, there's one drawing in this book drawn by an artist. It cost me $250.00.

So it's best to look for the so-called copyright-free illustrations, known as clip art.

I obtain these copyright-free illustrations from Dover Publications, Inc., in New York, from which I have bought several books of clip art. But there are other clip art book publishers. Here' are three clip art book publishers:

Dover Publications, Inc.
31 East 2nd St.
Mineola, NY 11501

Artmaster/Art-Pak
500 N. Claremont Blvd.
Clarement, CA 91711
(714) 626-8065

Wheeler Arts
66 Lake Park
Champaign, IL 61821-7101
(217) 359-6816

Some of Dover's titles are *Treasury of Animal Illustrations from Eighteenth-Century Sources* (edited by Carol Belanger Grafton)*; Men: A Pictorial Archive from Nineteenth-Century Sources* (selected by Jim Harter); and *Dore Spot Illustrations* (by Gustave Dore).

Request a catalog for its listing of these books.

Common Mistakes. There are some common mistakes to avoid in interior design. Two of the don'ts are as follows:

1. In typesetting, don't put two spaces after a period. The period creates a big space between ends and beginnings of sentences. The reason is that in typeset books, every letter has a different width to make reading easy, not like in typewritten manuscript in which an extra space after a period is a necessity. It's because the typewriter type is mono-spaced and all the characters have the same width.

2. Don't underline words to emphasize them. This underscoring is commonly used in typewritten material, but not in a typeset book. Instead, italicize the words.

ISBN and Bar Code

The ISBN (International Standard Book Number) and the bar code are needed in books.

ISBN. You can request an ISBN number from the ISBN Agency:

The ISBN Agency
245 West 17th St.
New York, NY 10011
(212) 337-6975)

The ISBN number will also be used in the creation of a bar code. If you request an ISBN for your book, you'll be given a series of numbers that you can use for each of your books.

The ISBN is used on invoices, catalogs, order forms, and the book itself because it is an identifying mark for book buyers, libraries, and others.

LC Catalog Card Number

Your book must also have a Library of Congress catalog card number (LCCN). You may request a pre-assigned LCCN number from the Library of Congress:

Library of Congress
Cataloging in Publication Division
Washington, DC 20540

You need this number for cataloging purposes by the Library of Congress. It is also a requirement for inclusion in the *Advance Book Infor-*

mation (ABI) requested by the R.R. Bowker Company for listing in the *Books In Print.* It is also to be placed on the copyright page of your book.

The LC catalog card number is needed for cataloging purposes required by librarians for sorting books with classification codes.

The bad news is that the Library of Congress has a backlog of books by small publishers not participating in the Library of Congress CIP program to be catalogued. (Publishers who have published at least four books are the only ones who can participate in the LC CIP program.) This is due to the emergence of too many small publishers as a result of the proliferation of desktop publishing.

The good news is that a company, Quality Books, Inc., a library distributor mentioned in this chapter, professionally services small publishing companies that are not participating in the Library of Congress CIP program. This company prepares a *Publisher's Cataloging in Publication.*

Quality Books, Inc. provides an appropriate Library of Congress classification number in P-CIP records. This is the portion of a library's call number that reflects the subject of a work. A library can add an author code, a date, a copy number, etc., to the classification number to create a unique call number for each title.

An example of a P-CIP prepared by Quality Books is on the copyright page of this book.

Quality Books, Inc., provides an appropriate Dewey Decimal classification number in P-CIP records. As with the LC classification number, this number reflects the subject of a work. Specific item information may be added to create a unique call number.

In short, Quality Books, Inc., provides P-CIP records based on standard library cataloging rules set forth in *Anglo-American Cataloguing Rules,* 2nd edition, revised (AACR2, rev.).

The Quality Books, Inc. fee schedule for the preparation of a P-CIP, which is sent camera ready, is as follows:

Regular service: 30 calendar-day turnaround, $30.00; priority service: 10 business-day turnaround, $50.00; express service: 3-business day turnaround, $75.00. Any service with Federal Express or Express Mail is $10.00 additional.

To obtain an application for a Publisher's - Cataloging in Publication (P-CIP), write to:

Quality Books, Inc. P-CIP Dept.
918 Sherwood Drive
Lake Bluff, IL 60044-2204
(708) 295-2010

Bowker ABI Form

In order that your book will be listed in the *Forthcoming Books in Print* and *in Books In Print,* published by the R.R. Bowker Company, you must request a copy of the ABI from:

R.R. Bowker Data Collection
    Center
P.O. Box 2068
Oldsmar, FL 34677-0037

(Bowker's general headquarters is at 245 West 16th Street, New York, NY 10011)

Types of Bar Codes. There are two types of bar codes: the *Bookland EAN bar code* and the *supermarket-type UPC bar code.*

If you intend to sell your books to bookstores, you should use the Bookland EAN. The UPC bar code can be used for books sold in supermarkets or other mass-merchandising stores. If you're selling to both markets, then you can use both of them.

How the Bar Code Works. The bar code is a necessary tool in book marketing as it speeds the distribution of books. Bar codes on books are required by book chains, such as B. Dalton Books, Waldenbooks, Crown Books, and other bookstores.

Here's the bar code of one of my books:

For this particular bar code, the first three digits (978) tells the scanning computer that this is a Bookland EAN bar code, and not a UPC bar code. The following nine digits are the same as the first nine digits (4th to 12th digits) of the ISBN with the hyphens deleted. The last number, (the 13th digit), is the computed EAN check digit. The vertical lines printed on a book identify the ISBN which, in turn, identifies the publisher, title, author, and edition (soft cover, etc.).

Example: ISBN 0-931613-05-1 converts into

Bookland EAN 9 780931613050

As you can see, the ISBN itself has been placed above the bar code in the OCR-A (optical character recognition, font A). To the right is a smaller block, which is the "price extension." The "5" indicates U.S. dollars and the next four numbers indicate the price.

Sources of Bar Code Film Masters. There are several manufacturers of bar codes. A few of the providers of bar code film masters, which cost from $20-$30, are as follows:

Symbology, Inc.
P.O. Box 1362
Saint Paul, MN 55113-0262
(612) 631-2100
(800)328-2612

GGX Associates
11 Middle Neck Road
Great Neck, NY 11021
(516) 487-6370

Landy & Associates
5311 N. Highland
Tacoma, WA 98407
(206) 752-5099

For a complete list of bar code film master suppliers, contact:

ISBN Agency
245 West 17th Street
New York, NY 10011
(212) 337-6975

Choosing a Book Printer

When you go to press, select a book printer, not a commercial printer that does all kinds of printing. Select a printer that does nothing but print books as its specialty.

Short-Run Printers. Whether you have a print run of 250 or 10,000 copies, go to a company that is known as a short-run book printer.

All of these printers accept camera-ready copies; some of them even accept manuscripts on disks.

I have my books printed in Michigan by short-run printers, which are well-known throughout the country. They are especially used by small- and medium-sized publishers, including university presses.

Here's a list of several book printers:

McNaughton & Gun
960 Woodland Dr.
P.O. Box 10
Saline, MI 48176
(313) 429-5411
Fax: (313) 429-4033

Malloy Lithographing, Inc.
5411 Jackson Rd.
Ann Arbor, MI 48103-1865
(313) 665-6113

Thomson & Shore, Inc.
7300 West Joy Rd.
P O Box 305
Dexter, Michigan
(313) 426-3939

BookMasters
638 Jefferson St.
P.O. Box 159P
Ashland, OH 44805

Delta Lithograph Co.
28210 N. Stanford Ave.
Valencia, CA 91355-1111
(805) 257-0584

For a complete listing of book printers, see a copy of John Kramer's *Directory of Short-Run Printers* at your local library.

It is also available from:

Ad-Lib Publications
51 N. Fifth St.
P.O. Box 1102,
Fairfield, IA 52556-1102
(515) 472-6617.

Develop a Good Relationship with Your Printers. You must develop a good relationship with at least two printers. In case one is busy, then you can go to the other one.

Be sure that you aren't delinquent in your payments.

At first, as a new customer, a printer will ask for a down payment before it accepts your book for printing. But as you develop your good relationship with the printer, you may obtain a net 30-day payment terms, or even net 60 to 90-day payment terms, without any advance payment involved. It depends on the volume of business with the printer and your good credit standing.

In the publishing business, the printer should be one of your best partners, besides the distributors and the book dealers.

IV. Marketing Your Book

As your book comes off the press, you must promote it.

"I'm an Author! I'm an Author"

You'll shout to the world: "I'm an author! I'm an author!" You are the happiest man or woman in the world.

The first thing to do is to send a copy to the United States Copyright Office for registration. The form that you will need is the TX Form, which covers "nondramatic literary work," which is used for fiction, nonfiction, poetry, periodicals, textbooks, reference works, directories, catalogs, and compilations of information.

Submit a copy of the book and the filled-in application form and a check for $12.00 to:

Register of Copyrights
Library of Congress
Washington, DC 20559.
(202) 287-8700

Promotional Materials

Even before you go to press, you must prepare a flyer about your book. Also, prepare a good sales letter if you will sell books by direct mail.

Photographer. As soon as you have the mockup of the cover of your book (to be provided by your graphic designer) or a copy of your first printing, have the book photographed by a photographic service who specializes in book photography, such as

Publishers' Photographic Services
10319 Pine Ridge Drive
Ellicott City, MD 21042
(480) 966-4880

This company specializes in black and white and color photographs for flyers, brochures, and catalogs for small publishers.

However, it usually prints only a few copies.

For black and white photo reproduction, contact:

Copley Photo Service
350 Camino del la Reina
San Diego, CA 92108
(619) 293-1883

From your original photograph, the company can make from 10 to 10,000 photocopies.

Flyers. If you're printing a full-color flyer, which may be 8 1/2 x 11 or 14 x 17 inches, you may not have it printed by your local printer. Contact companies that specialize in producing full-color flyers at a low cost.

Here are two companies that serve the publishing industry.

Econocolor
The Nielsen Company
7405 Industrial Rd.
Florence, KY 41042-2997
(606) 525-7405
Fax: (606) 525-7654

Tu-Vets Corp.
5635 E. Beverly Blvd.
Los Angeles, CA 90022
(213) 723-4569
Fax: 724-1896

Ask for price quotations from these companies and compare them with your local printers.

Review Copies

Before you take your book to a printer, you must have your galleys ready for submission to magazine reviewers. You need reviewers to help expose your book to future readers.

Bound Galleys. Galleys are called *bound galleys* or *reader's proofs,* which are actually books you make and distribute prior to the printing of your book. These galleys are required by *Publisher's Weekly, Library Journal,* and other book review magazines three months in advance of your publication date.

You can make your own bound galleys, but they may not be properly made according to current standards. If you wish it to be professionally done, contact a company that manufactures bound galleys. It will print and bind the copies you want. All you must do is to have your camera-ready pages photocopied or printed on your laser printer and then send them to a company that does this job for a print run of 10 to 20 copies. It may cost you about $40 per copy, more or less, depending on the size of the book and the copies needed.

You may try to have the bound galleys made by Graphic Illusions Corp./ Crane Duplicating or any other duplicating company. To be printed on the cover are the title, the subtitle, and the name of the author. Reviewers like this kind of cover, without the actual cover design of the book with graphics. They need books which are not yet actually printed. You may first call Graphic Illusions if you wish it to make your bound galleys.

Graphic Illusions Corp./Crane Duplicating
17 Shad Hole Rd., P.O. Box 99
Dennisport, MA 02639-0020
(508) 760-1321

Printed Copies. Of course, if you don't submit galleys, you can still submit finished books from your printer to some magazine reviewers or freelance reviewers. For one, *Booklist,* a publication of the American Library Association, accepts finished books for possible reviews.

Here are the four major book magazine reviewers:

Publishers Weekly
249 West 16th St.
New York, NY 10011-5301
(212) 463-6758

Booklist
American Library Association
50 East Huron St.
Chicago, IL 60611
(312) 944-6780

Library Journal
249 West 16th St.
New York, NY 10011-5301
(212) 463-6816

School Library Journal
249 West 17th St.
New York, NY 10011-5301
(212) 463-6757

Call the above magazines and ask for the names of the appropriate book review editors. Then send copies to those editors.

Besides the mentioned magazines, there are other publications that review books.

Follow-ups. You must follow-up your sending of review copies to the appropriate editors. If you don't want to make telephone calls to reviewers (and if you can afford it), you may hire a publicist. Ask other publishers about names and addresses of publicists with whom they have had business relations.

Here are two publicists serving small publishers nationally:

KSB Promotions
Attn: Kate & Doug Bandos
55 Honey Creek NE
Ada, MI 49301
(616) 676-0758

Marilyn and Tom Ross
About Books
P.O. Box 213
Saguache, CO 81149
(303) 589-8223

Before you sign a contract with any publicist, ask what he or she can and cannot do regarding the promotion of your book. Most importantly, be clear about what the services will be and the total fee involved in any specific project. You may specify only one or two services. Services may include writing press releases, sending copies to review editors, and making follow-ups.

You must know, however, that the success of any publicity doesn't depend only on who conducts it, but on the saleability of your book. A publicist can only help expose and promote your book, but he or she can't make miracles for it!

V. Distribution Channels

Long before you think of writing your book, you must determine if your book will sell in bookstores.

In an article published by Publishers Marketing Association, the organization's Trade Distribution Selection Committee found out from bookstores the reasons why many books are unacceptable for bookstore sales.

Some of the most-cited reasons for rejection are:
■ Lack of national appeal
■ Bad cover and interior designs
■ Marketplace already saturated with this type of book
■ Too specialized a topic
■ Too regional in approach
■ Lack of author's credentials on the subject
■ An excellent library book, but not a bookstore book
■ Book's marketplace hard to define.

If you think your book will sell through bookstores, look for the so-called master distributors, and select one that is best for distributing your kind of book. Remember that bookstores won't deal with small publishers, especially the one- or two-book publishers.

The Difference between Distributors and Wholesalers

Master Distributors. Master distributors are organizations that launch books each season with a catalog and a sales force. They distribute to other distributors, wholesalers, bookstores and other markets.·

A distributing company may have its in-house sales force (paid by salaries) or outside sales representatives groups which are paid commissions.

Publishers consign books to them: they stock books, get orders, deliver the books, and send bills to and collect payments from book buyers. Then they send checks to publishers, minus the amount representing their discounts. They send out monthly sales reports to publishers they represent.

Wholesalers. Wholesalers are organizations that fulfil orders to bookstores and libraries quickly. Much reorder business comes from wholesalers. Wholesalers may get books from distributors or direct from the publishers. They do not have their own sales forces.

There are those companies that claim to be distributors, but actually they are wholesalers.

How to Find and Select a Master Distributor

It's hard to select a master distributor. The reason is simple: once you select one, you're stuck with it for quite some time, depending on what is stated in your contract. Sorry, if you select the wrong distributor, you will be very disappointed, especially if it's your first one.

A few months before a book is published, its cover design, table of contents, and editorial fact sheets are submitted to your master distributor. However, this happens only if you already have a distributor and have proven that you are a reliable publisher.

If you're publishing a book for the first time, you can't submit a cover design, the table of contents, and

some sample chapters to a distributor for the book's approval for distribution. You must submit a printed book.

But once a distributor has sold your book successfully, all of your books (with certain exceptions, of course) will be marketed by your distributor.

Here are some master distributors that sell to wholesalers, bookstores, and other retailers:

Publishers Group West
4065 Hollis Ave.
Emeryville, CA 94608
(510) 658-3433

Consortium Book Sales
    & Distribution
287 E. 6th St.
St. Paul, MN 55101
(612) 221-0124

Independent Publishers Group
814 N Franklin St.
Chicago, IL 60610
(312) 337-0747

The Talman Company, Inc.
150 Fifth Ave., Ste. 630
New York, NY 10011
(212) 627-4282

Publishers Distributing Service
6893 Sullivan Rd.
Grawn, MI 49637
(616) 276-5196

National Book Network, Inc.
4720 Boston Way
Lanham, MD 20706
(301) 459-3366

Login Publishers Consortium
1436 W. Randolph
Chicago, IL 60607
(312) 733-8228

Atrium Publishers Group
P.O. Box 108
Lower Lake, CA 95457
(707) 995-3906

These master distributors ask for exclusive distribution. Normally, direct sales and premium sales (and some nontraditional markets) are exempted from a distribution contract. You may also request that certain markets be exempted—markets that the distributor doesn't cover.

The standard discount given by masters distributors to wholesalers is 50% discount. The discounts to bookstores vary from 45% to 48%.

Master distributor discounts from publishers vary: from 24% to 35% of the net sales. Gross sales (based on retail price) - discounts = net sales. Actually, master distributors who have no in-house sales representatives ask much larger discounts.

Here are examples of how master distributors give discounts to wholesalers and bookstores:

(Sales to Wholesalers)

Total sales at retail price: $3,000
Less 50% discount: $1,500
Total net sales billed: $1,500
Amount retained by distributor (based on 24% of net sales): $360.00
Amount paid to publisher: $1,140.00

(Sales to Bookstores)

Total sales at retail price: $3,000
Less 48% discount: $1,440
Total net sales billed: $1,560
Amount retained by distributor: $374.40 (based on 24% of net sales)
Amount paid to publisher: $1,185.60

The standard time of payment for books sold is 90 days. But some distributors pay after 90 days (or even up to 120 days). Once your book is distributed (and hopefully sells), you'll receive your monthly check.

A good distributor has a business relationship with national and regional accounts, particularly the major chains, such as B. Dalton Books, Waldenbooks, and Crown Books.

To find a good master distributor, ask other publishers who distributes their books. Know the names of these companies and inquire about their financial standing. It can happen that a distributor may go under. However, you may like a distributor, but it may not like your book. Because distributors are very competitive, they have a lot of books to choose from.

Develop a Good Relationship with Your Distributor. When you have a company distributing your books, develop a good relationship with it. For instance, in carrying books, the distributor will give you a deadline to meet.

For instance, those books published for the spring season (published from February to June) are sold by distributors' sales representatives to the major and regional accounts even if the books are not yet in print.

Sales meetings for sales representatives are held by December. These representatives, armed with sales catalogs and other promotional materials, then go out and sell the new and backlist titles.

With regard to deadlines, here's an example for the *1994 Publishers Deadlines* set by my distributor, Publishers Group West.

Fall 1994 Season

1. New titles announcement card due: 1/14/94
2. Completed editorial fact sheets due: 2/11/94
3. Graphics due: B&W-1 Color-2: 03/25/94
4. Sales Conference: 05/13/94

Of course, if you are a new publisher, you don't have to stick to these deadlines. You simply submit a sample of your book to the distributor's screening committee. Once you are an established publisher releasing and shipping books on time, you must adhere to the deadlines set by your distributor. The beauty of it is that your book may be sold even if you're still writing it. The important thing is that you must have your books shipped on or before the ship date you gave to your distributor.

The Library Distributors

Libraries are a great market for many books. Although there are books that sell both in bookstores and in libraries, there are also books that sell only in libraries and not in bookstores.

You can also consign books to library distributors that ask for 55% of the gross sales (or selling price).

Two known library distributors are:

Quality Books, Inc.
918 Sherwood Dr.
Lake Bluff, IL 60044-2204
(708) 295-2010

Unique Books, Inc.
4230 Grove Ave.
Gurney, IL 60031
(708) 623-7238

Direct to Wholesalers

You may also sell books direct to wholesalers. You can usually do that if you have no master distributor to sell books to wholesalers. In selling to wholesalers, you'll be normally paid in 60 to 120 days. You don't consign books to them. You just make shipments on accounts.

Just remember that wholesalers are not distributors. They have no sales representatives who solicit orders. All they do is wait for orders from their customers (bookstores, libraries, and institutions) and they fill the orders.

A wholesaler may be operating nationally or regionally. There are also wholesalers specializing in specific categories of books.

Here are some of them:

National Wholesalers

Baker & Taylor
Box 6920
652 E. Main St.
Bridgewater, NJ 08807-0920
(908) 218-0400

Ingram Book Company
Box 3006
1125 Heil Quaker Blvd.
La Vergne, TN 37086-1986
(615) 793-500

Brodart Company
500 Arch St.
Williamsport, PA 17705
(717) 326-2461

Regional Wholesalers:

Pacific Pipeline
19215 66th Ave. S.
Kent, WA 98032-2180
((206) 872-5523

the Distributors
702 S. Michigan
South Bend, IN 46618
(219) 232-8500

There are also wholesaling companies that carry books on certain categories. Here are some of them:

Specialty Wholesalers

New Leaf Distributing Company
5425 Tulane
Atlanta, GA 30336-2323
Specialty: New age, self-help

Nutribooks
Box 5793
Denver, CO 80217
(303) 778-8383
Specialty: Health food stores and other non-bookstore markets

VI. Mass Market Outlets

Books may also be sold to other mass market outlets, such as wholesale buying clubs (such as Price Club), discount stores, grocery stores, etc., throughout the country. It all depends on whether your book, is appropriate for this market.

Other Mass Market Distributors

Supermarket Book Distributors
12 S. Middlesex Avenue
Cranbury NJ 08512-9556
(609) 655-8335

Computer Book Service
4201 Raymond Drive
Hillside, IL 60162-1786
(708) 547-4400

Handleman National Book
   Distributors
500 Kirts Blvd.
Troy, MI 48084
(313) 362-4400

VII. Other Markets

Besides bookstores and other mass market outlets, your book may be sold via mail order, direct marketing (classified and display ads in magazines), direct mail, catalogs, gift shops, and premium and incentive sales. (Mail order, direct marketing, magazine classified and display advertising, and direct mail are discussed in Chapter 13, *Savvy Marketing: How to Sell Your Products or Services,* page 113, and in Chapter 16, *How to Start & Operate a Mail Order Business,* page 147.)

Catalog Sales

You may also find well-circulated catalogs that may sell your book. Although finding the right catalogs is not easy, you may try this market. You should approach catalogs that only carry books.

Resources:

The Catalog of Catalogs III
Woodbine House
5615 Fishers Lane
Rockville, MD 20852
(800) 843-7323

Directory of Mail Order Catalogs
Grey House Publishing
Pocket Knife Square
Lakeville, CT 06039
(203) 435-0880
The Wholesale-by-Mail Catalog
HarperCollins Publishers
10 E. 53rd St.
New York, NY 10022

Gift Shops

If your book can be a good gift, then gift shops may be another market for you. Through mailing lists, you can find gift shops, mostly in hospitals.

Premium and Incentive Books Sales

A premium or incentive product, is used to obtain and/or increase sales or promote goodwill. In short, a book can be a premium or incentive product. It can be used in different ways, some of which follow:

• *Customized Premiums.* This may be considered as a book rights sale. A company or an institution may buy rights for the reprint of your book to enhance its image or to promote its products. It may change the cover to include its company name, its logo, and its address, most probably on the back cover. The payment to you maybe involve an "outright sale" for the use of your book, or an advance payment on royalty. (Of course, your contract may involve only the distribution of the book to a specific market.)

Free Gift. A bank or another company may give your book as a free gift to its new customers or clients.

Pre-packaged Premiums. Your book may be also pre-packaged with a certain product. Sometimes this may be arranged with the product's manufacturer or with the retailer. Usually, the book is "shrink-wrapped" with the merchandise.

Charitable Premiums. Your book may also be an ideal fund-raiser by a charitable organization to its members or to the general public.

Book Clubs

If your book is a book club's main or alternate selection, it will gain recognition and possible big sales. A book club usually may reprint your book and you'll be given a royalty or it will buy books from you at a low cost to sell to its members.

As an example, my book *How to Teach Your Child* has been made a selection by the Homeschooling Book Club.

Here are two book clubs:

Book-of-the-Month Club
Time-Life Building
1271 Avenue of the Americas
New York, NY 10020-1368
(212) 522-4200

Quality Paperback Book Club
1271 Avenue of the Americas
New York, NY 10020-1368
(212) 522-4200

For a complete listing of book clubs, consult the *Literary Marketplace* in your local library.

VIII. Business Operations

You must be well-disciplined to run your daily business operations. You must learn how to say "no" to friends or relatives when you're researching or writing.

Time Management

There are only 24 hours a day. And you must have each day well spent.

As a one-person company, I operate out of my home. I have two computers and printers, a voice mail, a fax machine, a laser printer, and four cabinets. I do not write to individual bookstores; however, I do write and send book samples to book buyers in central offices of big and small chains and to clubs or organizations to help my master distributor market my books. For single, unsolicited direct orders, I require prepayment. In this way, I save paper work.

Fulfillment Software

Use a fulfillment software program to automate your operations. To save paperwork, choose a software program that once you make an invoice, it will automatically adjust inventory, customer history, total sales, etc.

Two of these programs for small and medium-sized publishers are as follows:

PIIGS
(Publishers' Invoice and
    Information Generating System)
Upper Access, Inc.
P.O. Box 457
Hinesburg, VT 05461
(800) 356-9315

Publishers Business System
RH Communications
P.O. Box 301177
Escondido, CA 92030
(612) 480-5641

Both of these programs can do order entry, royalties, inventory control, consignment, backorders, mailing lists, and other tasks.

Currently, I'm using PIIGS, which I find to be user-friendly. It's menu-driven and simple to manage. Upper Access, the publisher of PIIGS, also sell books by self-publishers through its catalog. The company provides a toll-free 800 number (for credit card orders only) that you can use if you wish to promote your book via TV or radio interviews and direct mail. In short, you can place its 800 number on your flyer, invoice, and other promotional materials. But remember, the order goes to Upper Access, not to you. So before you advertise its 800 number, be sure that you have a stock of your book in its hand.

Ask for a demo from either or both of the above companies, after receiving information from them, and see which program you are comfortable with.

Networking

You can't do it alone. You must join publishing associations that publish newsletters about publishing and hold annual seminars if you are serious in becoming a successful self-publisher. But in attending some conferences and seminars you will hear speakers tell about their experiences and techniques about self-publishing.

Two of the associations that are worth joining are:

Publishers Marketing Association
2401 Pacific Coast Hwy., Ste. 102
Hermosa Beach, CA 90254
(310) 372-2732

Cosmep
(The International Association of
   Independent Publishers)
P.O. Box 402703
San Francisco, CA 94142-0703
(415) 922-9490

Both of these associations publish newsletters and offer yearly seminars.

Also, you may join a publishers' association in your state.

In attending meetings and seminars, you may network with other publishers. Learn what they do and how they do it. But it's a two-way street; you must also share your experience and knowledge with them. That's the way how networking works.

Publishers Marketing Association and Cosmep both provide cooperative advertising in national magazines, such as *Publishers Weekly* and *Library Journal.* These two associations get big discounts (from 58 percent to 60 percent discounts) from the above magazines. They occupy several pages of ads to feature their members' books. PMA also offers cooperative mailings to libraries, bookstores, and book reviewers.

Resources

As a small publisher, you may buy several books authored by book publishing experts. Two companies that are good sources of publishing and marketing books are as follows:

Ad-Lib Publications
51 1/2 West Adams St.
Fairfield, IA 52556
(515) 472-6130

Para Publishing
P.O. Box 4232
Santa Barbara, CA 93140-4232
(805) 968-7277

You may also subscribe to one or more publications that provide current date information on book publishing marketing.

Two of these publications are:

Book Promotion Hotline
Ad-Lib Publications
51 1/2 West Adams St.
Fairfield, IA 52556
(515) 472-6130

Book Marketing Update
Open Horizons Publishing
   Company
P.O. Box 205
Fairfield, IA 52556-205
(515) 472-6130)

*Towers Club USA Info Marketing
   Report*
Towers Club USA, Inc.
P.O. Box 2038
Vancouver, WA 98668
(206) 574-3084

The yearly subscription to *Book Promotion Hotline* is $150.00. This hotline provides a lot of resources, including current listings of TV shows, distributors, wholesalers, bookstores, newspapers, and magazines.

A yearly subscription to *Book Marketing Update* is $60.00. But a subscription to *Book Promotion Hotline* will entitle you to a $30.00 yearly subscription to *Book Marketing Update*.

A yearly subscription to *TOWERS Club Info Marketing Report* is $95.00. Jerry Buchanan, who writes and edits this newsletter, has been publishing it for the past twenty years. (See the TOWERS Club story in chapter 19 entitled *How to Publish a Newsletter*.)

Subscribing to one or two newsletters is like having a staff of researchers doing the job of seeking marketing leads and resources for you.

Awards and Recognitions

One way to enhance your company's image and to give recognition to your company is to enter book publishing competitions. Awards and recognitions can give credibility to your company and your books!

In 1990, I not only won the "1990 Small Press Publisher of the Year" from Quality Books, but I was also the recipient of three awards: best cover design, best interior design, and best graphics illustrations for my book *Improve Your Grades*.

Those awards were followed by a 1991 Benjamin Franklin Award and a 1993 Benjamin Franklin Award from the Publishing Marketing Association, the sponsor of the prestigious Benjamin Franklin Awards competition held every year.

Here are some book awards competitions.

Benjamin Franklin Awards
Publishing Marketing Association
2401 Pacific Coast Hwy., Ste. 102
Hermosa Beach, CA 90254
(310) 372-7232

IACP Cookbook Awards
International Association of
   Culinary Professionals
304 W Liberty #201
Louisville, KY 40202
(502) 581-9786

Midwest Book Awards
Midwest Independent Publishers
   Association
9561 Woodridge Cir.
Eden Prairie, MN 55347
(612) 559-4800

Hawaii Travel Journalism Awards
Hawaii Visitors Bureau
2270 Kalakaua Avenue #801
Honolulu, HI 96815
(808) 923-1811

National Jewish Book Awards
Jewish Book Council
15 E. 26th St.
New York, NY 10010
(212) 532-4949

Children's Choices
Children's Book Council
568 Broadway
New York, NY 10012-3225
(212) 254-2666

Gold Medallion Book Awards
Evangelical Christian Publishers
    Association
950 W. Southern Ave. #106B
Tempe, AZ 85282
(602) 966-3998

Getting Testimonials

Testimonials are favorable comments about your book. On certain occasions, some readers offer comments to publishers about the usefulness of the book or how they liked it.

If you don't receive testimonials, asked for them. For instance, in 1989, I sent a sample copy of my book to Albert Shanker, president of the American Federation of Teachers, and I asked for his comments about the book.

He sent me a letter praising it. His comments follow:

> Bautista's *Improve Your Grades* is both an encyclopedic and a common-sense approach to improving school performance. An eclectic approach akin to Dale Carnegie, Norman Vincent Peale, and Masters and Johnson, *Improve Your Grades* offers a positive attitude, helpful techniques, and enlightening anecdotes to those who feel the need to improve it.

With his permission, I put Shanker's comments on the back cover of *Improve Your Grades,* along with other testimonials.

Don't despair if your book is not reviewed by a major book reviewer. You may send out copies of your book to the professionals known in the particular field of your book.

As an example, when my book *How to Teach Your Child* didn't have any reviews in the major review magazines, I sent free copies to about two hundred school principals and other educators. I asked for their opinions about the book, whether it's a good teaching tool or not, and/or whether it's a good resource for parents.

Many of them sent comments, mostly praising the book. Hence, I received a lot of testimonials, some of which I used in my promotions.

You can do the same, but be sure that you ask for their permission to use their comments.

Remember: Like the cover, testimonials do help sell books!

Revise and Expand It!

A newly revised book needs a new ISBN, a new bar code, a new price, and a new improved cover design.

In short, revised books are sold as new! Buyers of your old book may buy it again! Libraries will love it; your competitors will hate it!

Like in promoting other products, you'll say in your promotion, "New! Improved!" "Completely Revised and Expanded!"

So you see, you may sell your book again and again, month after month, year after year!

Hiring Consultants

Once in a while, if you have some problems and can't solve them, you can hire a publishing consultant. However, you must specify which service you want him or her to do.

On two occasions, I hired two consultants to do a marketing survey for me regarding the sale of my book *Improve Your Grades*. I specifically asked them to make a survey report, consisting of about five pages, discussing resources, steps, and techniques in selling my book to a particular market. If I remember correctly, I paid $250 each for the report. I once paid $25.00 for an initial market survey. In other words, the fee depends on the simplicity and the complexity of a certain project.

Before hiring a consultant, ask some publisher-friends if they know of someone. It's best to test the consultant by assigning a small project; for instance, a marketing survey consisting of several pages of a report.

In case you're considering to hire one now or in the future, here are a few publishing consultants:

Dan Poynter
Para Publishing
P.O. Box 4232
Santa Barbara, CA 93140-4232
(805) 968-7277
Specialty: Nontraditional market

John Kramer
Open Horizons Publishing Co.
P.O. Box 205
Fairfield, IA 52556-0205
(515) 472-6130
Specialty: Search for best market for books

Jerry Buchanan
TOWERS Club USA
P.O. Box 2038
Vancouver, WA 98668-2038
(206) 574-3084
Specialty: Publishing and direct marketing of reports, newsletters, and books

John Huenefeld
The Huenefeld Company
P.O. Box U
Bedford, MA 01730
(617) 861-9650
Specialty: Revamping publishing programs

Nat Bodian
5 Henley Ave.
Cranford, NJ 07016
(201) 272-5810
Specialty: Direct marketing and scholarly/technical publishing

Cliff Martin
Interpub
144 Buck St.
PO Box 555
West Linn, OR 97068
(503) 655-5010
Specialty: International sales, premium sales, and direct marketing

Marylyn and Tom Ross
About Books
P.O. Box 213
Saguache, CO 81149
(303) 589-8223
Specialty: Complete marketing promotions

IX. Bottom Line

A poorly written and poorly produced book won't sell! So produce good books and look for a good master distributor to market your books to wholesalers and bookstores and one or two library distributors. You do the writing and publishing and let your distributors do the marketing.

Mine is a one-person company, yet it operates like a big one because I run it with the cooperation of big distributors and printers. I hire only professional editors and graphic designers.

Don't be disappointed if you call my phone (810) 489-8640 and get voice mail. Maybe at that moment, I'm doing research work, or on my way to the post office or the bank (which I enjoy most), or window-shopping in a mall with my wife.

This chapter is a recap of what I think a self-publisher should do to be successful. My other writing and publishing techniques (and secrets) are contained in my book, *How to Run a One-Person Book Publishing Company.* Based on experience, that book is yet to be written.

How to Publish a Newsletter

19

■ Newsletter publishing is a multi-billion dollar industry. In fact, there are about 5,000 commercial newsletters grossing over more than $5 billion every year, according to *The Newsletter On Newsletters* of Rhinebeck, New York.

Newsletters cover wide-ranging subject areas: investments, business, health, education, psychology, science, etc. Besides these newsletters, there are thousands of newsletters published by schools, professional associations, corporations, etc.

A newsletter is an informal publication that is simple in format. It is defined as a specialized information publication for a defined audience, which is supported by subscription sales.

The old newsletters were known as "corantos"—single-page collections of news items from foreign journals. They were published by the Dutch in the early 17th century. Then English and French translations were published in Amsterdam. In the English American colonies, the *Boston Newsletter* was published in 1704. It was known as the first American newspaper.

In 1904, Roger W. Babson of Massachusetts introduced an investment advisory letter. It was followed in 1918 by the *Whaley-Eaton Report.* The *Kiplinger Washington Letter,* begun in 1923 by Willard M. Kiplinger, is still in existence today.

Newsletters are not supposed to have advertising. However, some newsletters do accept advertising but usually in the form of classified ads. Also, not all newsletters are published on a paid subscription basis.

Off the Press!

Some newsletters are published by entrepreneurs to promote their products or services. They are normally sent to readers free of charge or they are offered at a nominal charge to cover mailing costs.

A newsletter is different from a newspaper. While a newsletter can be written and published by a single person, a newspaper is staffed by reporters, editors, and production people. In short, a newsletter is what it says—a letter or a small publication that provides news (tips, advice, etc.). A newspaper, published daily or weekly, provides more news, views, features, and other information of interest to a larger segment of the population.

The beauty of this is that a newsletter can be published by a single person. He or she is its expert, compiler, writer, editor, financier, and marketer.

There is a big difference between writing a book and writing a newsletter.

A book is longer to write. It may take you three months, six months, a year, or several years to write, depending on its subject matter and content. It may be 50 pages or 300 pages in length. But once it is published, it may take two or three years before you revise it. (If it is a directory, however, it must be revised every one or two years.) With a few revisions and additions, you can make the book new again.

Meanwhile, a newsletter must have new material every issue. It may be published every week, every two weeks, once a month, or once every two or three months. It's up to you.

But you must issue it regularly. So it's a never-ending process: researching, interviewing, writing, and publishing.

However, as mentioned in this chapter, materials contained in a newsletter can be compiled and transformed into books, as has been done by some newsletter publishers who became authors of books.

I. Case Histories

Many people—stock market gurus, investment counselors, and other experts—are making big money in publishing newsletters. There are also ordinary people with their own interests and abilities who have thought of special ideas and researched much on a certain subject to become experts themselves. As experts, they have published newsletters and succeeded in it.

The Tightwad

Amy Dacyczyn, a self-compulsive tightwad, had an idea to help other tightwads make life more enjoyable and profitable. A graphic artist by profession, she thought of publishing a newsletter for tightwads. But the question was, "Would tightwads fork over money for a newsletter?"

"Let's see!" she might have said. So in June 1990, she published the premier issue of *The Tightwad Gazette* (with the subheading "Promoting Thrift As a Viable Alternative Lifestyle").

Two years later, Amy who writes, edits, and illustrates the newsletter herself, had over 100,000 subscribers.

Not only that. She has written a book entitled *The Tightwad Gazette,* published by Random House, that gave her a "substantial six-figure book advance." The book, by the way, is a compilation of articles and other material covered in the first two years of her newsletter.

Amy is now making big money—although she still is a tightwad!

The Book Marketer

John Kramer is successfully publishing a newsletter entitled *Book Marketing Update*. Known as an independent publishing expert on marketing, Kramer publishes a lot of resources in his newsletter, besides giving some other important tips and information.

Among resources usually found in his newsletter are chain stores, distributors, booksellers, newspapers and magazines, consultants, etc.

Since the newsletter is about updates it includes new magazines, new distributors, new editors, and other new changes among publications.

Serving small- and medium-sized publishers, Kramer, with Marie Kiefer, has compiled and published a book entitled *Book Publishing Resource Guide,* which may be considered the best resource on small press book marketing.

Kramer, a frequent speaker in independent publishing seminars, also serves as a consultant to self-publishers and other small publishers. Naturally, whatever he says in seminars may appear in his newsletter and other books, or vice versa.

Newsletter for Information Marketers

A specialty educational salesman tired after 24 years of making house calls to sell business, college, and home study courses. In 1974, he decided to write a book on selling intangibles and to start a follow-up newsletter, which he named *TOWERS Club, USA Newsletter.* (The book was titled *Writer's Utopia Formula Report,* which taught how to sell one's unique knowledge, instead of giving it away as most people do.)

Today, 20 years later, the only thing that has changed is the name of the newsletter. It is now the *TOWERS Club Info Marketing Report.* The salesman is Jerry Buchanan of Vancouver, Washington.

Recalling his bygone days, Buchanan says, "I started with an old IBM Executive typewriter and I had no idea of what it took to produce a monthly newsletter. But in my second year, I took in $249,000 in my mail box, and the newsletter has helped me find my unique niche in life. I live a relatively stress-free lifestyle and my bank account continues to grow and support me while I help my readers become better salespersons and self-publishers."

Buchanan's Description of a Newsletter Publisher's Duties. Buchanan discusses the duties of a newsletter publisher as follows:

A newsletter publisher serves a very useful purpose to special interest groups. He doesn't sell advertising space, so must charge a little more for his publication. But what he mails out in each issue is a digest of valuable information aimed directly at his own unique market of readership.

The benefit to the subscriber is time saved and important news delivered. The benefit to the newsletters is in being able to stay home and do the work without the hassle of freeways, regimented work hours, and possible employment layoffs from time to time.

Who Should Consider Starting a Newsletter? Buchanan advises that newsletter publishing is best suited to those people who fall into the following categories:

1. Don't mind reading reams of research materials.

2. Can write succinctly without omitting important details.

3. Have good keyboarding skills.

4. Have some experience in the field they choose to feature.

5. Stay current on the marketing skills necessary to keep the newsletter perking, year after year.

6. Are willing and able to meet deadlines no matter what personal problem may pop up in their lives.

7. Are adequately equipped with enough time, money, and intelligent persistence to stay with the job until it begins to pay off (one to two years, average).

Experiences. Talking about his experiences as a newsletter writer-publisher, Buchanan says, "I've been publishing my paid-subscription newsletters for a full twenty years now (December 1993) and plan to continue until I die. It has been a very rewarding enterprise, allowing me to avoid those daily trips by freeway to a downtown office to work for a salary. But newslettering requires a very special mind-set and regimen. The deadlines must be met, month in and month out, no matter how many personal problems may crop up in one's life. Choosing a universal theme and a way to reach potential subscribers for it can tax your brain. And the money does not come pouring in by the wheelbarrows from the first git-go! It takes time to build a loyal readership from wise knowledge of gaining favorable free publicity."

The *TOWERS Club Info Marketing Report* is published monthly (12 issues a year, ten pages, typeset, illustrated) for the world of entrepreneurial self-publishers. Annual subscription is $95.00. Editor/publisher is Jerry Buchanan. (TOWERS Club USA, Inc., P.O. Box 2038, Vancouver, WA 98668. Phone: (206) 574-3084. Fax: (206) 576-8969.)

II. Subject Matter

As a beginner, you may select a simple subject matter for your first newsletter geared toward a particular targeted market.

As in publishing books, you may start small but think big. As a start, my first publication was a 32-page booklet. Later, it expanded to 90 pages. Then eventually, I revised and expanded it into book form, containing 272 pages.

Knowing Your Competition

First of all, learn your competition. See what types of newsletters are already being published. See where you can fit in.

A good source of information on newsletters is the *Gale Directory of Newsletter*s. Also check on the *Encyclopedia of Associations* and the *Gale Directory of Publications*. They may be available in your local library.

See what markets they serve. Also, you may select a targeted market and try to serve that market.

Then you may think about what topic you should choose in publishing a newsletter.

Using Your Knowledge

Know yourself. There are many questions to be answered. What is your educational background? What are your interests and hobbies? What are your special skills? What special training have you undergone in school or at work? What are you good at?

Becoming an Expert

If you're not yet an expert in something, become one. Select a topic that you are interested in and do something about it. Make a thorough research about the subject, talk with people involved in it and learn everything about it. You can become an expert in something if you do all those things and hobnob with the experts.

As in writing newsletters, know what people need. Do they need to straighten up their financial affairs? Do they want to know how to raise their children the right way?

If you're already an expert, then write the newsletter. Whether you're an amateur or professional writer, it's best to have an editor. Or if you think you can't write it, hire a writer and provide him or her with the necessary materials.

In writing a newsletter, make it interesting, authoritative, and informative. Without inviting the readers' interest, you'll not gain enough readership.

Getting Help from Other People

For instance, if you want to publish a newsletter on how to raise children the right way (and you're good at it), you must interview some experts on the subject (and mention their views in your newsletter), do research, and communicate with parents who have problems in raising children. There are also those who have their own system in guiding their children to adult life. Many of these people will share their ideas with you and your readers.

In short, if you start a newsletter on raising children, let it be the mouthpiece of parents revealing their problems and how they are solving them. Encourage readers to ask questions. Maybe there are readers who can answers those questions. Parents, with your newsletter, can network with each other even if they live in California, Minnesota, or Virginia.

III. Design

As in books, you choose a design and format that suit your needs.

Size

Your newsletter may consist of single 8 1/2 x 11-inch sheets (stapled) or 11 x 17-inch sheets (folded in half, giving a size of 8 1/2 x 11 inches).

Format

The three basic formats are *single-column, two-column,* and *three-column* pages.

If you are using a typewriter or a simple word processor in writing your newsletter, a single-column format is ideal.

If you're using graphs, charts, and photographs, the two-column format may be the right choice.

But when you have long articles in a variety of subjects, the three-column format is best.

Masthead

The masthead is the part of the newsletter at the top of the first page. It gives the name and address of the editor or the publishing company, the year and the issue number, and the ISSN. The ISSN (International Standard Serial Number) is given by the Library of Congress.

You may send your request for information about the ISSN to the Library of Congress, 101 Independence Avenue, SE, Washington, DC 20540. The ISSN, like the ISB (International Standard Book Number) is needed for easy classification by researchers and librarians. Some publishers don't bother to do it. But if you plan to sell to libraries and researchers, you must obtain the ISSN.

Logo

As what many companies do for their businesses, you need a logo for your newsletter, which may be done by a graphic designer. A logo is a graphic symbol that represents an individual, a company, or a product. Select a logo that's easy to remember. If people remember it, they will remember your newsletter.

Typefaces and Alignment

As in publishing books, you may choose from a variety of typefaces to use in publishing a newsletter.

(See Chapter 18, *How to Run a One-Person Book Publishing Company*, page 175.)

IV. Production

Whether you use a typewriter or a computer in writing your newsletter, you must prepare it camera ready for the printer.

If you have a computer, then it is easier because there are several good word-processing software packages available, such as *Microsoft Word* or *WordPerfect*.

Or you may buy a desktop publishing program such as *Aldus Page-Maker, FrameMaker,* etc.

Choosing a Printer

Select a good printer for your newsletter.

Visit several printers in your area and ask for price quotations and samples of printing from them. While thinking about prices, it's best to evaluate the quality of their work.

While you may have your newsletter printed out of state, it's better if you can find a quality printer in your area. The reason is simple: You may visit it anytime, see the company's facility, and have a good relationship with its personnel.

Price Based on Specifications

You may use white or colored paper for your newsletter. A colored paper is more expensive than a white one. Remember that prices are quoted based on several specifications: for example, the type of paper to be used (depending on thickness, weight, smoothness, or roughness), the number of ink colors (whether in one color only or in two or more colors), and the print run. In printing, the greater the quantity, the lesser the price per copy.

Print Run

While you still have no subscribers yet, you may limit your print run to 1,000 copies to test the water. While you'll save money (per copy) on a larger print run, it's a waste of time, money, and effort to do so if your newsletter will gather dust in your office or basement.

V. Marketing

Publishing a newsletter is not enough. You have to do your marketing. You don't have to sell your newsletter door to door or in bookstores. Look for your subscribers.

You may sell your newsletter through subscriptions. That is, you may receive a payment for six months, one year, or two years. The beauty of it is that you can get the whole amount even if you only send one issue and then mail the succeeding issues later.

The newsletter subscription should be reasonably priced. For instance, a few pages of newsletter published every month may cost the subscriber from $6.00 to $200.00 a year, depending on the uniqueness or importance of the newsletter. The most expensive newsletters are those concerning investing, business, and financial management.

Also, know what other publishers of similar newsletters are charging to gauge how much you may price your own newsletter. If yours is the only one of its kind in the world and it can help thousands of people, then you may set a higher subscription rate.

Direct Mail

One of the best tools for marketing a newsletter is via direct mail. You choose a targeted market; for instance, working mothers. You may rent a list of subscribers to *Working Mother* magazine.

Your job is to look for working mothers who are seeking more ways to balance their lives as a mother and an employee (or worker). Let your newsletter be a networking medium for mothers throughout the country. In short, you may also get materials from your readers; for example, tips on saving time in household chores and in shopping.

Via Classified Ads

An inexpensive way of contacting potential subscribers is to place classified ads in magazines. In the classified ad, you may offer a free sample copy of the newsletter to the first 100 or 200 inquirers. Or, you may offer a sample copy at $3.00 or whatever price.

Other Promotions

For complete information on promotions and marketing, see Chapter 13, *Savvy Marketing: How to Sell Your Products or Services,* page 113 and Chapter 16, *How to Start & Operate a Mail Order Business,* page 147.

You may also participate in cooperative mailings by companies selling books with topics similar to yours. Also, your flyer about your newsletter may be included as a package insert in shipments done by other publishers and other mail order dealers.

VI. Bottom Line

Newsletter publishing is a very profitable business if you select a newsletter with the right topic at the right time. Become an expert in a certain subject matter by researching it, interviewing the experts, and involving yourself in it as a career.

While there are successful newsletters launched by one-person operations, there are also many newsletters that folded up after one, two, or several issues. You must prepare a definite business plan on how you'll write it, finance it, and market it.

If you think that this is the right business for you, start small and grow big!

To get help and to learn what's going on in the industry, you may join the Newsletter Publishing Association, 1401 Wilson Blvd., Ste. 207, Arlington, VA 22209, (703) 527-2333.

Diversification: Obtaining an All-Season Business

20

■ Diversification is a process by which you may establish an all-season business, month after month, and year after year.

With diversification, your one-person business may survive and prosper, even during rough economic times.

However, you need to diversify your business operations, not at your company's infancy but at its time of growing or during declining sales.

There are three types of diversification: *product,* or *service diversification,* and *market diversification.*

I. Product Diversification

When you are operating a product-oriented business, there may come a time when you must diversify by adding new products or by offering other services to your clients.

What Causes Diversification

Reasons for diversifying may be based on the following facts:

■ The business can't grow with its limited line of products; therefore, it must add new ones.

■ Its current products are seasonal; for instance, their peak sales are during the opening of school classes or the Christmas season.

■ Sales of current products are declining, which may be attributed to stiff competition, saturation of market, etc.

■ The entrepreneur wants to set a bigger targeted sales goal (for example, $100,000, $500,000 or $1,000,000 a year).

When to Diversify

I started diversifying my line of books after I had published two books: *The Book of U.S. Postal Exams* and *The Book of $16,000-$60,000 Post Office Jobs.*

After writing and publishing these books, I could not think of any other postal book. Hence, I decided to diversify and released educational books. Later, I shifted my attention to business books.

Since I cater to the mass market, I know my books could penetrate each market because I rely on my network of distributors and dealers in marketing my books.

In other words, different lines of products can be successfully marketed if you form alliances with a master or national distributor (if there is one in your industry) or with different independent distributors specializing in different items.

Diversifying Your Line

When adding new products, you may not only offer high-priced luxury goods, but you may also introduce some less-expensive products. That's because luxury goods may not be marketed successfully during hard economic times and they may be available only to those who have the money to buy them. Hence, the solution is offering some less costly products.

The fact is, whether in good or bad times, it's a good idea to offer both high-priced and low-priced products. The reason is that some people can only afford to buy inexpensive goods.

Adding a New Business

Another way of diversifying is to establish another type of business in your one-person company.

Another Source of Income. If you are engaged in a mail order business, why not try to import some of the products you're selling or import new products you may introduce to your market? Hence, you become an importer. Again, distributors are your allies in marketing them through department stores, grocery stores, etc.

Author/Publisher/Literary Agent. An example of an entrepreneur who has diversified his operations is a friend of mine. Let's just call him Johnny.

Johnny is an author and publisher of a successful series of travel books and a successful series of self-published humor books. A lawyer by profession, he is also a literary agent presenting authors' manuscripts to major publishers in New York for possible publication.

As a one-person business owner, Johnny also speaks at publishing conferences and seminars.

Buying a New Business

You may also buy a new business to diversify your one-person operations.

Granting that you are a publisher of career books, you may buy a small company that specializes in a different line of books, such as travel books for instance.

In that way, you'll avoid the pre-production processes of publishing: researching, writing, editing, typesetting, and layouting.

Seasonal Products

There are also different kinds of products you may sell during certain seasons. During the Christmas season, for instance, gift items are saleable products. In July and August, educational books, supplies, and materials are the products of the season—the opening of the school year.

The Dangers of Diversification

Diversification at the wrong time, however, may bring your business to disaster. It's because diversification needs additional outlay of capital for production or inventory and costs of promotion and marketing.

So before you start to diversify, you should determine if the business is already on its right footing, and decide 1) if it's the time to expand your business and 2) if you have the money to finance it. Determine if your profits can finance your expansion (by adding new products) or if you can obtain money from elsewhere. Maybe it's time to review your short- and long-term goals for your business.

When adding new products, you must have simplified accounting and inventory systems so that your operations won't be complicated.

A fulfillment software program may provide you this service. As an example, select a computer program that, when you make the invoices, your inventory figures and other sales reports automatically readjust themselves to indicate the current stock, total current gross sales, or value of goods on accounts or consignment.

Ask business persons in your industry what software programs they are using. If it's only a buy-and-sell business, then perhaps a program in an office supply store or a computer store may be the right one for you. Or if your business is different, you may

wish to have your software program customized. But there may be an available program that is right for your type of business already developed.

II. Service Diversification

If your business is service-oriented, you may also add new services to diversify.

Offering New Services

Offering new services doesn't mean you have to be a jack-of-all-trades. It simply means that you offer similar or related services to individuals or companies.

If you're giving a single service to a company, why not think of other services that you can offer to it?

As a service provider, you may offer services in the homes of your clients. If clients can't come to your office, perhaps you can go to their homes when it is convenient for them. It's your decision as to whether you charge extra for home service.

Adding Products to Services

Besides selling services, you may also sell some products that may be needed by your current customers that are related to your services.

If you are a consultant or an expert in a particular field, you may give seminars or record your speeches on tapes and sell those tapes to people who may not be able to attend your seminars or workshops.

There may also be a time that you write a book on your expertise. You may have to publish it yourself or you can have it published by a book publisher. After your speech during a seminar or a workshop, you may sell this book to attendees.

III. Market Diversification

Normally, the word *diversification* refers to product diversification. However, it can also refer to market diversification.

Market diversification simply means you seek other markets for your product, whether it's a book, a tool, or a gift item.

When you look for other markets, research how crowded the markets are. Decide whether your product can compete with existing products offered to a particular market. See if another supplier is needed to serve that particular market. You must also evaluate how different your product is from other products sold to a particular market.

Other Markets

While my book *How to Teach Your Child: Things to Know from Kindergarten through Grade 6* sells in bookstores and through mail order, I knew there were other markets.

Hence, I joined an association of school suppliers and rented its mailing list. I then contacted teacher and school supply stores to resell the book. (I could penetrate this market because my master distributor's sales representatives don't cover it and this market is excluded from our contract.)

Different Discounts

I offered teacher and school supply stores different discounts: a 50% discount to consignment orders (all returnable when not sold); a 55% discount on net 30 to 60-day terms, and a 60% discount on prepaid orders (with a check or a money order).

So they can obtain my book on whatever terms they want: if they don't want to invest money in it, they can resell the book at a lesser profit; if they want to get a larger profit, they obtain it on 30 to-60-day terms. To have a much larger profit, they must invest money upfront, with no returns.

Other Clubs or Organizations

I also sought out book clubs. One club, The Homeschooling Book Club, made one of my books a selection to offer to its members.

You may offer your products to clubs and organizations that may need them. It's better to contact such clubs or organizations than to spend too much money in trying to obtain retail sales. With a few exceptions, it's best to sell on wholesale, not retail.

Nontraditional Markets

Seek nontraditional markets. Will your products sell in gasoline stations, toy shops, garden shops, office supply stores, etc.?

There are many such shops that may be just the right places for your products.

IV. Bottom Line

Diversification can give you an all-season business. Therefore, you should sell some products or services for all seasons; other products for certain seasons (Christmas season, for instance); other products with high or low prices; and still others for different markets.

However, capitalization is a very important factor in business. Most often, new small businesses, particularly one-person businesses, are undercapitalized. If you don't plan for future diversification, you may have difficulty in expanding your operations.

Diversification takes time. It may take months or even years before it can become fully successful. Also, be prepared to know what steps to take if your diversification fails or causes you trouble. What emergency measures will you take if diversification screws up your business?

As a precautionary measure, add new products or services, one or two at a time. And most important, investigate what the market will be for these products or services. Know if products will be sold to traditional markets or to nontraditional markets, or to both of them.

If properly managed, diversification can give you a continuous flow of big profits to your business! But if it is improperly done, it may drive you to bankruptcy! (It's good if it doesn't drive you nuts!)

How to Do Consulting: Part Time or Full Time 21

■ One of the most ideal one-person businesses is consulting. According to *Venture*, more than half of all consulting firms throughout the country are one-person operations. Why? Because consulting can provide a part-time or full-time consultant with high income, charging clients per hour, per day, or per project.

A consultant's success depends on his or her expertise and on types of fields served.

I. Types of Consultants

There are three types of consultants: the *moonlighting consultants*, the *full-time company consultants*, and the *full-time practicing independent consultants*.

As a person engaging in the consulting business, you'll be either a *moonlighting consultant* or a *practicing independent consultant*.

As a consultant, you'll be either a *generalist* or a *specialist*. On one hand, a generalist has accumulated knowledge of business operations and functions in different industries, which may involve reorganization, streamlining of operations, integration of marketing methods, etc. On the other hand, a specialist provides high-tech knowledge and expertise in certain functions, as in the case of a consultant who specializes in mergers and acquisitions.

Moonlighting Consultants

Moonlighting consultants have a business of their own or have a regular job either in a consulting firm or in another type of company.

Become a Consultant

Moonlighters are usually corporate executives, financial and investment experts, lawyers, accountants, engineers, and others who are employed and are doing consulting work as a sideline to support their financial income and to achieve professional excellence. Some who are consulting as a sideline come from research firms, universities, and public agencies.

It is not uncommon that many of these moonlighters, in some stage of their lives, do their own private practice in consulting.

Full-Time Company Consultants

Full-time company consultants are employed by large, medium, and small firms. The number of consultants in each organization depends on the size and complexity of operations.

Full-Time Practicing Independent Consultants

Full-time independent consultants are people who are not employed by any company.

Full-time practicing independent consultants may be former moonlighters, fired or laid-off executives or employees, or company consultants or executives who decided to strike out on their own. That is, they decided to engage in their own independent consulting business.

II. Consulting Specialties

Many companies, especially the small ones, cannot afford to hire full-time consultants. That's why these firms just call in consultants for certain problems, which may involve reorganization, automation, marketing, or evaluation of a company's performance, plans, or future projects.

For instance, a one-person company needs consultants from time to time. (As an example, I've hired consultants at least four times in my publishing business, which all pertained to marketing.)

Some consulting specialties are as follows: *organization and management, plant operation, finance*, and *marketing*.

Organization and Management

Organization and management involve the structure of a business establishment, defining the functions of officers, management, and employees of a company.

It may also involve office procedures, business plans and surveys, data management, and office management.

Plant Operation

Among those areas covered by plant operation are *plant location and design, plant management*, and *inventory management*.

Location and design involve the selection of a plant site and its design.

Management covers equipment selection and purchasing, plant production, and overall factory management.

Inventory management covers quality control, shipping, and distribution.

Finance

Finance involves, among other things, financial planning, capital investment and expenditures, accounting, collection, and taxes.

Marketing

Marketing covers the defining of markets for products and services. It involves promotion and distribution and the selection of subcontractors, distributors, wholesalers, and dealers.

III. Skills Required

You need certain skills to be a successful consultant. Among them are *technical skills, business skills, communications skills,* and *public relations skills.*

In determining your skills, think of your educational background and training, past employment experiences, and lifestyle. Here are some questions to answer: *What did you do in college? What are you good at? What did you do as an executive or as an employee? What do you most enjoy doing? Do you enjoy traveling?*

Technical Skills

You need technical skills to be a successful consultant and to be of help to small- and medium-sized companies.

A consultant, in his field of expertise, not only has to use tried solutions to problems, but also must be creative. That is, the consultant must be innovative and create new solutions to current problems. Of course, if you are a computer consultant, you must know how computers work, how software programs run, and how different operating systems function.

Business Skills

Overall, as a consultant, you must know how businesses operate, such as the different functions in organization, production (or service), promotion, and marketing. For instance, how can you automate a business operation when you don't know how the company conducts its business or how it sells its products or services?

Having experience in business is a plus. But knowledge in business can be obtained in several ways, such as:

■ Reading books, magazines, newsletters, and other publications related to different industries.

■ Interviewing or talking with executives on how they operate their companies and how employees do their jobs.

■ Talking with financial experts, lawyers, accountants, and other consultants.

Communications Skills

Communications skills, whether in verbal or written form, are important. Being an expert in something doesn't guarantee your success in the consulting business.

You must be a good communicator. A good example of how one may communicate refers to the story of two school teachers.

One is a summa cum laude graduate of a great university. He is a talented teacher. He knows what he's talking about when he gives lectures. But most of his students don't like him because they cannot understand him well as he talks too fast. When he explains a certain matter, he expects his students to fully comprehend what he's saying. "Why can't you understand? It's easy." he often asks. But some of his students may say, "He talks like a parrot" or "He 's like a tape recorder." The reason is that he doesn't know how to teach.

The other teacher, who was an average student in college, explains clearly what he teaches. He thinks of every student as himself (while he was in school). He knows that not every student can immediately grasp what he's trying to say. Hence, he explains every process of how things work or why certain things happen. His students are learners! It's because he knows how to teach.

Therefore, in your consulting, you must learn how to communicate with your clients. It's because, as a consultant, you're a teacher! While mentioning technical terms in writing a report or in talking with your clients, you must learn how to translate these technical terms into layman's words so that they'll understand what you're saying. The reason is simple: you're teaching!

You need to present reports that are concise, direct to the point and understandable. Of course, you try to eliminate redundancies and errors in grammar and usage.

Public Relations Skills

Public relations skills relate to how you interact with your clients, your colleagues, other professionals, and the general public.

Your integrity and credibility will also depend on your public relations skills, your educational credentials, and your professionalism in dealing with clients and colleagues.

If you have a good performance record, you'll be referred to other possible clients.

IV. Marketing

No matter how good you are and even if you are an expert in some areas, you won't be a successful consultant unless you know how to market yourself and your services. (See Chapter 13, *Savvy Marketing: How to Sell Your Products or Services*, page 113.)

In consulting, you're not selling a real product; you're selling your knowledge and expertise to solve some company problems. You'll be paid for your diagnoses of business diseases or problems and the prescription for their treatments or solutions. You'll be selling reports in the forms of verbal communications and/or written reports containing the problems and their diagnoses and solutions or recommendations.

Direct Marketing

Direct marketing involved in consulting may include the so-called "free-offer consultation." This free offer means a client doesn't have to pay during a first consultation in order that you may know what his or her problems are and how you may solve them. You receive inquiries for your services by placing classified ads in your local paper or magazine.

In the first brief consultation, you ask what the problems are and merely indicate some possible solutions. However, don't talk too much. Reveal solutions to simple problems, but hold comments or possible solutions to the complicated problems.

Also, you may place classified ads that offer a free booklet or brochure. If the problem is easy, then you may give the complete solution. But if the problem is complex, you may indicate some possible alternatives of solving it. Then, perhaps if the inquirer is satisfied, he or she may contact you for future consultations.

Networking

As a consultant, you must develop a network of contacts, which may include colleagues, friends, executives, and current and former clients. In other words, you need referrals from your contacts.

To obtain these contacts, you need to join professional civic organizations and attend social functions.

As a one-person business operator, you may contact other solo practitioners who may help you in your work when you are overloaded with projects. That is, you charge your client a fee and pay your co-practitioner from your own fee.

There are times, though, that you may receive some subcontracting work from fellow consultants during weeks or months that you have only a few projects. It's a give-and-take situation. It makes sense to consider other consultants, especially solo practitioners, not as your competitors but as your friends and colleagues during both good and bad times.

(See Chapter 24, *Effective & Smart Networking,* page 245.)

V. Consulting Fees

You may charge your client by the hour, the day, or the project. You may charge $25 to $75 per hour, $200 to $600 per day, or $2,500 to $15,000 per project.

The determination of fees depends on many factors. It may depend on your educational background, your experience, and your reputation as a consultant. It may also depend on the simplicity or complexity of the project.

The best way to determine fees is to know how much other practitioners charge their clients. Another way is to ask for rate information for management consultants at various experience levels from the following association:

ACME-The Association of
      Management Consulting Firms
521 Fifth Ave.
New York, NY 10175
(212) 697-9693

ACME, founded in 1929, is the grandfather of management consulting groups.

For a list of other consulting associations, see *The Encyclopedia of Associations*, published by Gale Publications, in your local library.

Calculating the Daily Rate

There is a way to calculate the daily billing rate if you charge an amount equal to your salary as an expert, such as a computer systems analyst.

Suppose that you're receiving an annual salary of $50,000 as a computer systems analyst. To receive such an income as a starting consultant, you must count the number of working days a year. Although there are 365 days in a year, there are 104 Saturdays and Sundays. So 365 days minus 104 days equals 261 days.

Then:

$50,000 divided by 261 equals $191.57. Hence, $191.57 should be the daily rate.

$191.57 divided by 8 hours equals $24.00. Hence, $24.00 should be the hourly rate.

(To double your income to make it $100,000 a year, just double your hourly billing rate.)

A fee of $24.00 per hour is reasonable because you'll earn at least $191.57 per day to earn $50,000 a year. (But you must also remember that there are overhead expenses to deduct from $50,000 when running your own business. In other words $50,000 is your gross income, not your net income.)

Moreover, while you're guaranteed work of eight hours a day in a regular job, you can't be sure that you'll work eight days in consulting. You still must run your business and do promotion to get clients.

Therefore, based on the fact that you're not sure whether to do consulting eight hours a day, you must increase your daily rate if it won't be too high, based on your experience level.

Moonlighting

As a start, the best way to do consulting is to do it first as a sideline. In the publishing business, $75 per hour is the standard fee. Usually, publishing consultants do it by telephone consultation and/or by submitting a report or a survey that details problems and solutions or recommendations. If a neophyte publisher talks with a consultant in half an hour, he

or she will be billed $35.00 or half of whatever amount is agreed upon. But almost all publishing experts moonlight only as a consultant. They depend on their main line of business as publishers.

VI. Case Studies

Many consultants start on a part-time basis. But some experts start consulting as a full-time business.

Due to the proliferation of computers, computer experts and consultants are having good times in their businesses.

Computer Consultant

One consultant, Garry R., whose company is based in Ontario, Canada, specializes in handling systems integration of multimedia and graphics applications. Once in a while, he does project management for clients. "I enable them to produce their own presentations," he was quoted as saying in *Business Start-Ups* magazine (November 1993). In doing so, that business brought in more than $100,000 in sales last year!

The key to success, according to Garry, is having enough operating capital and contacts in your area of expertise.

"You have to be prepared to carry yourself for three to six months," he says, "and you should have an idea of what your first job will be—or you should already have it."

Garry uses a 386DX/33MHz computer, a fax modem, several phones and "tons of software" in conducting his business.

The Moonlighter

Thomas Ewald has a regular job and moonlights as a computer consultant. Specializing in MS-DOS systems, he also does ZIP + 4 encoding of databases.

Thomas advertises himself as "an independent consultant, giving you the individual attention a large agency just can't offer."

There are days when he earns more than his pay per day as an employee. He says that he looks forward to the day when he'll earn more in consulting than being an employee in a regular job. That will be the time that he can quit his job.

After work (4:30 pm) he changes from his working clothes to a suit and visits his clients—as a consultant.

Ewald says that "between needing more money, disliking my regular job, and getting near 40, I decided that I had better get something going!"

Ewald, holder of degrees in bachelor of arts and master of arts in linguistics from Oakland University in Michigan, says his technical skills are nearly all self-taught.

He studied computer programming at the International Data Processing Institute. Being very logical, good with books, and able to type well, when computers became available, he took to them naturally.

With his degrees, he was able to teach college-level courses, including computer programming, one semester at the Detroit College of Business.

To know how businesses operate, Ewald has done a lot of reading and listening to cassette tapes.

Ewald's story, as told by himself follows:

My first consulting job was a *pro bono*, that is, without pay. The need I generally fill is to correct others' mistakes. A computer system has three components, any one of which can be the problem: hardware, software, and user. In one case, another consultant had changed memory chips on his client's computer, but had neglected to format the system correctly. That was a hardware problem. I straightened it out. In another case, the treasurer of a local city had set up a system for the department of public works (DPW). But it was not set up correctly, and he kept putting off the DPW manager. I don't know if he was busy, lazy, or just didn't want to face the fact that he was in over his head. That was a software problem. Another time, I trained a school principal in using the system she had been issued. That was a user problem, as her prior computer training had been inadequate.

Ewald, who serves small businesses and individuals, to get business contacts, joined the Greater Detroit Chamber of Commerce. He also does some networking with other consultants, mostly by phone and fax. He also gets information from others via service lines such as CompuServe, GEnie, and Internet.

Here are some tips from Ewald for those wanting to be moonlighting consultants:

■ Time is the biggest problem for a part-time consultant. That is, decide when you will do marketing and *do it*.

■ You take some jobs more for the experience than for the money. Will the job increase your knowledge, experience, expertise, reputation?

■ A separate phone line is not a luxury, but a necessity if you are operating from home. If a potential client calls, you don't want your kids answering. That may be cute, but it's very unprofessional.

(Ewald's company name is Ewald Computer Consulting, P.O. Box 706, Hazel Park, Michigan 48030-0706, telephone/fax 810/547-7567.)

MBA Graduate

I have a relative, Casiano E., whose business is consulting on a full-time basis.

An MBA graduate, Casiano was working as an accountant/finance officer of an insurance company in the suburbs of Detroit. He was forced to be a consultant when the insurance company closed shop.

Rather than seek employment, he decided to do consulting as a business. He now enjoys his business because of its financial rewards. The only disadvantage is that he travels a lot, mostly seeing his clients in Chicago, where he spent most of his employment years before he moved to Detroit. It is there, he says, that he has a lot of contacts.

Now he is a successful consultant!

VI. Contract

A contract between a consultant and a client may be in the form of a simple letter of agreement. Or, it may be a formal contract with clauses and other provisions.

Generally, a simple letter of agreement will do. The agreement outlines the projects, sets the deadlines, and sets the fees.

However, when it involves a large project, a contract should be drawn with the help of a lawyer to avoid any legal problems in the future.

For small jobs, you may ask for a 50% payable upon completion of the job. However, for larger projects, you may start at 1/3 down at the beginning of the project, another 1/3 at the halfway point of job accomplishment, and the remaining 1/3 upon the completion of the job.

VII. Enhancing Image

To enhance your image as a consultant, you may have some speaking engagements. Many consultants speak in seminars, giving the impression that they are experts in certain fields. You may also hold seminars of your own, with you being the main speaker.

Another way is to write a book and self-publish it. (See Chapter 18, *How to Run a One-Person Book Publishing Company*, page 175.) Being an author will enhance your image as a consultant.

Also, be active in community activities and join civic and professional organizations.

VIII. Daily Operations

A consulting business is like any other business. It involves the naming of your business, whether it's a single proprietorship or a corporation.

You must establish your office and buy the necessary equipment, including a computer, to effectively run your operations. You must have a simple accounting system to monitor your income and expenses. See other chapters in this book for information on how to run your one-person business.

First Client

The first client is the hardest to get. Once you have served a client and have done your job well, that will be the starting point of a possible bright future career in consulting.

You first diagnose a client's problem, whether it's an organizational or marketing problem. "As of now," you may say to your client, "I don't know the solution, but I'll find it out if you let me do it."

Job Portfolio

If you have installed a new computer system for the automation of a company, have yourself photographed with the owner in front of the computer system. This photograph, with a caption, should be included in your job portfolio.

Have a three-ring binder with a leather cover with your name embossed in gold on it. In it, include your resume, letters of recommendation, testimonials, press releases, and other promotional materials.

If possible, have some of your press releases published. Whether published or not, include them in your job portfolio.

If you do a good job for a client and he or she doesn't write a letter of recommendation for you, then ask for it. If a client is satisfied with your job, he or she probably won't hesitate to give you such a letter if you request it.

IX. Bottom Line

Consulting can be a lucrative business for a one-person company. To be a successful consultant, however, one must possess technical skills in particular and business skills in general.

If you don't yet have these skills, you must pursue further education and experience.

A continuous flow of business spurred by referrals is the lifeblood of consulting. Hence, establishing a network of contacts, is the key to a successful career in consulting!

Tools and Systematization: Keys to Time Management

22

■ The use of tools and systematization is the one-person business owner's keys to time management to get things done in the shortest time possible.

Ambitious and successful entrepreneurs control time; they don't let time control their lives.

We have only 168 hours a week for sleeping, eating, working, leisure, and entertainment.

Usually, eight is the standard number of hours an employee works. If you are a full-time business person, you can work eight hours or more, or even less, depending on how you conduct your business.

At the early stage of your business, if you have a regular job and work only as a part-time entrepreneur, you have only a few hours to work each day. Therefore, you need to use your time wisely. In other words, plan your work and work your plan.

Among other things, time management may involve the following: *planning, setting priorities, setting deadlines, operating management systems, setting vacation time,* and *balancing your overall time.*

I. Planning

The first thing to do is plan your days, weeks, and months. For instance, what will you do in the morning, the afternoon, or the evening? tomorrow? the whole week? the whole month? next month?

Scheduling

Scheduling is an important tool in working your plans. You may divide your planning into three major periods: short range, mid-range, and long-range based on your overall business plan.

Short-range planning may cover the period from the present to six months, mid-range from six months to two years, and long-range from two to ten years. You must make your schedules based on this planning.

Listing

Listing may involve the use of a *time log*, wherein you list what you'll do every hour of the day. For instance, at what time do you wake up? What time do you start working in your office? What are your appointments during the day? If you're a service-oriented business-person, how many clients are you going to meet each day? Do you have a lunch appointment?

And the list goes on and on: every day, every week, every month.

If you're a part-time entrepreneur holding a regular job, what can you accomplish before you go to work? Do you need to wake up at 5 o'clock to do some writing or to answer some letters?

You may have a small appointment book that you carry at all times.

Traveling

Plan your commuting activities in advance on your daily *Things To Do Today* list. You may schedule a one-time trip to the bank, or to the post office, or to another shipper, such as the United Parcel Service (UPS). If you have several packages for delivery every day, you may arrange with the UPS for pick-ups.

How to Make Your Systematization Work

When you travel, instead of listening to news or music, listen to cassette tapes on self-motivation or how to be successful in business. Listen to tapes whose titles may be *How to Make Your Dreams Come True; If You Want to Succeed, Then Go for It!* or *I'll Succeed before I Die!*

A phone in your car may be a good investment, especially if you are a service-oriented provider. A portable tape recorder may also be of help if you want to record something while you're stalled in traffic or while on an airplane.

II. Setting Priorities

An entrepreneur, especially the one-person business owner, has so many activities to do in any given time period. Some of these activities are more important than others.

When you prioritize, it means you rank the tasks to be done in their order of importance.

The most important things to be accomplished in a given day should be done during your most productive time. That is when your mind is fresh and fully awake.

Your Most Productive Time

Some of us are morning people; some are night people. Morning people are most productive early in the morning while the night people are most productive in the evening or late at night.

I consider early morning as my most productive time. It is during this period that I write my books. Of course, the time is not always the same. I usually wake up around 9 a.m. because I also work late at night. However, I sometimes do my writings when I wake up at 3 a.m., 5 a.m., or 7 a.m. Some of these wake-ups are by accident. I may hear the ringing of an alarm clock of one of my children. Or my wife may wake me up to tell me she had a terrible dream, etc.

When I have written from two to three hours a day, I always feel that I have already accomplished so many things in a given day. (Of course, there are days when I postpone my writing because of unscheduled activities.)

When are you at your best period? Early in the morning? In the afternoon? At midnight? Monitor your periods of productivity. Try to do the most important activities during your most productive periods.

Rescheduling Undone Activities

As much as possible, make your schedule for each day in advance. And don't get frustrated when you don't finish all the work to be done in a particular day. You may reschedule them for the next day. But as much as possible, schedule only activities that you believe may be completed. And remember, you can only do certain things in a given time period.

III. Setting Deadlines

You may set realistic deadlines for activities and projects. Without the deadlines, it will be difficult to accomplish certain things in any given time frame.

When you make a commitment to do something, set aside a reasonable amount of time to accomplish it. As an example, if I plan to have a book released in the fall of any given year, I have to look at the "Publishers Dead-lines" set by my distributor.

The deadline periods may be as follows:

New titles announcement card due, January 15; completed editorial fact sheets due, February 12; graphics (black and white, 1, and color, 2), March 26; and sales conference, May 13.

Hence, my book, which is to be released in August (fall), should be in my distributor's warehouse by July. In other words, the book should have been printed by the early part of July.

What I do is go backward from July to determine my schedule of producing the book. Hence, I have to do the scheduling of researching, writing (how many chapters to be written in a month, for instance), indexing, etc., until I bring the camera-ready copy of my book to my printer for printing.

So, to make your schedule meet a deadline, you must count backward. If you plan to set a deadline for the accomplishment of a project in a year's time in the month of December in a given year, you start from there going backward to November, October, and back to January of that year.

IV. Operating Management Systems

Systematization is the key to doing things quickly and effectively. It's the sure-fire method for a one-person business owner. Hence, you must adopt your own system for managing every phase of your business.

Organization

Organize your office well.

Workstation. Set up your U-shaped or L-shaped workstation against two or three adjoining walls. This workstation should contain your computer, dot-matrix printer, laser printer, fax machine, voice-mail or answering machine, typewriter, and any other office machines. This workstation may be bought from an office supply store such as Office Max or through mail order catalogs. On your desk, everything should be organized: pens, paper clips, rubber bands, scissors, etc., should be in containers. Letter-head stationery and other papers should be properly placed in a com-partmentalized organizer.

Sorting Tables. In addition to this workstation, you may add several tables for sorting papers and for other purposes, which may be formed in a U-shaped opposite the workstation. In other words, you're surrounded by tables where all things should be within your reach. That is, you don't have to look for your things in every corner of your house or office.

Wall Calender. Install a calendar board on the wall near your work-station. This calender must contain the fifty-two weeks of the current year. Divided by weeks, you can write on the white plastic surface with a felt-top pen. Include important deadlines, appointments, and other things you should not forget. Make a color code; for instance, red for deadlines, blue for seminars or conferences, green for travel or vacation, etc. This calendar may be obtained from any mail order catalog or try the office supply store. If you wish, you may buy a monthly calendar for each month's activities.

Also, installing a cork board is a must. It may be purchased from an office supply mail order house. On it, you can stick important documents or notes within your reach.

In such an office, you are like a spaceman operating a space ship by remote control and coordinating your business activities with contractors, distributors, wholesalers, dealers, and other contacts.

Numbered Sorting boxes. Most entrepreneurs use filing cabinets for all their files. Uncovered compartmentalized boxes are important, too. (The boxes should be made of wood in compartments, standing on four feet, like stools. Or you can use the so-called literature organizers in multi-compartments, which are like pigeon-holes. They are sold by office supply catalog houses, such as Quill Corporation.)

While cabinets are good for permanent files, sorting boxes are ideal tools for temporary files. These thirty-one numbered boxes, representing each day of the month (yes, including Saturdays and Sundays) should be set up along the wall anywhere in your office but not far from your sorting tables.

As you receive mail, you can drop the bills, appointments to be made, deadlines to be met, and letters to be answered into the proper boxes. That is, if you want to mail the payment for any bill on the 15th of the current month, you drop it in the number 15 box.

Two Other Special Boxes. Set up two other special boxes. The first of these boxes should be for bills, letters, and other important papers for the next month (following the current month). This should be marked as the *Next Month Box.* At the end of the current month, you have to sort out the papers in the *Next Month Box* to be dropped in the 31-day boxes.

The second special box, to be marked *For Future Months Box*, should be for any future months. Papers in this box should be reviewed and sorted every month to know if they are ready to be dropped in the next-month box and later in the 31-day box.

Naturally, the contents of the 31-day boxes should later be permanently stored in a filing cabinet. (Of course, there are papers to be thrown away, such as invitations, etc.)

The use of open compartmentalized boxes, instead of filing cabinets, for temporary files is a convenient system. You don't have to open and close filing cabinet doors to search for or store files.

(Other sorting boxes for your bookkeeping and accounting are discussed in Chapter 26, *Single-Entry Bookkeeping for Simplified Accounting,* page 261.)

Large Garbage Container. Near one of my tables is a large plastic garbage container. Into this container, where the jumbo plastic bag fits, I throw away all my junks: catalogs, letters of solicitations, etc.

Office Procedures

You must also use some system in other office procedures. Here are some things you can do.

Take Action, Now! Most of the time, take action as soon as you receive letters. To answer a letter, you may just call the person who wrote you for inquiry or whatever reason. That saves time. Also you may write notes in the margin of the letter you receive and mail it back to the sender. Fax it, if the sender has a fax machine. Of course, there are important business letters that you must answer on your letterhead. That may be done in your convenience, on the weekend for instance.

Telephone Calls. You may receive calls something like these: "Hey, the weather's fine! How about going with me to play golf?" If you're busy, you must learn to say, "No! I'm really busy," or "I have a deadline to meet," or "I have an appointment."

Realize that you have the right to say no and don't be defensive about it. Most of the time, especially people who solicit something from you and you say "no", they ask why. For instance, when I say "no," the other person asks, "Why?" "I just don't want it: Period." is my usual answer.

Of course, you may say "no" politely and pleasantly, especially to friends. You may say, "I can help you some other time, but not now."

If you're busy working in your office, screen your calls by hooking up the voice-mail or answering machine. (My voice mail, with four mail boxes, is always hooked up, but I can always answer the phone if I want to or if I already know who the caller is.)

By screening calls, you can simply answer the calls later.

Make your telephone calls short.

Instead of asking, "How's your mother-in-law?" or "How's your bowling?" just say you called to know if the deal is to be closed or if the trip is to be postponed. In other words, just talk business after asking, "How are you?"

The Uninvited Guest. Sometimes people just come to your office or house. He or she may be a neighbor, a friend, or a relative. If that happens, and it's possible, don't offer a seat after opening the door. Just ask, in a polite manner, the nature of his or her visit. And then close your conversation and say you're about to go somewhere or are waiting for a client or a customer.

V. Setting Vacation Time

Schedule a vacation time. A vacation may be a pleasure trip or a combination business and pleasure trip.

When you take a vacation, at least once a year, you may say, "Hawaii, here I come!" or "Las Vegas, here I am again!" (The last time, you might have said, "Las Vegas, I shall never return!")

Vacation time energizes your body and your mind and refuels your ambition! Such a vacation is your own reward to yourself for doing an excellent job in running your business. When you go back to your own work, you're refreshed and more determined to pursue your goals and succeed in your business.

VI. Balancing Your Time

As a one-person business owner, you must have time for everything.

Most single business operators start their own one-person business as a part-time endeavor. So we'll presume that if you're a new business person, you're also are holding a regular job.

If you have a regular job, that takes about 8 hours of your 24-hour day. You add at least one or two hours to that eight hours for traveling time. If you add one hour, you've already spent nine hours of your day.

Work Time

Devoting some hours to your business, before or after work, is a must if you have a regular job.

Once you're a full-time entrepreneur, you may devote at least eight hours to your business, sometimes less, sometimes more. It all depends on the nature of your business.

When I quit my job in 1988 to devote my full time to my business, I would usually go down to our basement at 8 a.m. At exactly 5 p.m., I would come from the basement and tell my wife, "My day is over, I'm off now." It was like having a day on the job.

But all that changed when my business became well established. Now my work schedule is staggered. I may start at 2 a.m., 8 a.m., or at 10 a.m. and may end my day at 5 p.m. or midnight. It all depends on my workload and on my mood to work.

In short, my work hours are flexible. If I feel sleepy during any part of the day, I just sleep. (Why force my eyes to open when they want to be closed?)

Leisure Time

Even if you're busy with your work, allocating a time for leisure is a necessity. Leisure may mean just a trip to the mall with your wife or husband to do window-shopping (or real shopping) and to have a snack at a mall coffee shop. Leisure time may also mean a trip over the weekend.

Leisure time is a time for joy and relaxation and having a good time with your spouse and children.

VII. Bottom Line

Having a list of *Things to Do Today* is a must for every entrepreneur. However, it is not necessary to have an hour-by-hour schedule for all your activities, although it is a great idea. Just remember what you'll do in the morning, at lunch, in the afternoon, or at night. As has been said, set priorities and do the most important things first. (Of course, you'll have to keep your appointments.)

It's not necessary that you work 8 or 16 hours a day. But you must use tools and systems for your operations. If you work smartly, you won't take that long to work in your office every day, especially if your business is an established one. As the saying goes, "Work smart, not hard!"

I don't work eight hours a day in my office. I only work regularly from three to four hours a day. In spite of this, however, my operations cover the United States. It's because I'm using the resources of other companies in running my business.

Smart Ways to Manage Your Company's Cash Flow

23

■ *Cash flow*, which involves the cycle of receipts and expenditures of a company, is the lifeblood of any business. Simply defined, cash flow is the actual flowing of cash into and out of a business.

If more money comes in than goes out, the business will most likely succeed; if more money goes out than comes in, then the business will eventually fail. It's as simple as that!

Cash flow involves the spending of current available cash for costs of goods and materials, labor, and overhead to produce products or services, which are later sold to generate enough cash to continue the cycle of cash flowing into and out of a business. It's like the pumping in and out of blood by the heart to keep the human body alive and moving!

It's a common saying that to have enough cash for a business, one must control costs and increase sales. But remember that without the collection of sales, called receivables, there won't be money for operations of a business.

The circulation of cash flow, which keeps business moving, depends on the supply and demand of three factors: *receivables*, *expenses*, and *inventories*.

To keep your business going, you must have *cash reserves* for *expenses* and *inventories* to come from your *receivables*. These cash reserves are discussed in this chapter.

I. Receivables

Receivables are the amount of money that a company expects to receive for invoices of goods or services sold. Receivables pay for daily operational costs, goods, subcontractors, etc. Without them, a business will not survive.

"Small businesses focus on building sales, which is perfectly appropriate, but it's not enough," James Howard, chairman of the board of

Asset Growth Partners, Inc., a New York City financial-consulting firm for small businesses, was quoted as saying in the August 1992 issue of *Nation's Business*.

"It is entirely possible for a business to make a profit and still go out of business," Howard says in reference to the problem of inadequate controls over receivables and inventory.

He adds, "Just by managing receivables well in a small company, you can generate tremendous amounts of cash. In today's economy, maximizing cash is the name of the game."

Collections

To actually receive your receivables, you must adopt ways to improve your company's collections.

In the *Nation's Business* issue of November 1992, Bruce W. Barren, chairman of the EMCO/Hanover Group, Inc., a merchant banking company in Santa Monica, California,

made the following suggestions to improve a company's collection of receivables:

- Set uniform terms for credit and collection.
- Keep individual files on each customer—including all action and follow-ups—in case of a dispute.
- Start monitoring collection from customers halfway through the term (whether 30-day, 60-day, 90-day, or 120-day credit terms).
- Make room for bad debts because, realistically, not everyone pays 100% of the time.
- Consider hiring a collection service to devote more effort in recovering stray receivables.

Other Measures

Other measures that you can do to improve receivables or to avoid non-collection of many receivables, based on my experience and the experiences of others, are as follows:

- Invoice immediately and send the invoice to the right person.
- Send the statement of accounts every 15 days, instead of only once a month.
- Ask for prepayments of small orders for products or services from new customers or clients.(For example, I require prepayments of orders for one to five copies of my books from wholesalers or dealers.)
- Set a strict policy on credit for new accounts and require a complete application to determine credit worthiness.
- Set a credit limit, depending on the volume of business you receive from your customers.

■ Check references carefully to see the promptness of a customer in making payments.

■ Make frequent checks of the right contact person in a company who is authorized to charge products or services.

■ Follow up your statements and collection letters with telephone calls, especially the large accounts.

■ Hold shipments of products or stop rendering services to companies that give you a hard time in collections until pending payments for previous orders or services are received.

■ Offer a discount for payment within 30 days, or charge interest on payments after 30 days or 60 days (whichever term of payment you agreed upon).

II. Expenses

To have a business that is smoothly operating, you must monitor your expenses and your success or failure in generating more income. You apply the so-called *rule of two-thirds*: to put two-thirds of your energy into reducing costs and one-third into increasing income.

The point is that you know what your expenses are or will be, but you don't know exactly if you'll succeed in increasing your income. So the rule is that you control more the things you know, such as reducing or eliminating some expenses. It's a fact that it's harder to control certain future happenings, such as predicting your income. It's because there are many things that may screw up your plans and projections: The economy may worsen or more competing new products may come into the market.

As a general rule, to preserve a good cash flow, manage your cash effectively. Cash management means that you know how much money you have, how it's being spent, and how it should be spent in the future. It simply means that you are fully aware of how much is coming in and how much is going out.

Regarding reducing costs, there are many ways to reduce costs, whether they are for buying supplies and equipment, for the promotion of your products of services or for other overhead.

Supplies and Equipment

Be aware of the costs of supplies. For instance, mark the cost of each item, such as push pins, paper clips, pens, etc.

Be sure that you have a storage place for your office supplies so that they won't be misplaced or completely lost. Proper safekeeping is the name of the game. Sometimes we misplace things, and we ask, "Where's that rubber cement? I just placed it here." And then we buy extra cans of rubber cement, only to find out later that it had been covered by papers in the waste basket.

Many people have asked me, as soon as they know that I'm a publisher whether I have a printing press to print my books. They say that I'll save money if I print my own books. They don't know that you don't need a printing press to be a publisher.

If I establish a printing press, I must buy costly equipment and hire workers. (If I hire employees, then my company won't be a one-person business anymore.) And what do I do after printing my books on my printing press? I must seek printing jobs to make use of my machinery and workers. And I'll be tied up in supervising people and handling all the problems of an employer. Publishing is my business, not printing.

To have my books printed, all I need to do is to ask for a price quotation from my printer or printers, and approve the price of say $2.00 or $2.40 per book. Then the books will be printed and bound, and most of them shipped directly to my distributors. After that, I'll just have to pay my printer after 30, 60, or 90 days, depending on the credit terms agreed upon.

In other words, evaluate if you really need to buy equipment. For example, do you need a copier for your copying needs? Is it not practical if you just go to your library or a local quick printing shop for your copying needs? Or how about leasing equipment instead of buying if you don't yet have the money to put into it. However, there are certain exceptions. For a one-person business, you need general office equipment, such as a computer, an answering or voice-mail machine, a fax machine, etc.

Promotion

Keep track of your expenses in travel, entertainment, and advertising. Set a budget for promotion that you can afford.

Travel. Here are some questions to be answered: Do you really need to fly to California from your office in Maine to negotiate and sign a contract with a distributor? How about using a telephone and a fax machine or the Federal Express for that purpose? Do you need to attend a seminar to be held aboard a ship in the Bahamas to learn something about importing or publishing? Proceedings in some seminars, such as the ones given by some industries, are tape recorded. Then these tapes are sold to those who were not able to attend the seminar.

Of course, you attend important conferences and seminars to hear some good motivational speakers and to network with other entrepreneurs. However, although expenses for such occasions are tax deductible, it doesn't mean that you must attend every seminar sponsored by your trade association. You must be selective.

In deciding to attend a seminar, you must know beforehand who the speakers are and their fields of expertise and what the subject matters will be. If you think that you'll learn a lot from such a seminar and will meet old friends and establish some new contacts, then, by all means, try to attend it.

Entertainment. It's costly to entertain people. But there are times that you must take a prospective client or customer to lunch and to talk about business. You also need to entertain some executives to get the business of a company. But control your expenses. Don't go to expensive restaurants just to impress your prospective clients or customers. Of course, it depends on whom you're dealing with.

If you're entertaining a supplier from abroad who gives you much business, then, by all means, give him or her the necessary treatment for a major contributor to your business.

Advertising. If you have a new product or service, it's not smart spending if you advertise in several magazines or newspapers at the same time. Run a classified ad or a small display ad and analyze the results. If it pays for itself, then try a much larger one. Then monitor the results. Don't believe ad salespeople who say you need to advertise your product or service several times before it gets results. Repeat ads, without immediate good results, are done only by large and institutional advertisers to expose their products to the general public and to make profits in the long run.

Other Expenses

You must also control your overhead expenses. You can do this by maintaining good records. As a one-person business owner, you must have adequate bookkeeping. If yours is a single-proprietorship, use the single-entry, cash system of accounting instead of the double-entry, accrual system of accounting. (See Chapter 26, *Single-Entry Bookkeeping for Simplified Accounting,* page 261.)

III. Inventories

Excessive inventories are a major drain on your cash flow. Many entrepreneurs produce a great volume of products to save cost per unit. In other words, they manufacture a larger quantity at one time to lower

the cost per unit. Usually, when you produce in larger quantity, you can lower the price of your product per piece. For instance, a book may cost $2.30 per copy with an order of 5,000 copies. With an order of 10,000 copies, the cost may go down to $1.95 per copy. This also applies to prices of other products. It's easy to tie up capital in inventory. But what if the product doesn't sell well? In short, manufacture only the products that your distributors and wholesalers need or what you believe you can sell.

Control Your Expenses

Must Fill the Need. Common sense dictates that you must not manufacture in large quantities or buy in bulk if you don't have enough buyers for the products. You'll have time to go to production again if the market demands it! As an example, if any of my books run out of stock, a mere telephone call to my printer will have my book reprinted in four weeks!

With regard to books to be released for the first time, I usually call my distributors to the trade and libraries to ask how many orders they have received (original books are sold through catalogs and cover color graphics even though they are not yet actually printed). Then I ask how many copies they need. If they need a total of 5,000 copies for the first order, I usually will print only about 7,000 copies, which will give me a reserve of 2,000 copies for my other dealers. I always do this in order not to tie up much capital in inventory. Anyway, it's easy to have a reprint. This can also be done with regard to other products.

But there are times when you must ship larger quantities of your product to your distributors and wholesalers, such as when they expect that there will be a great demand for your products. At this time, you must deliver what they need.

Warehousing. Naturally, if you stock larger quantities of your products, you need a warehouse. It may be your garage, your basement, or a self-storage area near your home or office.

But the best warehouse for your products is your distributor's warehouses. Most of my books are stocked in my master distributors' warehouse. My master distributor orders larger quantities, from 2,500 to 5,000 copies per order, while my small distributors order from 50 to 300 copies. These books are shipped directly from my printer to my distributors' warehouses on a consignment basis. I like shipping my books direct from the printer because of the carrier's policy of giving big discounts to larger shippers (such as my printer). If I ship books to my distributor, I must pay the full rate.

So if it's possible, have your products shipped directly from your manufacturer to be warehoused in your distributor's compounds. It saves time, money, and effort on your part.

You must manage your inventory efficiently. It can be done efficiently if it is tracked with a good computer software program.

My software program, PIIGS, beeps whenever I make out an invoice and the stock is low, as if saying, "You'll be out of stock soon, so go to press now!" It's because my software is set to beep when my inventory goes down to a certain level, 500 copies of each book for instance.

IV. Inventory Cash Reserve

There must always be a reserve cash fund for inventories. This may be deposited in a savings account, separate from your business account. If not, you may have occasional problems in manufacturing products or buying products for resale from your sources.

When There is No Reserve Fund for Inventories

One of the most memorable times of my life as a publisher happened in 1990. I had a printing of 12,000 copies of my book *The Book of U.S. Postal Exams* shipped to my distributing company in California on consignment. The approximate cost of printing the book was over $28,000.

Within one month, my master distributor sold out the books, together with some copies of my other books. Therefore, the company ordered 5,000 more copies. The trouble was that I was out of stock of this book. The books shipped to wholesalers and bookstores were invoiced by my distributor. But the books, of course, were on credit. I didn't know my distributor's credit terms with wholesalers or bookstores.

Still, I had not sent any money to my printer for the cost of 12,000 copies previously printed on credit on 50% 30-day, 50% 60-day payment terms. So I couldn't order a reprinting of the 5,000 copies requested by my distributor. It's because I had not yet received the payment for the 12,000 copies shipped to my distributors' customers. My distributor, based on our agreement, pays me 90 days after I receive my monthly sales report.

Having that kind of problem was too much to shoulder. I didn't know where to borrow the money to pay for a reprint because the money coming in for the next two months would be paid for the previously ordered books.

What I did was to bring to my printer my distributor's bulky computerized sales report detailing where all the 12,000 copies and other copies of my books were shipped or sold. The money that my distributor would send me after 90 days totalled $60,000. (That's sure money because my dis-

tributor is always up-to-date in making payments to me.) I showed the sales report to my printer and I asked for a 90-day credit for the new order. In short, my sales report somewhat became a collateral for a new reprint. In 90 days, I was able to pay for the 12,000 copies and the 5,000 reprint!

This can happen to you, whatever your products. When a product becomes a hot item, and you may not know why, your distributor will order it from you. You can't say, "Sorry, it's out of stock!" or else the company may say, "If that's the case, then we'll see you in court!"

Yes, that may be a violation of your contract because you must supply them with products when they are needed. Remember, distributors spend money in marketing that may include catalog costs, payments to sales representatives and their office staffs, etc.

That incident in my life as an entrepreneur became a lesson to me. From that time on, I always put money in a reserve fund for inventory, unlike when I relied on forthcoming receivables to pay for my printing. You can do the same if you want to always have money for your inventory!

Easy Explanation

It's easy to explain why we sometimes run out of money for inventory. Whenever we receive payments for products sold, we tend to spend all the money to buy additional equipment, supplies, etc. We forget the cost of the products sold.

The solution is that if the payment you receive involves the sale of 2,000 copies of a book or pieces of a product, set aside an amount for the cost of the item ($2.00 each for a book for instance) and place it in a reserve fund for inventory. You do this for every sale.

Therefore, if you go to press or go to any other manufacturing process or purchase of goods for resale, you have the necessary funds to pay for them.

In other words, the money collected is not all profit. Spend only the profit for operations and set aside the capital.

V. Expense Cash Reserve

Another thing that you may do to avoid shortage of cash for other expenses is to put a certain amount of your collections into an emergency cash reserve fund. Deposit it in a separate savings account, possibly in another bank. All money withdrawn should be returned when you make collections. Such a fund is for emergency business expenses that may crop up.

VI. Cash Flow Planning

Businesses may have profits but be out of cash. The reason is too much money in inventory or equipment or on credit.

To avoid disaster, you may process a cash flow projection, a cash flow chart, and a financial statement consisting of a balance sheet and a profit-and-loss statement.

Cash Flow Projection

Managing a company's cash flow projection takes planning and follow-through. Plan and take action. That's the rule of the game.

One such measure is to prepare a monthly cash flow projection. By doing this, you estimate your receivables for the next one or more months and your expected expenses. In other words, your expenses should be based on what you'll collect. And of course, place money in your cash reserve funds for inventory and expenses.

Review your past monthly cash projections and compare the estimate and actual income and expenses received and incurred during the past months. Then you'll have a basis for your future cash flow projections and you'll know where your business is going.

Cash Flow Chart

A cash flow chart may contain the beginning of a month's balance, receipts, total income, and cash disbursements. To know the end of the month's balance, you may total income minus the disbursements.

Disbursements may include supplies, maintenance or repair of equipment, advertising, rent, utilities, telephone, etc.

Financial Statement

A financial statement involves the preparation of a *balance sheet* and a *profit-and-loss statement.* (See examples in Chapter 26, *Single-Entry Bookkeeping for Simplified Accounting,* page 261.)

Balance Sheet. The balance sheet contains the *current assets* (which include accounts receivables, inventories, and expenses) and *liabilities.*

Liabilities include accounts payable, notes payable, and sales tax payable, loans, etc.

Income Statement. The Income statement, sometimes called the profit-and-loss statement features the net sales and total expenses and the profit or the loss. In short, the net sales (gross sales minus discounts) minus the expenses equals the profit or the loss.

VII. Net Working Capital

There are several ways to measure the flow of cash and a company's ability to maintain cash or liquid assets that can be converted into cash, if needed. One way is to compute the company's *net working capital.*

You can determine working capital by deducting current liabilities from current assets. Current assets are those cash on hand, accounts receivable, inventories, and short-term investments, such as bonds, stocks, etc., that can be converted into cash. Remember that current assets are different from fixed assets, such as buildings, equipment, etc. The difference between assets and current liabilities is the net working capital. Of course, the value of the net working capital changes from time to time. It's because some money comes in and some money goes out. It's the smart managing of cash flow that can make your business succeed or fail.

VIII. Bottom Line

In a nutshell, here are the measures that you can do to manage an effective cash flow:

■ Have control of your inventories. Manufacture or buy only a certain volume of your products that you need for your distributors or wholesalers and other dealers.

■ Establish two reserve funds (one for inventories and one for emergency business expenses). Deposit money in the two reserve fund accounts whenever you receive any collections.

■ As much as possible, don't pay your bills in advance. Wait until the due date.

■ Use other people's money. Seek long-term credit from your manufacturers or suppliers. In other words, if possible, sell the products before you pay your manufacturers or suppliers. (In my case, I obtain 30-day, 60-day, and 90-day credit terms from my printers. Sometimes I pay after 30 days, 60 days, or 90 days. There are times, though, that I request 50% after 30 days, and 50% after 60 days. Occasionally, the payments are 1/3 after 30 days, 1/3 after 60 days, and 1/3 after 90 days. It depends on my current circumstances.) So you may seek different credit terms if you already have a good relationship with your manufacturers or suppliers. Anyway, they also get good credit terms from their own suppliers.

Effective & Smart Networking

24

■ Small business owners, especially one-person operators, should practice *networking* to compete with the Goliaths of their industries and succeed in their businesses. Networking, if effectively used, can show you the road to finding subcontractors, distributors, wholesalers, customers, and other business contacts.

Networking simply means meeting people with the same interests as yours in order to profit from the connections. Sales leads and productive ideas may crop up in these connect-ions, particularly if you network with people who are already successful.

Networking, however, will be successful and productive only if people share their own knowledge, expertise, and resources with each other to help one another in marketing their products and services.

Networking is a two-way street. You give and receive. In other words, reciprocity is a fundamental requirement of networking.

Networking may be divided into three kinds: *informal, semiformal,* and *formal.*

I. Informal Networking

Informal networking is everywhere: at cocktail parties, in churches, on golf courses, aboard airplanes, etc.

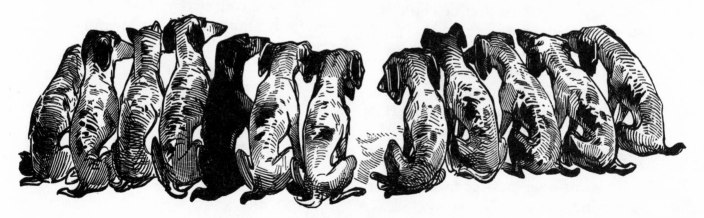

Networking Is a Way of Life

When you call a colleague-friend in New York or in Pennsylvania to ask for resources or information, you're networking.

When you strike up a conversation with someone sitting next to you in an airplane, you're networking. Who knows, he or she may be an entrepreneur doing the same business as you.

"You Call Me" or "I'll Call You"

Informal networking may also occur when someone calls you to talk about business.

But to call an entrepreneur, or be called by one, should be done in such a way that it will be of benefit to both of you.

Picking One's Brain

A man who introduced himself as a new publisher called me a year ago.

The man told me, "I've heard that you're a successful publisher, so I want to meet with you to pick your brain!" He suggested that we meet in a certain place so that he could pick my brain.

Those words irritated me. There was a man who wanted to learn something about publishing in an hour's meeting with me so that he could be successful like me.

His approach should have been something like this: "I'm also a publisher. I think we can share our ideas and resources about publishing. How about having lunch with me?"

A Four- or Five-Member Group

Organizing a four- or five-member group in your locality is a good idea. You might meet once a week or twice a month just to have lunch and talk about how you'll succeed in your own businesses. It's somewhat like a support group—supporting each other in times of need.

Of course, you'll form this group only if you share the same goals and dreams. Don't invite a negative thinker to your group.

Networking via On-Line Services

By subscribing to so-called national commercial on-line services, you may not only send and receive some information but you can also network with other entrepreneurs around the world.

This is done by the use of a computer and a modem, from your home or outside office. You can send or receive information by hooking up your computer with other computers and national networks through your modem by means of telephone lines.

You can do the hookup by using a special software program that is usually provided free by on-line services. Also, on-line services can link you to Internet. Internet is a network linking libraries, research centers, and universities.

If you like electronic mail, you may send any short document to your addressee's mailbox if you know the number.

Three biggies of the major commercial on-line services are as follows:

CompuServe
P.O. Box 20212
Columbus, OH 43220
(800) 484-8199
(DOS, Windows, Macintosh)

America On Line
8619 Westwood Center Dr. Ste 200
Vienna, VA 22182
(800) 827-6364
(703/448-8700
(DOS, Windows, Macintosh)

Prodigy Information Service
445 Hamilton Ave.
White Plains, NY 10601
(800) 776-3449
(919) 993-800
(DOS, Windows, Macintosh)

II. Semiformal Networking

Semiformal networking can be achieved by joining national and local trade associations of your industry. By joining such associations, you may know of the latest equipment or computer software for your particular industry. And you may know how members of the associations are running their businesses. As a self-publisher, I am a member of two national associations.

Usually, organizations for small businesses are geared toward how to compete with large competitors.

Of course, you can also join civic clubs, such as the Lions, the Rotary, and your local chamber of commerce if you think that those will be good networking groups for you. It depends on the nature of your business. Joining these clubs is especially important if you are in a business-consulting or computer-consulting field.

To me, joining such clubs is not important, because I can't get any business for my publishing company. In other words, joining such clubs is

only a waste of time for me. Of course, you may join one or two of those clubs if you can get some business from them or if you want to be of service to your community.

Education and Training

Find out what your industry's trade associations offer in terms of education and training. For instance, does your association conduct seminars on how to be successful in your industry? As an example, for the independent publishing industry, the Publishers Marketing Association holds its Publishing University seminars during the annual convention of the American Booksellers Association.

Don't forget the marketing potential of trade associations. Usually, they hold trade shows to show the industry's products to distributors, wholesalers, and dealers.

Where to Find Associations

You can find trade associations in the *Encyclopedia of Associations,* published by Gale Research, Inc., in Detroit. It lists more than 25,000 national organizations, arranged by subject. You may also ask friends, accountants, and other people if they know of a trade association for your industry.

Networking through national trade associations may be done only once or twice a year during their annual conferences, seminars, or shows. However, some of these associations may also have local chapters.

Local Associations

It's important that you join your local trade association. Some associations hold meetings once or twice a month.

In a local association's meeting, it usually starts with a 30-second introduction by each member, especially if the association is small. Each member tells his or her name and the company's name and business. Usually, the members wear name tags.

"I'm So and So! So you're So and So!" In these meetings, business cards are exchanged. One member may say, "I'm John Brooks, president of One-Person Electrical Service, doing business day and night." Another member, may introduce herself as, "I'm Michelle Thomas of Interior Designers."

It's a good idea to be at the meeting place at least 15 minutes or so early so that you'll have time to interact with other members. Also, it's wise to stay 10 or 15 minutes after the meeting is over. In that way, you'll have time to meet other members of the group you have not yet met.

In attending meetings, you can expect to receive some sales leads or resources. However, you should also provide some referrals or resources to some or many of your association's members.

Brainstorming. Brainstorming is a session during a meeting, a conference, or a seminar during which problems are presented and recommendations are offered. For example, in brainstorming sessions during a seminar, product package designs may be presented to get feedback from the audience. That is, the attendees make comments about the design and how it can be improved.

Joining a Committee? Some people join committees of each organization to really get involved in an association's activities. Some get themselves elected as officers of the association. However, there is no need to do so if you have no time for it.

Not all associations may give you sales leads or resources. That may depend on how such groups are run by its officers.

I've had this experience with a local association of my industry. There were only a few successful people in the group because most were just beginners.

I would always give resources of some "tips" at every meeting. I spent almost a whole day on the meeting because it was held far from where I live.

However, I didn't get anything from the association. Some members expected to receive vital information and sales leads, but they could not give any. Some expected to succeed in their business without doing any studying, researching, or attending seminars. Some just wanted to be spoonfed with information from co-members who had spent years of studying and learning the business.

Thinking that it was just a waste of time to continue my membership, I quit the association. In other words, it was not a two-way networking street as far as I was concerned. The association folded up and its members were forced to join a regional association.

In other words, effective networking dictates that you network only with people who can give, and not only receive ideas and resources.

III. Formal Networking

Many entrepreneurs join referral clubs. These are nonprofit organizations formed by business and community groups.

Networking Provides Sales Leads

Formal networking provides sales leads to its members. Usually, participants in these clubs are required to provide a total of at least 20 leads a year for other entrepreneurs in the association. Besides membership fees, members are also required to pay monthly fees.

New Type of Networking Groups

In the 1990s, a new type of networking groups have sprouted out in different parts of the country. These groups, known as referral clubs, consist of companies with diverse businesses serving the same types of customers or clients.

In other words, a referral club may consist of companies in a particular industry, such as a home improvement group. This group may include a kitchen remodeling company, an interior decorating company, a security systems company, etc.

Members of these groups refer their customers to their co-members or they refer members of their group to their customers or clients.

Birds of Different Feathers Do Flock Together

Companies with diverse businesses serving the same customers form alliances to help each other. If there is no such a group in your area, you may organize one.

Some of these networking groups or clubs are as follows:

Small Business Network
The Business Resource Groups
13713 Lynncroft Dr.
Chantilly, VA 22021
(703) 968-9610
(Northern Virginia only)

Business Network International
268 S. Bucknell Ave.
Claremont, CA 91711
(800) 688-9394
230 chapters nationwide

Creative Referral Networks
8700 Monrovia St.
Lenexa, KS 66215
(913) 492-1316
(Kansas City area only)

Le Tip International
4926 Savannah St., Suite 175
San Diego, CA 92110
(800) 255-3847
395 chapters nationwide

Ali Lassen's Leads Club
Box 279
Carlsbad, CA 92018
(800) 783-3761
300 chapters nationwide

Team Network Corporation
3734 Angelton Court
Burtonsville, MD 20866
(301) 890-8999
(Washington, DC metro area only)

IV. Bottom Line

■ Networking is both beneficial to product and service providers. But it should be a two-way street.

■ If you expect to receive marketing ideas, referrals, or resources, then you must give your own. Be sure that you have some tips and other valuable information before you attend your small group of networkers or your local or national organization's meeting.

■ If you just give but don't receive any information from your organization, then just quit the group.

■ There are some entrepreneurs who form state or local organizations just to use them as their market sources for their products or services.

Beware of these officers who use the organization only for their own benefit. The point is that they want more members to come in. The more members they have, the bigger market for their products and services.

■ The size of an organization does not necessarily count in effective networking. The quality of membership of a group, however small, is the most important factor.

■ All sales leads in networking should be followed up with telephone calls, letters, or fax messages.

■ Since networking is time-consuming, it's wise to be careful in selecting a networking group. Forget about nonproductive networking.

Networking Is a Two-Way Street

Using Other People's Brains　25

■ It is often said that "two heads are better than one." But the truth is, many heads are better than one, particularly when you operate a single-person business. Using other people's brains can make your dreams a reality!

In pursuing a dream to become a successful one-person business operator, you need to receive advice from experts and nonexperts. You cannot do it alone!

And there are two kinds of advice that you may obtain: the free advice and the paid advice.

Advice may come from either a group of people *encouraging* you or another group *discouraging* you. It's pure common sense that you listen to encouraging remarks and close your ears to discouraging statements.

I. Free Advice

Free advice may come from your spouse, friends, colleagues, and/or mentors. Paid advice may come from books, specialized magazines or newsletters, seminar speakers, and/or experts known as consultants. Consultants are supposed to have the credentials and the expertise in their own field of operations.

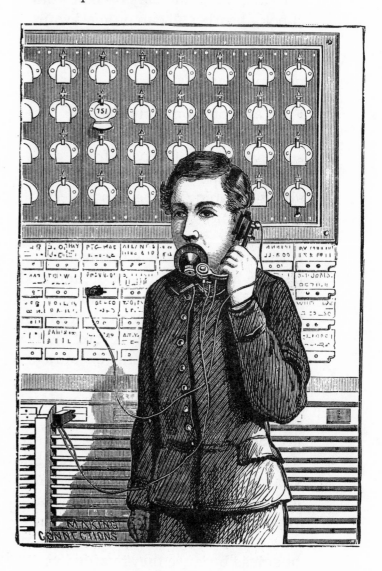

Can You Help Me?

Before you launch your business, you must share your dreams, goals and plans with your spouse. Probably, the best free advice you can get is from your spouse, particularly if he or she is in support of your business. Your spouse may give you encouragement, moral support, and most of the time, financial support. In times of success and joy, your spouse may be the first to congratulate you, and he or she may tell you, "I told you you'd make it!" In times of failures and frustrations, he or she may become your shock absorber. "Lean on me!" your spouse may whisper into your ear "Together, we shall solve your business problems."

Free Advice from Friends

According to many books, we must seek advice and feedback from friends, relatives, and/or coworkers about pursuing a business project. Yes, you may get an abundant supply of free advice from them. But the truth is that they sometimes themselves become hindrances to our dreams and undertakings. Of course, sometimes we may obtain some good advice from a few of them, but that is rare! Many of them can't give you the encouragement and good suggestions you need in operating a business unless, of course, some of them are entrepreneurs themselves. The reasons are simple: Some of them just ignore what you're doing; some of them may be jealous of what you're doing or what you've accomplished. Some of them may discourage you from engaging in business because they're afraid you may fail and lose money in it. And some of them may be just negative thinkers; they are not dreamers, like yourself, and they themselves are afraid to engage in entrepreneurship. They want only the security of a job for their livelihood. (However, in today's economy, as you know, no job is secure!)

As an entrepreneur, I don't rely on advice from relatives or friends (except from two or three friends who are my colleagues) regarding business matters. In fact, I'm not lucky in receiving good advice. Some friends even talk sarcastically when I talk about self-publishing as a one-person business. I don't have any hard feelings toward them. They just don't understand me and they don't understand what I'm doing. So while they're fishing or bowling during weekends, I do some "typing" at home. (That's what they say.) So in my acknowledgment in my book, *The Book of U. S. Postal Exams,* I wrote the following phrase: "I'm also grateful to a few of my friends for their nonencouragement and noncooperation. Without the noninterference of these people, this book would not have been written and published." (There are instances, however, that we meet in parties or gatherings where we can talk about most anything, but seldom about business.)

In the beginning of my career, a few friends ignored what I was doing and didn't give any encouragement or moral support. But when I received several national recognitions and book awards, they began to recognize me as an author-publisher. They began to encourage me in pursuing my other projects.

Such things can happen to you during your career as an entrepreneur.

Free Advice from Mentors

One of the best ways to be successful in your career as an entrepreneur is to look for people who may become your mentors. Seek people you admire and wish to emulate. Maybe you like their style of doing business, their resourcefulness, their own way of dealing with customers or clients, and their network of contacts.

In other words, look for teachers who can show you the way to independence and riches in life— teachers who have the ideas, expertise, and experience in your particular field.

In approaching a mentor candidate, in person, by letter, or a telephone call, say that you admire him or her as a successful person, and ask a few questions about your project or ambition. If he or she answers, then possibly you've found a mentor candidate. If there's no response, there's no door opened.

It's really hard to find an ideal mentor. It's like looking for a mate: A man may say, "I really love you. I want to marry you," but the woman may answer, "I'm sorry, but I don't love you!"

Moreover, many successful entrepreneurs don't let themselves be the mentors of anyone. Some of them, may be just busy; some may be just selfish; some maybe just won't give free advice. There are a lot of reasons.

But, in some instances, there are some successful men and women who want to share their knowledge, aspirations, and dreams to possible protegees. They may want to hand over to someone the knowledge that they have accumulated throughout the years of their lives before they are buried in the ground without their earthly possessions. I, for one, have given free advice to some people who were just starting.

If you're persistent, there's a possibility that you may find a mentor whom you like and who likes you. If that happens, then be a loyal protegee and a good follower.

A Marquette University professor once said that those looking for mentors should "identify someone who would be a clear communicator, would take a personal interest and is both competent and respected in the organization. Come up with an idea or new project and run it by them. If they respond in a helpful way, that's the start of a relationship."

According to surveys made time and time again, successful people have had one or several mentors in their lives—mentors who shared their ideas, insights, aspirations, dreams, and networks or contacts.

Free Advice from Suppliers and Distributors

You may get feedback from your suppliers, distributors, dealers, etc. The advice is free! They can give you fresh ideas and suggestions about product designs and packaging, products to be produced and marketed, advertising tips, resources, etc. They may want to help you because they need good products to sell for you! The more they sell, the more they earn. Of course, the more you earn, too. So it's a win-win situation!

As a book author-publisher, I get feedback from my distributors about proposed titles, book designs, marketing, etc. I ask, "What can you say about the title?" "Does the cover need a picture or an illustration?" "How about the back cover copy? Is it satisfactory to you?"

Once, I had a hard time composing the back cover copy of my book. Since packaging is very important for a product, I sent my rough draft for the back cover copy to my distributor, PGW for feedback. I said that if the copy is not satisfactory or if it lacks punch, then maybe the best PGW copywriter can help me improve it. The copywriter did it! The back cover copy had enough punch, was compact and concise, and told all about the book and its benefits to readers (all the things I wanted to say in a single page, but couldn't think of). Just remember that writing a sales or advertising copy is different from writing a book! An excellent job is done and it's free.

If you produce and sell products, you can do as I did. Ask feedback from your distributors and dealers about packaging designs, raw materials to be used, etc. You may ask "What do you think of the design of the packaging?" "How can we improve it?" "What do you think about the product itself?" "How different is it from products of the same type that you have sold?" Just ask, and they'll tell you their opinions.

Free Advice from Professionals

You may also get free advice from accountants, insurance agents, financial planners, and bankers if you have problems.

Some of them may expect you to return the favor; some do not. For example, you may obtain an insurance policy from an insurance agent or place money in an investment selected by a financial planner. An accountant may give you some tips; however, he or she may expect you to let him or her handle your accounting.

Most accountants may tell you that if you have inventories, you may use only the accrual system of accounting, with the complicated debit and credit terminology. That's because that is what they learned in school. You can use the cash system of accounting for tax purposes even if you have inventories. In fact, the best accounting system in the world, especially for a single-operated business, is the single-entry, cash system of accounting. I've been using this system since I started engaging in business more than ten years ago. (See Chapter 26, *Single-Entry Bookkeeping*, page 261.)

Be careful not to make any commitments to any of them. For example, it is costly to hire an accountant, and you may not be able to afford it, especially if you are new in business.

Free Advice from Competitors

You may not be aware of it, but you can also get unsolicited help from your competitors. Your competitors, especially the large ones, spend thousands and even millions of dollars in launching promotional campaigns. Study their techniques in running their businesses, scrutinize their ads that come out in newspapers and magazines prepared by well-known advertising agencies, and learn how they seek the help of distributors and sales groups to sell their products in the marketplace.

There are instances that you may ask for a copy of their latest catalogues by pretending that you are a dealer or a buyer. In that way, you may know what products they sell and how they sell them. You may ask how much discounts or commissions they give to wholesalers and retailers. You'll be given copies of their promotional materials, including brochures and salesletters. Study these promotional materials and get ideas from them.

Free Advice from Uncle Sam and Private Institutions

There are government and private agencies that can give you advice in starting and running a small business.

Among them are the U.S. Small Business Administration, Small Business Development Centers, Service Corps of Retired Executives, Department of Commerce, and the Department of Agriculture.

> U.S. Small Business Administration
> Office of Innovation, Research, and Technology
> 1441 "L" Street, N.W.
> Washington, DC 20416
> (212) 655-400

> Small Business Development Centers

The Small Business Development Center (SBDC) program is sponsored by the Small Business Administration. It is a cooperative effort by federal, state, and local governments with universities and the private sector. The SBDC provides management techniques and technical assistance to individuals and small businesses interested in entrepreneurship. The centers are located in universities and SBDC directors are from the college of business administration of universities involved in this program.

> SCORE
> (Service Corps of Retired Executives). Sponsored by the Small Business Administration. Find a SCORE branch in your area.

> Department of Commerce
> (202) 377-3181

The department of Commerce gives information and assistance in international trade.

> Department of Agriculture
> (202) 475-3418

The Department of Agriculture offers a number of trade-related information services to potential exporters of agricultural products.

Agency for International Development (AID)
(202) 647-1850
This agency can facilitate U.S. exports to developing nations serviced by AID programs. It gives information on upcoming purchases of AID-financed commodities by foreign purchasers.

II. Paid Advice

In case that you may not find a mentor who is willing to give you free advice, then read business books or subscribe to magazines or newsletters or hire a consultant.

Books, Magazines, and Newsletters

When you buy business books and subscribe to magazines, you're paying for the authors' knowledge, expertise, and experience accumulated for many years. In short, you're picking their brains!

Consultants

If you want fresh ideas and solutions to current problems, you may look for persons whose livelihood is giving advice. These people, known as consultants, charge fees for services rendered to clients.

Consulting fees depend on the simplicity or complexity of a problem or project. (See Chapter 21, *How to Do Consulting,* page 217.)

If possible, find a consultant appropriate for your needs who's willing to guide you for a certain period of time at a reasonable cost.

For instance, in the marketing of information business, including self-publishing, there's a consultant who charges $495.00 as a consulting fee for a whole year's advising on a particular project. I have had the opportunity to contract with him for a one-year consultation. I've also consulted with other publishing consultants.

Hiring a consultant doesn't mean you are an incompetent business person. No entrepreneur knows it all. More particularly so if you're just a neophyte entrepreneur. Even if we are experienced business persons and are already successful in our endeavors, there are consultants who are more successful and experienced than we are. They have the expertise and experience to help us in some aspects of business management, promotion, and marketing. Even giant corporations hire consultants when they launch projects or when they downsize. Entrepreneurship is continuing education. Economy changes, technology improves, people's needs change. In fact, everything changes because we're tired of the status quo. So we invent, reinvent, and invent again! Now, they are reinventing the corporation. Even Vice President Gore is reinventing the government! (And now, I'm trying to reinvent the one-person company.)

■ *How to Find a Consultant.* The leaders of particular industries usually provide consulting to entrepreneurs. If you are a member of a trade association, get in touch with these leaders by asking for some names.

Some of these experts give seminars where they lecture on business start-ups or business management, including promotion and marketing.

Attend some of these seminars if you think you can learn from them. However, before you do that, learn about the credentials of the speakers and how they're doing in their businesses. For instance, are they successful in the field in which they profess to be an expert?

Before I attend any publishing seminar in the field of writing and publishing, I first inquire about the expertise of the speakers, their backgrounds, and how successful they are. Here are my usual questions: "Are they successful in writing and publishing books for the general public?" "How many successful books they have sold? Do they have any bestsellers? How do they sell them? Through bookstores? Through mail order? Through non-traditional outlets?"

It is not unusual that some people giving seminars on business only read business books, interview successful people, and speak with emotion. They themselves do not operate their own successful businesses. In other words, they are not qualified experts and consultants. It's like a speaker who talks about *How to Make a Million Dollars a Year* when he or she, in fact, has not made a million dollars in his or her lifetime.

So be selective in attending seminars. If you're impressed about a particular speaker, then you may hire him or her as a consultant.

■ *When to Hire a Consultant.* Most of the time, entrepreneurs seek the help of consultants when problems have accumulated in running their business. It's like a family that sees a doctor when someone is already seriously ill, about to die. The best time to hire a consultant is during the early stages of a project.

You may seek the help of a consultant based on different occasions:

■ For a specific time period.

■ For a certain numbers of hours per month.

■ For a particular project or problem.

You may pay the consultant by hour, by the month or by the project.

■ *How to Negotiate with a Consultant.* Before you finally hire a consultant, you may negotiate with several consultant candidates.

The first thing to do is call or write your consultant candidates and ask about their backgrounds and business experiences. Then say something about your project or problem that needs solving and ask how much it will cost you to consult him.

Be specific in your proposal. For instance, you may say that you have a new product and would like to sell it to consumers.

Specify if you're looking for distributors or dealers or if you're selling it via mail order. You may also ask how you may sell it to nontraditional markets Also ask how much time he or she may devote to it and how long it will take him or her to submit a report with resources and recommendations, if what you want is a survey on marketing.

It will be easier and clearer for you and the consultant to agree on submitting a report or a survey, and to specify in your agreement the total cost for the project.

Of course, one way of consulting is by the hour on the telephone. But it's hard to explain everything on the phone and the consultant may have limited time to answer your questions. So a by-the-hour agreement may not be ideal for you, whether it's over the phone or making a survey. It's because it's hard to do an accounting of the hours and money spent by the consultant. You may not know what a consultant did at a certain time on a certain date. Hours are too flexible to be measured.

What I usually do when I consult with an expert is to ask how much it will cost for him or her to submit a report to me, probably consisting of three to four pages, single-spaced, about marketing covering a specific matter, the details of which I submit for review and evaluation. Then I set a deadline or ask at what date he or she can submit the report. That is a definite proposal.

Or you may agree to a month-by-month or year-by-year consultation. For instance, you may consult with an expert for one year. During this period, the consultant may advise you as you ask questions. But the question is, how many questions can you ask every week or every month? Is the consultation to be by phone or by written communications or both? Be specific in details so that there won't be any misunderstandings. Also, be specific about the terms of the pay-

ment. Is the total payment to be paid in advance? Fifty percent down and the balance on submission of the report? Is it on an installment basis as the consultation progresses?

Be realistic about the results of consultation. You may increase or not increase your sales after consultation. There is no guarantee on that. The success of recommendations by a consultant may depend how you implement the suggestions or how much money and effort you may devote to the project. Or it may depend on the product itself. Who knows? Maybe, the product needs some more improvement. Or maybe, only a hundred people may buy it, not the millions as you had expected. The sale of products depends on many things and circumstances. If you have the product at the right time, at the right place, and for the right market, then you may have a winning product!

IV. Bottom Line

Picking other people's brains is a very important factor in starting and growing your business. You can do it in many ways.

In a nutshell, you do the following when using the knowledge and experience of other people:

■ Don't rely on advice from friends and relatives in running a business, unless they are entrepreneurs themselves. Sometimes, they may only discourage you instead of encourage you. Or they may just ignore what you say and what you do.

■ Obtain a mentor who can nourish your dreams and desires, one who may help you all the way without waiting for any financial reward. Successful people, one way or another, have had mentors during their careers as professionals or as entrepreneurs.

■ Pick the experts' brains by reading their books and articles or news items in specialized magazines or newsletters.

■ Engage the services of consultants. It is a wise decision and one that will help you trudge the sometimes treacherous road to success. However, know the background, experience, and expertise of your consultant candidate before you hire him or her. The most important thing is to determine the rate of his or her success in a particular field.

■ Any consultant's recommendations are not to be followed blindly. Use your common sense and instinct in using some or all of the recommendations.

■ Your success as an entrepreneur depends on how you steer your commercial ship in the stormy sea of adventure to reach your own destiny. But you must be the only captain of your ship!

Single-Entry Bookkeeping for Simplified Accounting 26

■ Entrepreneurs, most often, find it hard to choose which accounting system should be used in running their businesses: whether the *cash system* or the *accrual system* of accounting. You must decide which one to use in the very beginning of your business. The point is, choose one that is appropriate for you as a one-person business owner.

The cash system features *single-entry* bookkeeping, while the accrual system features *double-entry* bookkeeping.

I. Accounting Methods

On the front page of IRS Schedule C (Profit or Loss from Business) for sole proprietors, is a line that asks about the accounting system one uses in doing business. The major accounting systems are *cash* and *accrual*. (There are also other permissible methods. See them as provided in IRS regulations discussed somewhere in this chapter.)

Cash System

Under the cash system, sales are recorded only when they are paid. At the same time, all accounts payables are recorded only after they are actually paid. In other words, sales are entered into records as such when payments, whether in checks, money order, or cash, are received. At the same time, accounts payables are recorded as expenses when they are actually paid.

In using this system, you may use the simple *single-entry bookkeeping system.* That is, a sale or an expense is recorded only once.

Accrual System

Under this system, you report your income or expenses as they are earned or incurred instead of when they are collected or paid. In other words, sales are included in that same taxable year, whether they are paid or not. The appropriate taxes for such sales are to be paid. Also, the accrual method provides a system for recording expenditures in a single installment but covering more than one period.

One feature of this system is that it uses *double-entry* bookkeeping. The double-entry system is complicated for non-accountants. Every transaction is entered twice in the books. For example, when a customer buys something from you, and he or she pays for it, your gross sales increase while your inventory decreases. So both changes must be entered into your records: one as a *debit entry* and the other as a *credit entry*.

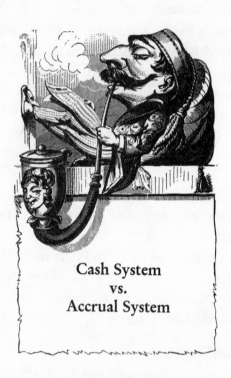

Cash System
vs.
Accrual System

The Current Debate

Before we further discuss the cash and accrual systems of accounting, we may see what the Internal Revenue Service (IRS) provides in its tax regulations regarding accounting systems and inventories.

II. IRS Tax Provisions

The Internal Revenue Service specifically defines the methods of accounting in the Internal Revenue Code.

Permissible Methods

Section 446 of the Internal Revenue Code gives the IRS a wide latitude in changing a taxpayers method of accounting. No single accounting method is required for all taxpayers; however, *if that method does not clearly reflect income*, that method can be changed by the IRS. A taxpayer can challenge this statutory authority only if the Commissioner has abused his discretion.

The regulation under Section 446 provides in pertinent part:

Section 446 (1986 Code). (a) *General Rule.*—Taxable income shall be computed under the method of accounting on the basis of which the taxpayer regularly computes his income in keeping his books.

(b) *Exceptions.*—If no method of accounting has been regularly used by the taxpayer, or if the method used does not clearly reflect income, the computation of taxable income shall be made under such method as, in the opinion of the Secretary, does clearly reflect income.

(c) *Permissible methods.* (1) In General. Subject to the provisions of paragraphs (a) and (b) of this section, a taxpayer may compute his taxable income under any of the following methods of accounting:

(i) *Cash receipts and disbursements method.* Generally, under the cash receipts and disbursements method in the computation of income, all items which constitute gross income (whether in the form of cash, property, or services) are to be incurred for the taxable year in which actually or constructively received... .

(ii) *Accrual method.*—Generally, under an accrual method, income is to be included for the taxable year when all the events have occurred that fix the right to receive the income and the amount of the income can be determined with reasonable accuracy. Under such a method, a liability is incurred, and generally is taken into account for Federal income tax purposes, in the taxable year in which all the events have occurred that establish the fact of liability, the amount of the liability can be determined with reasonable accuracy, and economic performance has occurred with respect to the liability.

(iii). *Other permissible methods.* Special methods of accounting are described elsewhere in chapter 1 of the Code and the regulations thereunder... .

(iv) Combinations of the foregoing methods. (a) In accordance with the following rules, any combination of the foregoing methods of accounting will be permitted in connection with a trade or business if such combination clearly reflects income and is consistently used...A taxpayer using an accrual method of accounting with respect to purchases and sales may use the cash method in computing all other items of income and expenses...

Limitations of Cash System

However, there are some limitations on the use of the cash basis of accounting. Section 448 was added by the Tax Reform Act of 1986 and this section limits the use of the cash method.

Four types of taxpayers cannot use the cash method of accounting for tax purposes. Instead, such taxpayers must use or adopt the accrual method of accounting.

The four types of taxpayers that are subject to this restriction are:

(1) "C" corporations
(2) Partnerships that have one or more C corporations as a partner or partners
(3) Tax shelters
(4) Trusts that are subject to tax on unrelated business income.

However, there are certain exceptions to this general rule. These are:

(1) Farming businesses
(2) Qualified personal service corporations involved in the performance in the following fields: health, law, accounting, engineering, performing arts, architecture, actuarial science and consulting.
(3) Entities with gross receipts of not more than $5,000,0000.

It is clear that with the above provisions, any C corporations and other entities with less than $5,000,000 gross receipts, can use the cash method of accounting. All of those with over the mentioned gross receipts, must use only the accrual system of accounting.

Another item to be considered in determining whether to use the cash or accrual system is the presence of receivables.

If those receivables are substantial (there is no rule of thumb on what is substantial) the accrual method is preferable. In other words, the use of the cash method may be subject to challenge, although the IRS may not challenge service-type business, such as professionals. For example, if you are in the roofing business or asphalt paving business and you use the cash method, although you have substantial accounts receivables and less than substantial inventories, you may face trouble. In this case, you should use the accrual method. The

IRS has successfully argued this service type business in J.P. Sheahan & Associations, T C Memo 1992-239 and in Asphalt Products Co., v. Commission, 796 F.2d 843 (CA-6, 1986).

In short, you can use the cash method even if you have receivables; but those receivables should not be substantial. But you'll be raising a red flag for the IRS if you include "bad debts" in your deductions from your gross income. It's because you're supposed to deal in cash transactions only; that is, payment is made in every transaction. Only those in accrual accounting can deduct "bad debts" from their gross income, together with the other expenses from 8 to line 27B of Schedule C.

III. Inventories

The IRS says when you have inventories, you must use the accrual method for purchases and costs of sales because you are required to take the inventories into account in figuring taxable income.

Inventory accounting is contained in Section 471. It states in part that the use of inventories is a necessity in order to clearly determine the income of any taxpayer. The regulation under Section 471 provides in pertinent part:

> *Need for Inventories.* In order to reflect taxable income correctly, inventories at the beginning and end of each year are necessary in every case in which the production, purchase, or sale of merchandise is an income-producing factor. Section 1.471-1, Income Tax Regulations.

Accounting books always emphasize that if you have inventories, whether you buy products for resale or have them manufactured for you, you have to use the accrual system of accounting. When you hire an accountant to do your bookkeeping or accounting, the accounting system to be used is always accrual.

Before we further discuss the advantages and disadvantages of each system, we may learn what books are supposed to be used in bookkeeping.

IV. Bookkeeping

In conventional bookkeeping, which is also known as recordkeeping, books are used by businesses, large and small. What books to use depend on the preference of each business. Some of them are the cash receipt journal, the cash disbursements journal, accounts receivable journal, the accounts payable journal, and the general ledger.

Standard Recordkeeping Tools

Cash Receipt Journal. The cash receipt journal should contain sales of goods or services. It lists the payments in either cash, checks, money orders received from cash sales or charges. In short, it lists the money that comes into the business.

Cash Disbursement Journal. The cash disbursement journal contains payments, whether in cash or checks for purchases, services, bills, debts, and other obligations. It lists the money that goes out of the business.

If you use the accrual system of accounting, you must enter each transaction twice in each of the above books, both as a debit and as a credit item.

Accounts Receivable Journal. The accounts receivable journal lists goods delivered or consigned to your customers or services that were rendered to businesses or individuals to be paid on particular credit terms.

Accounts Payable Journal. The accounts payable journal lists your bills and other obligations. In short, it's the money that you owe.

General Ledger. The general ledger is a record of all the summary and totals from all journals. It records transactions and balances of individuals accounts. The accounts are organized into five classes of individual accounts as follows:

a. *Assets.* Assets record the value of what company owns.

b. *Liabilities.* Liabilities record what the company owes.

c. *Capital.* Capital records the company's total equity.

d. *Sales.* Sales record all gross receipts for a specific accounting period.

e. *Expenses.* Expenses record all expenses incurred during a specific period.

Assets may include cash, inventories, machinery, etc. Liabilities may include notes payables, accounts payable, and other obligations and liabilities.

At the end of each accounting period or fiscal year, the individual accounts are totaled. After that, they are closed. Then the balances of the accounts are included in financial statements, such as the balance sheet and the income statement.

Single-Entry System

Whenever I attend seminars on financial management, the accrual system that uses the double-entry bookkeeping is always emphasized to be the right system. Speakers, usually accountants, say that in double-entry bookkeeping, there is a double-check of transactions so that errors are prevented. But the fact is, even with the use of the computerized ledger, you cannot always balance the books. Therefore you enter a bogus transaction to balance the books.

Once when I attended a financial management seminar, many of the attendees were disgusted by the speakers' insistence on the use of only the accrual system. In fact, the accountant-speakers gave samples of financial records used by large corporations, and not on the ones used by small businesses or one-person business owners. (Most of the attendees were self-publishers without employees.) The accountants lectured on the theories and not on the practicality of a simple system to be used by one-person business owners.

Since I started my one-person publishing company in 1985, I've been using the cash system of accounting that features single-entry bookkeeping. It's simple, practical, and it works for me.

I don't use the cash receipt journal, the disbursement journal, the accounts receivable journal, the account payable journal or the general ledger.

Instead of the cash receipt journal, I use a software program for publishers called PIIGS. This program records my sales and inventories and can generate reports such as customers' history and accounts receivable.

Instead of the cash disbursement journal, I use a spreadsheet for my computer to record my expenses or payments of bills and other obligations.

Numbered Sorting Boxes. To be easier for you to record your expenses, it's wise to set up numbered sorting boxes. These are uncovered compartmentalized boxes. Actually the boxes are made of wood in compartments, standing with four feet, like stools. The number of boxes depends on the number of accounts that you will set up. For example, box 1 may be for inventories, box 2 for advertising, box 3 for postage and freight, etc.

Accounts must be categorized based on Schedule C (Profit or Loss from Business) filed with Form 1040. For my own use, for instance, I changed some of the categories on Schedule C to suit my business needs. I include typesetting to replace Line 23 which is office repairs on Schedule C. I don't include non-applicable categories, such as uniforms, because I don't wear uniform while conducting my business. While there are 20 expense categories (plus some sub-categories) on the Schedule C, my accounts number 23.

If you have 23 accounts, then set up 23 standing sort boxes similar to pigeon holes. Number the boxes with your account or category numbers. Twenty-two of the boxes should be for expenses that you'll deduct from your gross sales. The last box number (23) is for undeductible items such as withdrawals and cancelled checks drawn for personal or family use. Number the boxes with your account number.

Whenever you receive disbursements receipts, throw them into the proper boxes. After you receive your cancelled checks from your bank, deposit each of them in its proper box, depending on its category; for instance, bank interest for box 13. So each box may contain cash disbursements receipts and cancelled checks.

In other words, the 23 boxes are for your expenditures. As much as possible, pay in checks because these are the ones to be placed in your sort boxes.

Of course, cash receipts are also to be placed in the boxes as back-ups in case the IRS questions a payment for any account. (In other words, such checks are paid for business purposes and not for personal needs.)

Spreadsheets. Instead of the cash disbursement journal, I use a spreadsheet with my computer to record my expenses or payments for bills and other obligations. Prepared by my computer science graduate son, the monthly spreadsheet contains dates, creditors' names, account numbers, check numbers, and amounts for all transactions.

The expenses add automatically from January to December, featuring the "total from last month and the up-to-this-month" figures.

If you have a friend who does programming, you may request him or her to program an expenditure program for you.

One-Write System. You enter these transactions on a single-entry book known as the DOME or any similar system, such as the one from General Business Services. These bookkeeping systems are available in office supply stores. Or you may consider buying the computerized versions of the one-write system DOME. The two versions are the DOME ABC (Dome Accounting by Computer), a software version of the popular DOME Simplified Weekly/ Monthly Bookkeeping system for computers, and the DOME Plus, which features 15 pre-established business categories. For information, write to:

Dome Publishing
10 New England Way
Warwick, RI 02887-9976
1 (800) 432-4352

For sales, if you don't have any computer, then you may purchase invoices from any mail order houses or from your local office supply store. Record the sales in any ledger of your choice.

Fulfillment Software Program. Your one-write system for expenditures cannot be used for making invoices and adjusting inventories.

If you have a computer, you need a fulfillment software program for your sales. Ask accountants and other business persons to recommend the ideal software for your particular line of business.

a. Quicken. For recording of expenditures, you may purchase the program *Quicken,* one of the bestselling finance software. It is ideal for small businesses and is available from your local school supply store or direct from Intuit.

Quicken manages personal and small business finances, including bills, bank accounts, investments, tax record keeping, credit cards, assets and liabilities, loans, and budgets. It also handles accounts payable and receivable, payroll tracking, income statements, balance sheets, cash flow planning, and more.

b. Quickbooks. One program used for small business is *Quick-Books.* It is available from office or computer stores or direct from Intuit, the manufacturer of *Quicken.* It can do all the things done by *Quicken* but it has a general program for fulfillment. In short, *Quickbooks* prepares invoices and other financial reports.

For more information about the two programs, write or call:

Intuit
P.O. Box 3014
Menlo, CA 94026
(415) 322-0573

Of course, there are several computerized accounting programs you may use. One of them is called *Money-Counts* from:

Parsons Technology
375 Collins Road, N.E.
Cedar Rapids, IA 52402
(800) 779-600.

The Program I Use. As I have mentioned, instead of the cash receipt journal, I use a software program called PIIGS. This program, created for independent publishers, records my sales and inventories.

Whenever I enter a transaction, whether paid or on credit, with the making of an invoice for that particular transaction, the inventory of any of my books adjusts itself; that is, it decreases in number based on the number of books invoiced. When I say "invoiced," that account may be paid in cash or on credit or consignment. With this program, I can prepare several reports. For instance, I can generate a report that details the accounts not yet paid (which are called receivables). It may also generate a customer's history and other matters.

In a nutshell, instead of using cash receipt journal, disbursement journals and accounts payable journal, I use a spreadsheet for my expenditures and a fulfillment software program for my summary of sales.

For accounts payable, I throw the invoices into the proper sorting boxes. Anyway, I have only a few bills to pay every month so I remember what they are and when they are due. Sometimes I stick invoices to be paid to my hanging cork bulletin board.

Cash Method vs. Accrual Method: Advantages and Disadvantages

Income and Expenses under the Cash Method. The beauty of the cash method of accounting is that you only count a transaction as a sale when money, whether in cash, money order, or check, changes hands. That is, the sale is made after the merchandise or the service is delivered or rendered and is paid, whether it's invoiced or not. Likewise, any expenses incurred (Line 8 to Line 27b of the Schedule C) should be deducted during a particular taxable year.

One big advantage of using the cash method is that it's simple to use and involves little work: only single-entry bookkeeping.

Income and Expenses under the Accrual Method. Under this system, any merchandise sold, whether paid immediately or in 30 to 90 days, are already considered as sales and their corresponding taxes should be paid the year they were invoiced. They are all considered as sales even if they are not yet paid.

Here's an example: Suppose that you have made a sale involving the shipment of products worth $50,000. It was invoiced December 15. You have to pay the tax on this shipment in the same taxable year. You are supposed to pay the tax on this sale immediately because you are to pay your estimated tax for certain goods sold in a quarter. In this case, you have to pay the estimated by January 15 of the following year.

But suppose the goods were not paid for even after 120 days. Then you must pay the unpaid appropriate tax by April 15. If you don't have extra money in the bank, then you're in trouble. (Under the cash method, you won't have this problem, unless you allocate to something else the amount for your taxes.)

One more disadvantage of the accrual system is that it's complicated and involves a lot of work and several accounting books. And you may need the services of an accountant. One advantage, as accountants claim, is that it minimizes the occurrence of errors because of its double-checking capability.

Costs of Inventories

Whether you use the cash or accrual method of accounting, you must use the accrual system in computing the cost of production or purchase of merchandise, which is known as the *cost of goods* or *cost of sales*. You compute this on page 2, Part III of Schedule C. You start with the value of the inventory at the end of previous year's closing inventory. Then you add your costs of production or purchases and other costs. Inventory at the beginning of the year plus your current costs minus the value of inventory at the end of the year equals the cost of goods sold.

You deduct the cost of goods sold (line 4 of Part I of Schedule C) from your gross sales or receipts (Part 1, Income of Schedule C).

There's a disadvantage in using the accrual method in the computation of cost of goods or sales. However, you can't do anything about it. You must use the accrual method in this computation, whether you use the cash or accrual method in your accounting.

The disadvantage in this system is that you cannot deduct all the costs of inventories the same year that they were incurred. You can deduct only the cost of goods sold, not the costs of the whole inventory. The methods used in inventory vary. You may determine the value of the inventory (cost of production or cost of pur-

chase) and other methods such as the lower of cost of market value. (In computing the costs of goods sold, I use the production cost of inventory per unit in determining the inventory at the beginning of the year and the inventory at the end of the year.)

A Combination of Two Systems

If you wish, you may use the cash method for expenses (Part II of Schedule C), such as supplies, rent, wages, and advertising. Then at the end of the year, when you prepare your income tax, you may use the accrual method for sales and purchases (cost of sales, Part I of Schedule C). By using the accrual method only for sales and cost of purchases (cost of sales), you are matching revenue and costs. Thus, gross sales minus returns and allowances minus cost of goods sold (as computed on page 2 of Schedule C equals gross margin or gross income. Gross income minus expenses (Part II of Schedule C) equals net profit or loss.

V. Depreciation

Depreciation involves the purchase of property that will decrease in value through age and usage. Depreciation is a deduction tool for entrepreneurs. Generally, the whole cost of a property used in a business for over a year is not deductible the taxable year it was purchased. Rather, its cost is recovered over several years through depreciation deductions. You can deduct them through yearly depreciation by means of the General Depreciation System (GDS) or the Alternative Depreciation System (ADS). Since these systems, even with instructions, are hard to understand, you may need the service of an accountant to fully understand them.

However, there's an easy way to depreciate a property the year that you place it in use. Now you can elect to expense certain tangible property up to $10,000 a year. That is, you can deduct up to $10,000 worth of property from your gross sales as part of your expenses. The property may be a car or any office equipment.

Office Equipment

If you buy a computer system worth $5,000, you can depreciate the whole amount and place this figure on line 13 of Part II (Expenses) of Schedule C and it will become part of your expenses that year. In other words, you can deduct up to $10,000 a year in depreciation cost every year, provided you have more income than your deduction.

Vehicle

If you buy a vehicle exclusively to be used for business use, you can't deduct the whole cost if it's more than $10,000. You can deduct the $10,000 and then carry over the balance to the next tax year. The election of this expense to be depreciated in a lump sum may be made as late as the time your return is filed, which generally is up to April 15.

VI. Business Deductions

There are a variety of expenses that are deductible whether you operate your business at home or outside your home. The expenses, however, should be necessary and connected with the operation of your business.

Allowable Deductions

The best way to know the allowable deductions is to look at Schedule C.

However, there may be specific expenses not indicated on Schedule C. These expenses depend on your business and may include postage, freight, direct mail and media promotion expense, post office box rent, and continuing education costs. Include them on line 27a of Schedule C (Other Expenses) or type some of them over expense categories applicable to your business. For expenditures, categorize them into several accounts.

Vehicle Expenses

For vehicle expenses to be deducted from your gross business income, you may keep all the receipts for its maintenance the whole year. You can deduct all the expense of maintaining it. But you must prove, with receipts, that they were actually expended.

There is a simple way to take advantage of a vehicle use as a business expense, you merely use the gasoline mileage rate allowed by the IRS. The 1993 allowance per mile is $.28. If your vehicle mileage per year is 15,000, then multiply that number by $.28. The answer is $4,200. You can write this on line 10 on Part II of Schedule C.

Home Office Deduction

One of the most controversial deductions that a home-based entrepreneur faces is the home office deduction. In general, the IRS stipulates that you may deduct a room or a space expense if that part of that home is exclusively used on a regular basis as your principal place of business.

Suppose your office space occupies 5% of the overall footage, then you may deduct 5% of your expenses for such things as overall repairs, maintenance, utilities, etc.

Supreme Court Ruling. A Supreme Court decision in January 1993, sided with the IRS that disallowed the home office deduction of approximately $2,500 made by a Virginia self-employed physician who used his home office from 10 to 15 hours a week.

In an 8-1 decision, the justices affirmed what is specified in the Federal Tax Code: The office in the home must be the "principal place of business" where revenue is generated.

In the case of this physician, while he did his billing and other paperwork in his home office, he worked as an anesthesiologist in different hospitals. In other words, since he performed his job outside the home, the Supreme Court decided that his home office was not his "principal place of business."

Doubts about Home Office Deductions. In view of this decision, more and more home-based entrepreneurs, especially those who work out of their home to conduct their business (pho-

tographers, interior decorators, etc.) now have some doubts about the home office deduction. This is aggravated by the fact that many people say that you'll be raising a red flag if you claim a home office expense deduction. While any home-based entrepreneur can claim legitimate home office deductions, only about 1.6 million taxpayers took the deduction in 1992 for the year 1991. They used the new Form 8829 for calculating the deduction. (Form 8829 makes it easier to identify and itemize valuable deductions. It works with the old Schedule C for the self-employed to itemize "direct" and "indirect" deductions.)

Whether you wish to claim home office deduction is up to you. The question is, how much money is involved? How much can you save in claiming office deductions? Several hundred dollars? Does it count to save, say, $500 if you experience sleepless nights figuring out whether the IRS may audit you because you have deducted office expenses in the home?

There's another reason why some legitimate home-office workers decline to claim the home office deduction. It's because if you have depreciated a portion of your house or condominium, that part is considered as a business expense and not as a residence. You have to pay tax on the prorated portion that represents the home office deduction if you sell your house or condominium.

Also, remember that the home-office deduction is available only to sole proprietors and not to one-person corporations.

It's Your Decision!

You may weigh the advantages and disadvantages in determining whether to take your legitimate deductions. Of course, even if you don't take home office space deductions, you're entitled to deduct all the legitimate expenses for office supplies and equipment used in your home-based business in figuring your income tax.

If you want to claim home-office space deductions, fill out and file Form 8829, together with Schedule C and other tax forms with the IRS.

VII. Federal Taxes

Income is derived by deducting your total deductible expenses from your gross income.

Income Tax

You must pay federal income tax if you derive an income from your one-person business. You must pay an income tax on your business, whether you engage in business part time or full time.

Sole Proprietorship. If your business is a sole proprietorship, you must report your income or loss on Schedule C to accompany your Form 1040. Submit them with your other tax forms, if you have some more.

Corporation. If your business is a one-person regular corporation (C corporation), you must report your income or loss on Form 1020. If your business is an S corporation, you must use Form 1120S to file your income tax.

Self-Employment Tax

Being self-employed, you must pay self-employment tax. It is similar to the social security tax paid by wage earners. Instead of withholding it from your check, you pay it yourself. However, if your business is a one-person corporation and you have a salary, you must withhold social security tax from your paycheck as a wage earner and send it, together with other deductions as both an employer and as an employee, to proper government agencies. As a general regulation, you must pay self-employment tax if you have earnings from your business of $400 or more per year. For more information, request a copy of IRS Publication # 533 (Self-Employment Tax).

Estimated Tax

Income and self-employment taxes must be paid immediately as required by the IRS. Instead of paying it once during the end of the income tax filing date (April 15), you must pay as income is generated. If taxes are not paid immediately, a penalty may be imposed on you.

As a business person, you must pay estimated income and

self-employment taxes in installments by the following dates:

April 15
June 15
September 15
January 15 (of the following year)

However, if you don't yet expect any income or if your income is only minimal, you don't have to pay estimated income and self-employment taxes.

Excise Tax

You may or may not be subject to an excise tax. But you must be aware of it. An excise tax is imposed on some products or services. For example, if you import, manufacture, or sell fishing equipment, your business may be subject to excise taxes. Or if you are an insurance agent doing business with foreign insurers, you are liable to pay such taxes.

For more information, request a copy of the IRS Publication #510 (Excise Taxes).

VIII. State Taxes

As an entrepreneur with sales from your business, you must pay state taxes.

Income Tax

Your income from business, which is included in your adjusted gross income on your IRS Form 1040, is reported on your state income tax form. In Michigan, the adjusted gross income from any of the Federal 1040 forms is reported on line 10 of the MI-1040.

Sales Tax

Most states require payments of sales taxes on goods sold within their state. If there's a sales tax in your state, then you have to pay the sales tax on every retail sale in that state. Usually, sales taxes are paid quarterly. But if you have only low sales in your state, you may file the sales tax form and payment only once a year, depending on what your state requires. If you want to avoid payment of sales tax, sell only products to distributors and wholesalers in your state. In other words, don't sell retail, only wholesale in your state.

Use Tax

The use tax is imposed on purchases from other states of equipment or products used for business. Michigan collects use tax. Verify if there is such a tax in your state.

Single Business Tax

The single business tax is imposed on self-employed individuals and companies. In Michigan, those subject to this single business tax are businesses with more than $40,000 gross income a year.

The appropriate forms must be filed with the Department of Treasury or the appropriate department of your state, whether the business has an income or not if the sales exceed the sales target that your state has set.

IX. City Taxes

Some cities require income tax payments whether you are a wage earner or an entrepreneur. Some cities merely require the payment of certain fees. Inquire about them before you establish a business, particularly about licenses.

X. Financial Statements

The types of financial statements are the *balance sheet* and the *income statement*, known also as *the profit-and-loss statement*. (However, there may be also some statements that you can prepare that may include a cash flow statement that identifies the sources and applications of cash.)

Balance Sheet

The balance sheet shows what you own and what you owe. It is a financial statement that records the condition of the business as of a fixed date, such as at the end of every quarter or at the end of the year.

The balance sheet contains three categories: assets, liabilities, and net worth.

Assets. Assets are everything owned by or owed to your company. They may include current assets (which can be converted into cash within a year), long-term investments, and fixed assets.

a. *Current Assets.* Current assets include cash on hand, whether in your bank or in your pocket, accounts receivable, inventories, and prepaid expenses, (which may include goods and services bought or rented prior to use).

b. *Long-term Investments.* Long-term investments may include special savings accounts to be maintained at least one year.

c. *Fixed Assets.* Fixed assets may include property, such as land, buildings, equipment, vehicles, furniture, etc. Land should be listed at the original purchase value, while buildings and other property may be listed at the current value (original cost minus depreciation).

d. *Other Assets.* There may be some assets that may not be listed above.

Liabilities. Liabilities are all the things that your company owes from your manufacturers, suppliers, banks, Uncle Sam, etc. They may include current liabilities and long-term liabilities.

a. *Current Liabilities.* Current liabilities may include accounts payable, short-term notes payable, taxes payable, etc.

b. *Long-term Liabilities.* Long-term liabilities may include mortgages and other loans to be paid over several years.

Net Worth. Net worth is sometimes called owner's equity. It may include original capital, and additional capital, plus profits after withdrawals.

To find out your net worth, simply use this formula:

Total Assets - Total Liabilities = Total Net Worth

To find out your total assets, simply use this formula:

Total Liabilities + Total Net Worth = Total Assets

Hence, total assets must equal the total liabilities and total net worth. That's why it's called a balance sheet.

(See a sample balance sheet on page 277.)

Income Statement

The income statement, also known as the profit and loss statement, shows the sources of your income and how you spent some of it over a specific period of time, such as monthly, quarterly, or yearly. This statement shows how your business is doing. (See an income statement on page 278.)

The income statement has five major categories: *income, operating expenses, net profit (loss) before taxes*, and *net profit after taxes*.

1. *Income*. The determination of an income undergoes several processes. First, determine your gross receipts, then deduct returns and allowances and the cost of goods sold, which results in your gross profit. After that, add other income from services or interest, which gives the gross margin, otherwise known as gross income (Line 7 on Schedule C).

a. *Gross receipts*. Gross receipts are the total revenue you get when you sell goods or services. It is sometimes called gross revenue.

b. *Net Sales*. Some goods are returned or services are cancelled. When you deduct returns and allowances from the total receipts, then you will get the net sales.

c. *Cost of Goods Sold*. As the words indicate, the cost of goods sold (line 5, Part I, on Schedule C) reports the cost of the goods sold during a specific period. In determining the cost of goods, simply determine the value of inventories at the beginning of the year, then determine the value of purchases, less the cost of items withdrawn. Then add the two items (cost of inventory and purchases) to get the total amount for inventories and purchases. Total cost minus cost of inventories at the end of the year equals the *cost of goods sold*. (See Form 1040, Schedule C for actual computation.)

d. *Miscellaneous Income*. Miscellaneous income may be derived from other sources, such as interest income or rendering services to clients or customers by a full-service-oriented business or a product-oriented business providing products and services.

2. *Operating Expenses*. Operating expenses involve the so-called controllable (or direct) and fixed (or indirect) expenses.

a. *Variable Expenses*. Variable expenses are sometimes called direct expenses. They are, in fact, direct costs for products or services. Such expenses may include costs for advertising, promotional materials, packaging, etc.

For instance, if you can't afford it, you can advertise a little; if you have the resources, then you can advertise a lot. In other words, you can control costs if you want to.

b. *Fixed Expenses*. Fixed expenses are sometimes known as indirect expenses. These expenses are not directly related to your products or services. They may include taxes and licenses, rental fees, loan repayments, depreciation allowances, etc.

3. *Net Profit before Taxes.* Net profit is derived by deducting the total expenses from the gross income

4. *Taxes Due.* Taxes based on your income are to be paid.

5. *Net Profit after Taxes.* You derive the net profit after taxes by deducting the total taxes paid or to be paid from the net before taxes.

(Note: Should you make any mistakes in categorizing expenses, whether they are controllable (direct) or fixed (indirect), don't worry about them. They are all expenses. The total expenses are deducted from your *gross income.*)

Cash Flow Statement

As discussed in Chapter 23, cash flow, which involves the cycle of receipts and expenditures of a company, is the lifeblood of any business. It is the actual flowing of cash into and out of a business.

To understand how you earn or spend money, you must prepare a cash flow statement. The statement should show an analysis of the cash inflows and outflows.

According to some books, in preparing a cash flow statement, you must know your working capital. You can determine the working capital by deducting your current liabilities from your current assets. Assets may be in cash, stocks, etc. In other words, the working capital may be in cash or in liquid assets—assets that can be converted into cash.

There's nothing wrong with that. But suppose you really don't have enough assets?

The simplest way to do to manage your cash flow is to prepare a cash flow statement that shows only the following: *cash on hand, guaranteed receivables, unpredictable receivables, allocated funds for expenses,* and *working capital.*

1. *Cash On hand.* Cash on hand is the total money that you have in the bank or somewhere in your closet.

2. *Guaranteed Receivables.* Guaranteed receivables are the checks you are sure will come in to you. These may include checks that come regularly every month from your distributors or wholesalers.

3. *Unpredictable Receivables.* Unpredictable receivables are money that you receive whether you like it or not. They come as payments for your products as a result of unsolicited orders.

4. *Allocated Funds for Expenses.* Allocated funds for expenses may be determined by knowing how much money you have and how much money you have yet to receive. Allocate only a segment of what you'll receive. In other words, watch your purchases. Purchases can be made one at a time, especially for equipment.

5. *Working Capital.* Working capital should be set according to your needs for operating expenses and inventories. In other words, you should set a minimum amount of working capital. This working capital may include money in two reserve funds for inventories and operating expenses.

CURRENT BALANCE SHEET

_____
Company Name
As of _____
Date

ASSETS		LIABILITIES	
Current Assets:		**Current Liabilities:**	
Cash in bank	$ _____	Accounts payable	$ _____
Petty cash	_____	Notes payable due	
Accounts receivable		within one year	_____
(Less allowance for		Taxes payable	
doubtful accounts)	_____	Federal income tax	_____
Short-term investments		State income tax	_____
(stocks, bonds,		Self-employment tax	_____
certificates, etc.)	_____	Sales tax	_____
Inventories	_____	Other taxes	_____
Other income	_____	**Long-term Liabilities**	
		Notes payable	_____
Total current assets	_____		
Fixed Assets:			
Land	_____	**TOTAL LIABILITIES**	_____
Building	_____		
Improvements	_____		
Furniture and fixtures	_____	**NET WORTH (OR OWNER's EQUITY)**	
Equipment	_____	Proprietor's capital,	
Vehicles	_____	beginning of period	_____
Other assets	_____	Net profit for the	
		period (less owner's	
		drawings)	_____
		Additional capital	
		invested	_____
Total fixed assets	_____	**TOTAL NET WORTH**	_____
TOTAL ASSETS	_____	**TOTAL LIABILITIES AND NET WORTH**	_____

Note: Total assets must always equal the total liabilities and total net worth. That is why it's called a _balance sheet._
Formula: Total Liabilities + Total Net Worth = Total Assets

INCOME STATEMENT
(Profit and Loss Statement)

_____
Company Name

For the Period Beginning _____ and Ending _____

INCOME

1. Gross receipts or sales

2. Returns and allowances

3. Subtract line 2 from line 1

4. Cost of Goods sold (See computation below)

    a. Inventory at beginning of period

    b. Purchases

    c. Add line a and b

    d. Inventory at end of period

    e. Cost of goods sold (Subtract line d from line c)

5. Gross Profit or Gross Margin (Subtract line 4 from line 3)

OPERATING EXPENSES

1. Variable Expenses (Direct)

    a. Advertising

    b. Contractual services

    c. Freight and Packaging

    d. Professional fees

    e. Miscellaneous direct expenses

2. Fixed (or Indirect) Expenses

    a. Taxes and licenses

    b. Utilities

    c. Rent or lease

    d. Loan repayments

    e. Miscellaneous indirect expenses

TOTAL OPERATING EXPENSES (add lines 1 and 2)

NET PROFIT (LOSS) BEFORE TAXES

TAXES (Estimated)

NET PROFIT AFTER TAXES

XI. Bottom Line

■ For a one-person company, it seems that the cash system, a single-entry bookkeeping, is the best to use. It is easy to use, especially if you have appropriate computer software programs for bookkeeping. With this system, you know exactly how much money you have. While you have receivables, you don't count them as cash yet, so you don't have to make purchases anticipating the collection of such accounts.

■ With the cash system, you don't have to pay estimated taxes for sales if you've not yet collected the receivables.

■ You may use the cash system of accounting in your bookkeeping for your expenses as outlined on Schedule C (including expenses not categorized in the form). Then shift to the accrual system to prepare the first part of Schedule C. The portion that you will use the accrual system for is Part I of that schedule which concerns gross receipts and cost of goods sold. It's because inventories are involved in this portion of the schedule. In using the accrual system for cost of sales, you're matching revenue and costs.

■ Make financial statements that you can understand, not complicated ones such as may be contained in many books that you cannot use. Make the financial statements for use by a one-person company, not those appropriate for a large corporation.

■ If you, however, want to obtain a loan from a bank, you must of course, pattern them from standard financial statements.

Of course, you may use the accounting system that you'll be most comfortable with. Who knows, you may invent another accounting system that will work for you.

Program Your Mind for Success

■ "Whatever the human mind can conceive and believe, it can achieve!" says Napoleon Hill in his classic book, *Think and Grow Rich*.

The Wright brothers conceived the idea of making machines that could fly and they did it!

A great many inventors conceived the creation of useful products and they did it!

I conceived the idea of successfully writing and publishing books in America (even if English is only my second language) and I did it!

All mankind's achievements originate in the mind. The mind is the engine and the driver of the human body.

You can make use of it and you can program it for success!

You are the master of your fate!

I. Ingredients of Success

There are many ingredients of success. But some of them come directly from the mind. But nobody can put them there except you. So you must do it!

By programming your mind for success, you can develop a positive mental attitude, you can ignite your booster rocket for ambition, and you can have high self-esteem, faith, enthusiasm, and persistence.

Thoughts Occupy Your Mind

Positive Mental Attitude

Thoughts occupy your mind: they are powerful enough to uplift your spirit and emotions in time of happiness or to paralyze you into immobility in times of failures and frustrations. If you're in control of your thoughts, you'll be in control of your emotions, dreams, and destiny.

Either you think positively or you think negatively; it's as simple as that. If you're a positive thinker, you'll move forward, however big the obstacles are. If you're a negative thinker, you're doomed to fail.

You can think positively if you dwell on past successes and not on failures, if you see the bright side of life and not the dark side, if you look at problems as challenges and opportunities. You can be a positive thinker if you think only about things that you can change, and forget about things you can't change. You can change the way you think, from negative to positive. You can improve your situation in life. You can exercise your mind as you exercise your muscle.

Positive thinkers always believe that through planning, determination, and perseverance, they can be whatever they want to be and achieve whatever they want from life.

Igniting Your Booster Rockets for Ambition

Almost a century ago, people recognized that rocket power was the key to exploration of space beyond the earth's atmosphere. Vehicles cannot be sent into space against the force of gravity without the use of powerful rockets.

To be a success in life, to do what you want to undertake, you need booster rockets to send your dreams into your own outer space.

"How can I ignite my booster rocket from within me?" you may ask. Think big and be ambitious! Think of the career you'll build, the money you'll accumulate, or the fame you'll achieve, and the booster rockets in your brain will launch your dreams. Then chase those dreams!

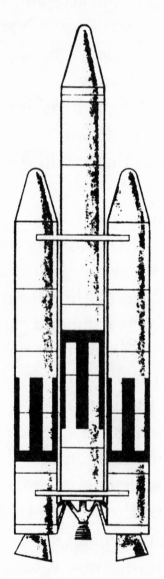

Launch Your Dream!

The Dreamer. Years ago, when I told some of my friends that I wanted to write and publish books in America, they laughed at me. A woman who's involved in selling books warned me that I would lose my shirt because I was too small to compete with the giant publishers in America. I didn't hear them; my desire was as hot as a glowing iron. No one could stop me. I failed during my first years of writing and self-publishing; few people bought my instant-printed and home-produced booklets on postal exams. Bookstores would not buy them; my friends and relatives would not buy them (they wanted them free). But I persisted, for I had faith in myself and in my product.

After five years, when I had enough money, I bought a computer, rewrote the manuscript, and produced it in book form.

Then I had the opportunity to contact the big book distributors that now sell my book to bookstores and libraries. My first book, *The Book of U.S. Postal Exams,* has sold more than 100,000 copies so far.

My network of distributors and dealers have sold thousands of my other books beyond my wildest dreams. Besides having accomplished my goal of receiving the gross income I earn each year, I've received various book publishing awards, including the prestigious "Small Press Publisher of the Year" award in 1990.

It is now that I fully realize that in order to succeed in life, you need the help of other people. You can't do it alone. You must share the job and you must share the rewards.

Now I'm writing and publishing books so that I can help others succeed in life.

The Clock is Ticking! Now is the time to set your booster rocket and push the launching button! With courage and will power, you'll be on your way to your destination.

Self-Esteem

Self-esteem may be defined simply as "You are what you think you are." All of us have self-esteem, but the degree depends on how we regard our own feelings, how we blame and hate ourselves when we make mistakes, and how we love and reward ourselves when we are successful.

You may have low, average, or high self-esteem. Since self-esteem is a conglomeration of all your feelings toward yourself, other people, and life itself, you must develop high self-esteem to have the self-respect and self-confidence so necessary in becoming a successful entrepreneur and a successful human being. In view of this, you should protect yourself from negative feedback from some of your friends, enemies, colleagues, coworkers, and all the people you encounter throughout the day, every day.

The lower your self-esteem, the more you'll have negative thoughts and failures, the more you'll feel down and believe you have nothing to live for, the more you'll think that you can't be a success in life.

On the other hand, the higher your self-esteem, the more ambitious and enthusiastic you'll be to set goals to pursue your dreams.

In the early 1970s, a father would throw his son a baseball. The son would catch it, and throw the ball back to his father. That became a routine. There was nothing unusual about it, except that the son had no right hand! He would catch the ball, flip his glove into his handless forearm, and throw the ball back to his father.

An ordinary human being would not dare to do what this young man envisioned, but he had high self-esteem; he believed in his ability and potential and his parents believed in him. He was not ashamed of himself just because of his handicap; he believed that he could accomplish whatever he dreamed of doing.

As a pitcher, Jim Abbot led the University of Michigan baseball team to two Big Ten championships. He also pitched for the United States in the Pan American Games, humiliating Cuba in Havana, and pitched for the U.S. team in the Seoul Olympics, where the Americans became world champions.

The left-handed Abbot was drafted by the California Angels. One day in March 1989 at age 21, he stood on the mound in the Oakland A's spring training park in Phoenix. He had two strikes on batter José Canseco, a one armed pitcher against a slugger. Abott threw the next pitch and Canseco swung and missed! On that day, Abbot became a winning pitcher for the first time as a professional. He dreamed it, and he made it! He is a positive thinker with high self-esteem!

Many people are not like Jim Abbot, however. Because they were born with a disability, because they were not born intelligent, or because they were born poor, they let others abuse them physically and mentally. Their lack of self-confidence erodes their thinking and interferes with their ability to set goals for themselves. Many people can't handle the failures in business or in personal relationships that diminish their self-worth and self-respect. It's too hard for them to learn from their mistakes and to go on living! For this reason, such people succumb to drugs, alcohol, and deep depression which sometimes drive them to end their lives.

People with high self-esteem think that failures are only temporary defeats. They feel that they can bounce back from their failures and disappointments.

Be responsible for your thoughts and actions. If you make mistakes, forgive yourself, admit that you're only human, and learn from those mistakes. If you do the right things, then you can reward yourself.

As you achieve small successes based on what you've planned—earning some profits, winning some awards, you'll know that you're becoming happier and friendlier and more content with life, an individual who has a mission to accomplish.

As you accomplish what is best for you, dreaming the right dreams, setting the right goals, and making the right choices and decisions, you'll know that there's a purpose in your life, and your self-esteem will rise further. You'll let go the guilty feelings about your mistakes, and you'll experience the fullness, not the emptiness, of life. No more blaming others, no more procrastination, no more backward thinking. What is left is peace of mind and your plan for your future. Like others, you're qualified for a place in society. You're entitled to success and happiness. But it all depends on your way of thinking. You are what you think you are, and you will become whatever you want to become! Onward to your destiny!

Faith and Enthusiasm

After you have written down your short- and long-term goals, it's time to take steps to achieve them.

When you pursue your goals in life, you're like a track-and-field athlete who has to jump over many hurdles. You jump over these hurdles one at a time, not all at once, in a continuing effort.

To achieve your goals, you must be inspired and enthusiastic.

A man once asked three laborers what they were doing. The first laborer said, "I'm laying bricks." The second laborer gave a similar response. The third laborer said, "I'm building a church!" The third laborer was enthusiastic; he was inspired because he was building a church.

Stimulating the Mind. Years ago, a mother took her son to the library to stimulate his interest in baseball. "He would get books about Babe Ruth and Ted Williams," she said, "and he would learn through reading. I would read to him first, and then he would read them."

That boy grew up to become the most valuable player in the 1984

World Series, when his team, the Detroit Tigers, clinched the world championship. He was Allan Trammel, the Tigers' shortstop, who also was voted the most valuable player in the American League in 1987.

Have Role Models. If you want to be somebody, it's good to have role models. Emulate the entrepreneur, the writer, or the speaker you admire. At first, copy his or her style of doing business, writing, or speaking. Later, you'll develop a style of your own.

Dr. Richard Morales, a psychiatrist and stress-management specialist who practices in Largo, Florida, says, "It is necessary to model yourself after others as a more effective way of learning what it is that self-made people do. Find a well-known personality who has done something you admire and read as much as you can about that person. If there are videotapes of the person, study them so that you can imitate his or her walk and the way he or she talks. Then find out as much as possible about that person's interests."

How can you have faith in yourself or in your goals? Why do you believe that you can achieve them?

If you have written down well-planned goals, if you have plans like architects' plans, if you have the map to be used in trudging some chartered and unchartered roads to your destiny, there's no reason why you can't believe in yourself and in your goals. In your imagination, you already have seen and conquered your obstacles and reached your destination. Yes, you can support your plans and written goals with affirmations and visualizations.

Emilie Coué, a French psychologist, taught his patients to make this affirmation: "Day by day in every way, I am getting better and better!" (His patients did improve!) Tell yourself the same thing. You'll have a good felling about yourself! You'll feel stronger and more enthusiastic and inspired, and you'll always think positive things.

This kind of self-talk is called *affirmation*. Affirmation is the process by which you talk to yourself, confirming what good things you have done or what good thoughts you have. When these thoughts are repeated again and again, your mind eventually accepts them as true. Then they make you feel good, giving you the enthusiasm and inspiration to push toward your goals.

Affirmation, coupled with visualization, can make your dreams come true. Visualization is the process by which you imagine that you are succeeding. If you want to become a successful entrepreneur, visualize yourself working in your one-person office with all the tools of modern technology. See yourself receiving checks from your distributors and dealers month after month after month. See yourself going to the post office and opening your mail box bulging with envelopes that contain checks from persons and companies you have never heard of before. See yourself receiving awards from organizations that recognized the outstanding achievers in your industry.

Play and replay these images on the screen of your imagination; feed them to your subconscious mind. If your subconscious mind sees them over and over again, even if they are not yet true, eventually it will believe that they are happening or have happened.

According to psychiatrist Richard Morales, achievers are able to picture themselves where they want to be and experience how it feels to be there. He says, "I call that instant preplay. Transport yourself into a successful experience, See it, hear it, feel it as if it were happening. Then take these fabricated experiences and store them in your memory for reference."

What Visualization Can Do. A man named Lyndon Johnson always visualized that he would be in the White House—and he was! When I was little, I always visualized that from the Philippines, I would go abroad (maybe to America) to pursue a dream—and I did!

Practice affirmations and visualizations every day, especially before you go to sleep at night or after you wake up in the morning. Fill your study room or bedroom with pictures and mottoes such as *If it can be done, I can do it,* or *Do it now!* In the private offices of many industrial leaders and businessmen are hung such slogans and pictures from great men of the past. F.W. Woolworth, who was called the Napoleon of business, was reported to have had a private office that was a replica of Napoleon's study. Leaders like Woolworth did such things to remind themselves that they could succeed in life just as those great men had succeeded in the past. If you do these things, you'll have constant reminders of your goals and you'll be inspired to act. You won't let things happen; you'll make things happen!

Persistence and Rewards

Sometime, somewhere, you'll suffer defeat in your quest for success. There will be times when you seem unable to find enough customers or clients for you to survive and succeed in business.

Don't let failures deter you; make them your stepping stones to learn. Don't be afraid to fail, because failures are a test of how tough-minded you are, how much self-discipline you have, and how well you can adjust to any unforeseen circumstances. Often, when we admire successful men and women, we see them only when they are already on top; we don't know that they stumbled many times on the way.

Sometimes, friends, relatives, and those close to you will judge or criticize you and say, "Don't do that, you'll only fail." "You can't make it as a businessperson because you have no money." "If it were a good idea, it would have been done by somebody else."

Friends and relatives love you, so they don't want you to fail or get hurt, but they don't know that you have set your own goals in life and that what you are trying to do is attainable. Sometimes, too, some of them are jealous; they don't want you to succeed and leave them behind.

Try again even if you fail! Failure is nothing but a temporary defeat; it is nothing but a chance to learn from your mistakes.

Thomas Edison suffered thousands of failures while doing his experiments, but he persisted. In everything he failed, he discovered one more thing that didn't work. Then all that was left was the only thing that worked. In this way, Edison found the path to success and became one of the world's greatest inventors.

The following verses sum up one of the laws of success.

You Can

If you think you dare not, you don't.
If you like to win but you think you can't,
It is almost certain you won't.

If you think you'll lose, you're lost.
For out in the world we find,
Success begins with a fellow's will—
It's all in the state of mind.

If you think you are outclassed, you are,
You've got to think high to rise,
You've got to be sure of yourself before
You can even win a prize.

Life's battles don't always go
To the stronger or faster man,
But sooner or later the man who wins
Is the man WHO THINKS HE CAN!

—Anonymous

Life's successes bring small and large rewards. Visualize these rewards if you have the ambition to succeed in business, imagining the day when you will become financially independent or rich.

Program your mind for success! Reinvent yourself if you think you should. Change your way of thinking, change your way of working, change your way of managing time—all of which should be for the better of you. Improve your relationships with your spouse, your children, and other people. Surround yourself with people who will inspire and motivate you. Then continue climbing your ladder to success and finding your destiny. You can be whatever you want to be!

II. Bottom Line

Avoid negative thinkers. Associate with positive thinkers and you'll be one too; associate with success-conscious people, and you'll be one, too.

Listen to inspiring tapes and read books that can help you to develop a positive mental attitude, high self-esteem, faith, enthusiasm, and persistence, and to launch your dream for you to achieve.

7-Point Success Formula for a Solo Operator 28

■ A formula is a method or a system for making or doing things; it is the key to an objective. Used efficiently, a formula for success will help you achieve your goals as a one-person business operator!

I've devised a seven-point formula based on my experience and on examples from case studies of other successful one-person business persons. You may adopt this success formula to help you succeed in your business.

1. Have a Dream and Chase It

A woman friend of mine once asked me what she should first do to launch a business. My answer was, "Have a dream and chase it!"

Yes, a dream results from an ambition, and without an ambition, there is nothing to look forward to and aim for in the future.

What is ambition? Webster's New World Dictionary defines ambition as "a strong desire to gain a particular objective; specif., the drive to succeed, or to gain fame, power, wealth, etc."

To have a dream, you must ignite your booster rockets for ambition!

Do you want to be an author? A graphic designer? A consultant? An importer-exporter? A seminar speaker? A global entrepreneur? Do you want a change in your career? Do you want a challenging endeavor now that you are retired? You need a burning desire to accomplish any of these endeavors!

What is stopping you from launching a dream to succeed? Are you deaf? Beethhoven, composer of immortal symphonies, was deaf. Are you crippled? Alexander Pope was crippled so painfully that he could hardly move, but he became a Goliath of English literature. Are you feeling old? Walter Damrosch wrote and conducted one of his greatest operas when he was 80. Victor Hugo produced his famous *Torquemada* when he was 80. The list goes on and on!

2. Program Your Mind for Success

You should program your mind for success. All mankind's achievements originate in the mind.

Program your mind for success so you can develop a positive mental attitude, ignite your booster rocket for ambition, and have high self-esteem, faith, enthusiasm, and persistence— all of which are the nuts and bolts for achieving success.

3. Set Short-term Goals and Long-Term Goals and Make Plans to Accomplish Them

If you already have a burning desire to become a successful entrepreneur, you must make plans and work according to those plans. An architect makes a plan for a house or a building. You, too, should make plans to build a successful one-person business.

Where Are You Going?

Once I asked a woman who was walking on the street, "Where are you going?" She looked at me, puzzled. I asked a man the same question and he answered, "It's none of your business!" In a place I know, when you meet a man or a woman on the road or anywhere else, you don't greet him or her with "How are you?" You ask, "Where are you going?"

Now I ask you: where have you been? What have you accomplished in life? Where are you going? What do you want to become?

Why not set short-term and long-term goals? Short-term goals may be goals for a day, a month, or a year. Long-term goals may be goals for two years, five years, or ten years.

Think small and you'll get small things; think big and you'll get big things.

Read the following lines, and you'll know what I mean:

I bargained with Life for a penny.
And Life would pay no more,
However I begged at evening
When I counted my scanty store.

For Life is just an employer,
He gives you what you ask,
But once you have set the wages,
Why, you must bear the task.

I worked for a menial's hire,
Only to learn, dismayed,
That any wage I had asked of Life,
Life would have willingly paid.

—Anonymous

Write down your short-term and long-term goals. Your goals should include the time at which you'll accomplish what you want, the business you want to pursue, and the exact amount of money you want to accumulate by the time you reach the age of 55 or whatever age you choose.

Don't forget to set a deadline for your goals.

Make a general written statement of destiny to read before you go to sleep and when you wake up. The idea of writing a statement was conceived first by Napoleon Hill, author of *Think and Grow Rich*, one of the most influential books ever published. Other writers of self-help books have adopted this idea, although they present it in different ways.

When you have written your statement, don't show it to your friends, to your wife or husband (if you're married), or to your boss (if you're employed). If you do, they may think you're crazy, so this is just between you and me. Read it aloud twice daily; feed it to your subconscious mind. Believe and feel as if you already possess the money. See it on the screen of your imagination. Later, you won't read the statement anymore; you'll be able to recite it because you'll have memorized it.

When you read or recite such a statement, it penetrates into the depths of your body and brain, giving it to the subconscious mind to work on even while you're asleep.

You're the Master of Your Fate. Whether you're in your forties, your fifties, your sixties, or your seventies, remember what poet William Ernest Henley wrote: "I am the master of my fate, I am the captain of my soul."

So don't let yourself float like a log, swept here and there in the River of No Return. Paddle your own canoe!

When you prepare your short- and long-term goals, be specific about what you want to be; whether you want to be a part-time or full-time business person.

Planning. Now you must make plans. Prepare a business plan as outlined in Chapter 3. Specifically, the plan should include the following steps:

■ A description of the business you want to launch.

■ An evaluation of your present situation. What resources do you have? What skills do you have? How would you reinforce your past experiences and knowledge?

■ A step-by-step procedure on how you should implement your plan.

■ A deadline for accomplishing your goals.

Start Now! Whatever resources you have, whatever interests and abilities you have or you don't have, you must start now! Survey the market and pick the right business—a business that you'll enjoy.

Then register your company name. If you register your business, that's the first step to launching a part-time or a full-time business.

Remember, in launching a business, you're like a hunter who goes to an unchartered territory to hunt for deer (or whatever). Arm yourself with the proper hunting tools and equipment. As an entrepreneur, you'll seek customers or clients for your products or services.

4. Make Use of Smart Technology

With today's advanced technology (computer, fax machine, voice mail, etc.), you can operate your business locally or internationally. You can even network with fellow entrepreneurs throughout the world by subscribing to so-called on-line services such as CompuServe and others.

5. Form Alliances with Subcontractors and Other Businesses

As large corporations downsize, they delegate to outside sources some day-to-day operations, such as data processing, and other matters that can be subcontracted. Nowadays, big and small companies are engaged in forging what is called "partnering." In such partnership, they may have a formal joint venture, a supplier relationship, a product development partnership, or a service or marketing relationship.

Delegate the Task of Production

The smart solo operators do the same; however, they delegate, as I do, the big task of production and marketing to outside subcontractors. The one-person owners also hire professionals who may do product designs and promotional pieces, such as salesletters or brochures.

Also, small or independent entrepreneurs are forming groups to be able to compete with their giant competitors in their industries. If you want to be a successful one-employee company, rely on your subcontractors, distributors, and dealers for the production and marketing of your products. You are the pilot of a commercial ship!

If you are providing service, make alliances with companies and people who can give you referrals. But first, you must provide reliable services to be recommended by them. (For more information on this, see Chapter 14, *Wise Ways to Manage Subcontracting & Partnering*, page 125.)

6. Use the Brains and Experiences of Other People

A wise entrepreneur receives free and paid advice from other people. You may be able to receive constructive criticism or feedback from fellow entrepreneurs by networking with them. If possible, find a mentor. If you can't find one, then you may use consultants for your particular projects or problems. You may find a good consultant through your trade organizations or through inquiry from some business persons using consultants. (See Chapter 25, *Using Other People's Brains,* page 251.)

7. Simplify Your Business Operations

One of the reasons why some people are afraid to engage in business is that they don't know how to do record keeping and accounting. They think that accounting should be done only by accountants and that they have to hire one if they engage in business.

Cash or Accrual System of Accounting. When you engage in a business, you have to use the cash system or the accrual system of accounting. In the cash system, you only enter a sale in your books if you receive the payment for a product or a service. But in the accrual system, you'll record the sale even if it's not yet paid. The cash system involves a simple system of record keeping, which is also called single-entry bookkeeping. The accrual system, however, requires double-entry bookkeeping.

In other words, as a solo operator, it's better to use the cash system, (which requires a simple or single-entry bookkeeping) than the complicated accrual system (which requires the double-entry system, known as *debit* and *credit).*

If an accountant does your accounting, he naturally will use the double-entry system. He or she may also tell you that if you have an inventory, you should use the accrual system of accounting. (See Chapter 26, *Single-Entry Bookkeeping for Simplified Accounting,* page 261.)

Simplify Your Work. Simplification is the best tool for a one-person operator. Don't engage in complicated operations. As an explanation, negotiate only and have dealings with a few people or a few companies in your operations, whether in production, promotion, or marketing. In publishing, for instance, engage the services of a master distributing company and let it sell your books to other distributors, wholesalers, and bookstores.

If possible, engage only in wholesaling, not retailing. And don't be afraid to divert from standard procedures in business. For instance, it is a common practice by companies to drop-ship for their dealers. Drop-shipping means that if you sell products to dealers, those dealers may request you to drop-ship products directly to their individual customers. They send you their payment for such shipments plus the cost for shipping, accompanied by shipping labels containing the names and addresses of your dealers, as if the products came directly from them.

I used to drop-ship books to my dealers' customers. But later, I stopped doing it because I had to pack a number of packages of their shipments. I didn't have to do this routine job, so I told my dealers that I had changed my company's policy and that I would no longer drop ship orders. (Packing consumes a lot of time.) Since they want to sell my books, they now all buy wholesale.

For single orders, require prepayment from dealers. Collecting single order payments may give you a lot of headaches. Imagine, the minimum time to receive the payment of a single- or few-copy order on credit is 30 days. And it may be extended to 120 days!

Use a Lot of Common Sense. There are lot of operations in business in which you can use common sense. For example, if you'll not get anything from networking with a particular group, then just discontinue it. Find another group association where networking is a two-way street; that is, you give and receive sales tips or resources.

Another thing, if your first ad in a magazine doesn't pay for itself, forget it. Don't listen to sales representatives who tell you that your ad will generate orders after a few placements. Nonsense! If your product is a winner or if your service is really needed, the first ad tells it all!

If a certain project doesn't click, abandon it. Go on with your life and pursue another project! Life is an adventure, so with business.

Don't be afraid to be a nonconformist. If some entrepreneurs are going to the west, you may go to the east. Sometimes you may forget about standard procedures, you may create procedures of your own. Don't forget to experiment—experiments have resulted in unbelievable useful products and outstanding accomplishments in the world!

Onward to Your Destiny!

Bibliography

Alexander, Roy. *Commonsense Time Management.* Amacom/American Management Association, New York.

Alvarez, Mark. *The Home Office Book: How to Set Up and Use an Efficient Personal Workspace in the Computer Age.* Goodwood Press, Woodbury, CT.

Bangs, David H. Jr. *The Market Planning Guide: Gaining and Maintaining the Competitive Edge.* Upstart Publishing Co., Inc. Portsmouth, NH.

Bangs, David H. Jr. *The Start-Up Guide: A One Year Plan for Entrepreneurs.* Upstart Publishing Co., Inc. Dover, NH.

Blake, Gary and Robert W. Bly. *Your Practical Primer to the Ins and Outs of Advertising and Publicity.* A Plume Book, New American Library, New York.

Bodian, Nat G. *How to Choose a Winning Title: a Guide for Writers, Editors, and Publishers.* The Oryx Press, Phoenix, AZ.

Botkin, James W. and Jana B. Matthews. *Winning Combinations: The Coming Wave of Entrepreneurial Partnerships Between Large & Small Companies.* John Wiley & Sons, Inc., New York.

Brabec, Barbara. *Homemade Money: The Definitive Guide to Success in a Homebased Business.* Betterways Publications, Inc. Crozet, VA.

Burgett, Gordon. *Self-Publishing to Tightly-Targeted Markets.* Communications Unlimited, Santa Maria, CA.

Burstiner, Irving. *The Small Business Handbook: A Comprehensive Guide to Starting and Running Your Own Business.* Prentice Hall Press, New York.

Cohen, William A. *The Entrepreneur and Small Business Problem Solver.* John Wiley & Sons, New York.

Dirks, Laura M. and Sally H. Daniel. *Marketing Without Mystery: A Practical Guide to Writing a Marketing Plan.* Amacom/American Management Association, New York.

Edwards, Paul and Sara, and Laura Clampitt Douglas. *Getting Business to Come to You.* Jeremy P. Tarcher/Perigee Books/The Putnam Publishing Group, New York.

Edwards, Paul and Sarah. *Working From Home: Everything You Need to Know About Living and Working Under the Same Roof.* Jeremy P. Tarcher, Inc. Los Angeles, CA.

Eyler, David R. *Starting & Operating a Home-Based Business.* John Wiley & Sons, New York.

Fleury, Robert E. *The Small Business Survival Guide: How to Manage Your Cash, Profits & Taxes.* Sourcebooks Trade/Sourcebooks, Inc. Naperville, IL

Gallagher, Richard R. *Your Small Business Made Simple.* Double Day, New York.

Goldstein, Jerome. *How to Start a Family Business & Make It Work.* M. Evans & Company, Inc. New York.

Halloran, James W. *Why Entrepreneurs Fail.* Liberty Hall Press/McGraw-Hill, Inc., New York.

Hodgetts, Richard M and Donald F. Kuratko. *Effective Small Business Management.* Harcourt Brace Movanovich, Publisher, San Diego, CA.

Kelley, Robert E. *Consulting: The Complete Guide to a Profitable Career.* Charles Scribner's Sons, New York.

Levinson, Jay Conrad. *Guerrilla Marketing Weapons: 100 Affordable Marketing Methods for Maximizing Profits from Your Small Business.* Plume/New American Library/Penguin Books, New York.

Loftus, Michele. *How to Start and Operate a Home Based Word Processing Or Desktop Publishing Business.* Bob Adams, Inc. Holbrook, MA.

Magrath, Allan J. *Market Smarts: Proven Strategies to Outfox and Outflank Your Competition.* John Wiley & Sons, New York.

Mancuso, Joseph R. *How to Write a Winning Business Plan.* Prentice-Hall, Inc. Englewood Cliffs, NJ.

Parson, Mary Jean. *Managing the One-Person Business.* The Perigree Books/The Putnam Publishing Group, New York.

Pinson, Linda and Jerry Jinnet. *Anatomy of a Business Plan.:.* Out of Your Mind...and Into the Marketplace. Fullerton, CA.

Sandhusen, Richard L. Marketing: A Streamlined Course for Students and Business People. Barron's Educational Series, Inc. Hauppauge, New York.

Shenson, Howard and Ted Nicholas. *The Complete Guide to Consulting Success: A Step-by-Step Handbook to Build a Successful Consulting Practice.* Enterprise/Dearborn Financial Publishing, In., Chicago.

Silver, A. David. *Strategic Partnering: How to Join Forces with Other Companies to Get Capital, Research and Development, Marketing, Product Testing, and Sales Support.* McGraw-Hill, New York.

Spira, Jeff. *Turn Your Ideas Into Money.* Chilton Book Co. Radnor, PA.

U.S. Government. *The State of Small Business. A Report of the President Transmitted to the Congress, 1992.* United States Government Printing Office, Washington, D.C.

Whitmyer, Claude and Salli Rasberry and Michael Phillips. *Running a One-Person Business.* Ten Speed Press. Berkeley, CA.

Wilson, Jerry R. *Word-of-Mouth Marketing.* John Wiley & Sons, Inc., New York.

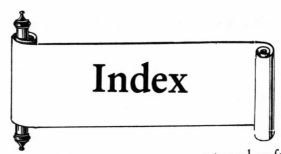

Index

Notes

Notes

About the Author

Veltisezar B. Bautista operates his own
successful one-person publishing company.
Named the Small Press Publisher of the Year in 1990
by Quality Books, Inc., he is the recipient of six other
book publishing awards, (including two Benjamin Franklin
Awards from Publishers Marketing Association).
A former journalist and the author of five books,
Bautista lives in Farmington Hills, Michigan.